Microsoft®
Office Excel 2003

Nancy D. Lewis

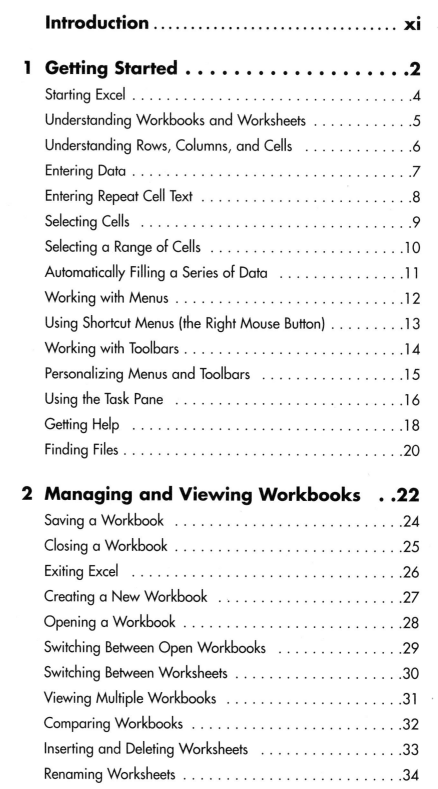

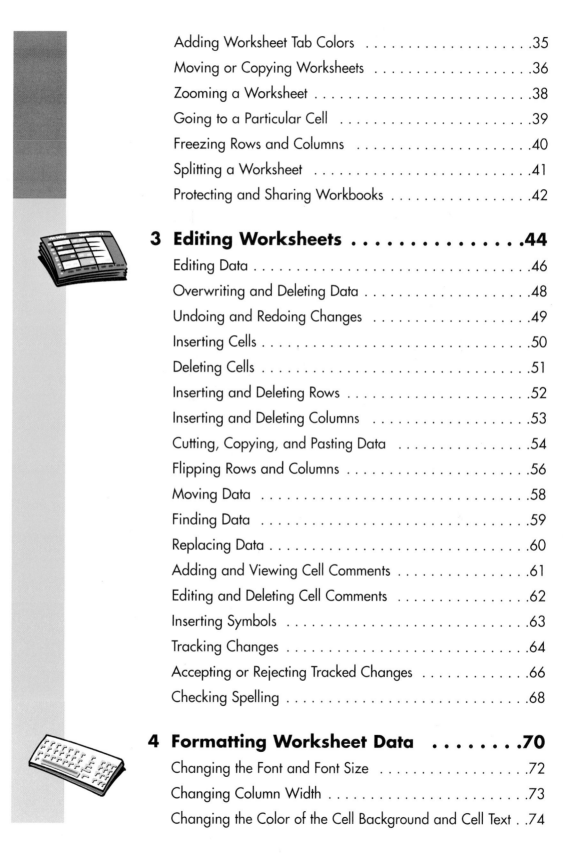

6 Working with Charts 132

Easy Microsoft Office Excel 2003

International Standard Book Number: 0-7897-2960-1

Library of Congress Catalog Card Number: 2003103665

Printed in the United States of America

First Printing: September 2003

06   05   04   03   4   3   2   1

Bulk Sales

Que Publishing offers excellent discounts on this book when ordered in quantity for bulk purchases or special sales. For more information, please contact

U.S. Corporate and Government Sales
1-800-382-3419
corpsales@pearsontechgroup.com

For sales outside of the U.S., please contact:

International Sales
1-317-581-3793
international@pearsontechgroup.com

Trademarks

All terms mentioned in this book that are known to be trademarks or service marks have been appropriately capitalized. Que Publishing cannot attest to the accuracy of this information. Use of a term in this book should not be regarded as affecting the validity of any trademark or service mark.

Warning and Disclaimer

Every effort has been made to make this book as complete and as accurate as possible, but no warranty or fitness is implied. The information provided is on an "as is" basis.

Associate Publisher
Greg Wiegand

Acquisitions Editor
Michelle Newcomb

Development Editor
Kate Shoup-Welsh

Managing Editor
Charlotte Clapp

Project Editor
George E. Nedeff

Copy Editor
Seth Kerney

Indexer
Chris Barrick

Proofreader
Linda Seifert

Technical Editor
Cari Skaggs

Team Coordinator
Sharry Gregory

Interior and Cover Designer
Anne Jones

Page Layout
Stacey Richwine-DeRome

About the Author

Nancy D. Lewis is a freelance writer, editor, and computer training consultant. Her books focus on computers, business, and real estate; her teaching focuses on computer users of all ages who want to learn the tricks (as well as the ins and outs) of the Office products' trade.

Dedication

To Sid ....

Acknowledgments

A special thanks to Michelle Newcomb for working so patiently with me and being a terrific Acquisitions Editor! In addition, I would like to thank Kate Shoup-Welsh for all her hard work and great suggestions; as well as George Nedeff, Seth Kerney, and Cari Skaggs for their edits.

We Want to Hear from You!

As the reader of this book, *you* are our most important critic and commentator. We value your opinion and want to know what we're doing right, what we could do better, what areas you'd like to see us publish in, and any other words of wisdom you're willing to pass our way.

As an associate publisher for Que Publishing, I welcome your comments. You can email or write me directly to let me know what you did or didn't like about this book—as well as what we can do to make our books better.

Please note that I cannot help you with technical problems related to the *topic* of this book. We do have a User Services group, however, where I will forward specific technical questions related to the book.

When you write, please be sure to include this book's title and author as well as your name, email address, and phone number. I will carefully review your comments and share them with the author and editors who worked on the book.

Email: feedback@quepublishing.com

Mail: Greg Wiegand
            Associate Publisher
            Que Publishing
            800 East 96th Street
            Indianapolis, Indiana 46240 USA

For more information about this book or another Que title, visit our Web site at www.quepublishing.com. Type the ISBN (excluding hyphens) or the title of a book in the Search field to find the page you're looking for.

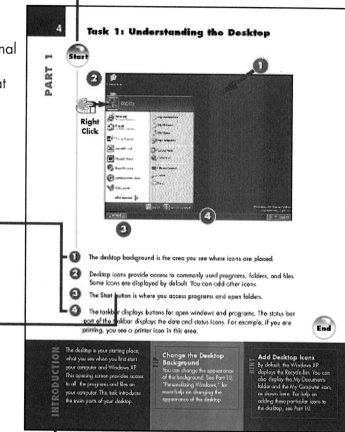

① Each step is fully illustrated to show you how it looks onscreen.

It's as Easy as 1-2-3
Each part of this book is made up of a series of short, instructional lessons, designed to help you understand basic information that you need to get the most out of your computer hardware and software.

② Each task includes a series of quick, easy steps designed to guide you through the procedure.

③ Items that you select or click in menus, dialog boxes, tabs, and windows are shown in **bold**.

drag

drop

How to Drag:
Point to the starting place or object. Hold down the mouse button (right or left per instructions), move the mouse to the new location, then release the button.

See next page

End

Introductions explain what you will learn in each task, and **Tips and Hints** give you a heads-up for any extra information you may need while working through the task.

See next page:
If you see this symbol, it means the task you're working on continues on the next page.

End Task:
Task is complete.

Selection:
Highlights the area onscreen discussed in the step or task.

Click:
Click the left mouse button once.

Double-click:
Click the left mouse button twice in rapid succession.

Right-click:
Click the right mouse button once.

Pointer Arrow:
Highlights an item on the screen you need to point to or focus on in the step or task.

Click & Type:
Click once where indicated and begin typing to enter your text or data.

Introduction

If you've picked up this book, you probably use or are thinking of using Microsoft Office Excel 2003 either in your home or business. Excel is the best-selling spreadsheet program available, and with it, you can create all kinds of financial documents—budgets, sales worksheets, income totals, expense reports, loan payments, and more. If there's something you need to do with numbers, Excel is the program for that job.

But Excel isn't your *life*. You don't want to learn every little function and feature. You want the basics, enough to get your job done as quickly and painlessly as possible. That's why this book is perfect for you.

Easy Microsoft Office Excel 2003 provides concise, visual, step-by-step instructions for all the key tasks. You can *see* how to perform each task. The book covers the most common things you do, and covers the best way to do them. You learn how to create, edit, format, and print worksheets. You also learn how to jazz up a worksheet with charts, pictures, links to Web sites, and more. As an added bonus, you can use Excel as a mini-database program; this book also covers the database features of Excel. And finally, you learn how to make some changes to how the program works. Just about everything you need in one *easy* book.

You can turn to a particular task and follow the steps for that task. You can read the book from cover to cover. You can use the book as a reference. You can turn to a particular topic (such as charts) and follow all the tasks for that topic. No matter how you use it, you will find the information you need to make learning Excel easy.

Getting Started

To learn any new application, it's a good idea to have some basic knowledge of how to start the application, what appears onscreen, how to ask for help, and how to find files in the application. If you are new to Excel, read this part so that you get a good understanding of these basic skills. If you have used Excel before, you might want to skim through this part to see what's new.

A *worksheet* is a grid of columns and rows. The intersection of any column and row is called a *cell*. Each cell in a worksheet has a unique *cell reference*, the designation formed by combining the row and column headings. For example, A8 refers to the cell at the intersection of column A and row 8.

The *cell pointer* is a white, cross-shaped pointer that appears over cells in the worksheet. You use the cell pointer to select any cell in the worksheet. The selected cell is called the *active cell*. You always have at least one cell selected at all times.

A *range* is a specified group of cells. A range can be a column, a row, or any combination of cells, columns, and rows. *Range coordinates* identify a range. The first element in a range coordinate is the location of the upper-left cell in the range; the second element is the location of the lower-right cell. A colon (:) separates these two elements. The range A1:C3, for example, includes the cells A1, A2, A3, B1, B2, B3, C1, C2, and C3.

Excel Workbook Desktop

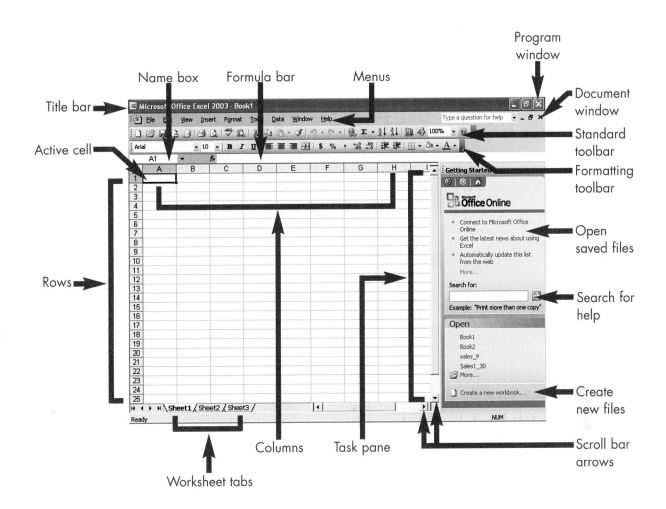

Title bar • Name box • Formula bar • Menus • Program window • Document window • Standard toolbar • Formatting toolbar • Active cell • Open saved files • Search for help • Rows • Create new files • Scroll bar arrows • Columns • Task pane • Worksheet tabs

Starting Excel

Start

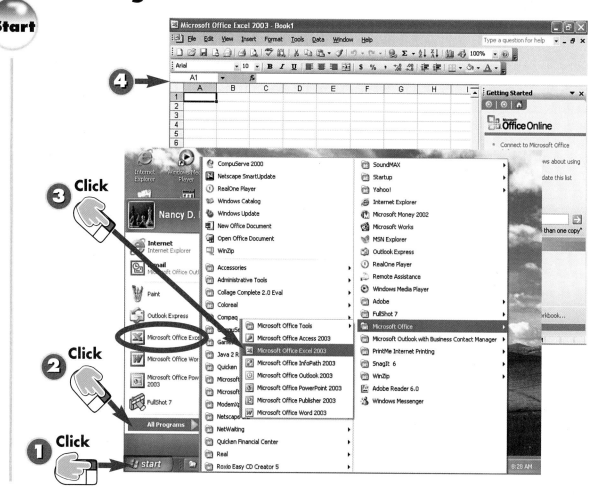

3 Click

2 Click

1 Click

1 Click the **Start** button.

2 Click **All Programs** and locate the **Microsoft Office** submenu. If you see **Microsoft Office Excel 2003** in the main Start menu, you can click it here instead.

3 Click **Microsoft Office Excel 2003** in the Microsoft Office submenu.

4 The Excel window opens with a blank "worksheet."

End

You start the Excel application the same way you do most other applications in Windows XP: using the Start menu. If you've recently used Excel, the application command might be visible on the first pane of the Start menu as well as in its normal location, in the All Programs submenu.

Using desktop shortcuts
Depending on your setup, you might have a *shortcut icon* for Excel on your Windows desktop. If you do, you can double-click it to start the program.

Starting Excel by opening a file
Another way to start Excel is to double-click on an existing Excel file—for example, in your My Documents window. Windows will automatically start the application and open the file you double-clicked.

Understanding Workbooks and Worksheets

 Start

③ Click

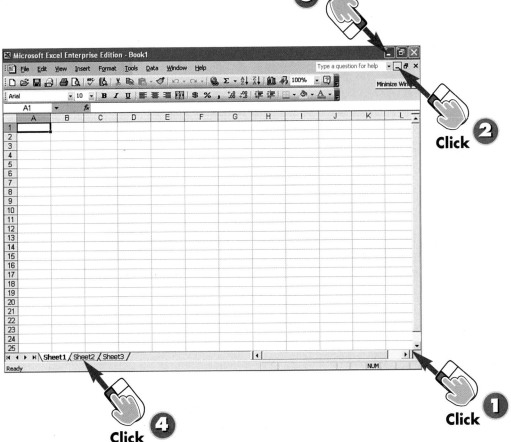

② Click

① Click

④ Click

① Click the **scroll bar arrows** that correspond to going left and right or up and down. The scroll bars allow you to scroll through additional rows and columns.

② Review the document window controls, which allow you to alter the viewable size of the workbook. Click the **Minimize** button to shrink the workbook to only the name of the file.

③ Review the program window controls, which allow you to alter the viewable size of Excel. Click the **Minimize** button to shrink Excel to a button on the taskbar.

④ Review the tabs at the bottom of the workbook (Sheet1, Sheet2, Sheet3). You can click on these tabs to move between the worksheets within the workbook.

End

By default, Excel workbooks contain three worksheets. In time, you'll learn to add more worksheets, rename them, delete them, color-code them, and much more. In this task, however, you'll focus on learning how to move around in workbooks and worksheets.

TIP

Resizing the window
Click the **Restore Down** button on Excel's document window controls and then click on the window border and drag it to resize Excel to whatever viewable size you like. To go back to full size, simply click the **Maximize** button.

TIP

Worksheet tab buttons
Each worksheet is named Sheet1, Sheet2, or Sheet3, by default. Another way to move through a workbook's worksheets is to click the next right or next left arrow buttons.

Understanding Rows, Columns, and Cells

Start

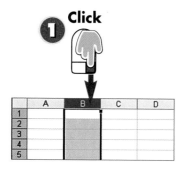

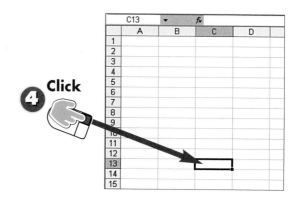

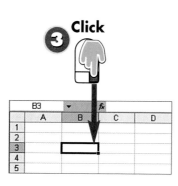

1. The letters along the top of the worksheet columns (A, B, C, and so on) are the *column headers*. Click on any one of these column headers to select an entire column.

2. The numbers along the left side of the worksheet rows (1, 2, 3, and so on) are the *row headers*. Click on any one of these row headers to select an entire row.

3. Click in the worksheet to select a cell. The active cell is B3 because it is where column B and row 3 intersect.

4. Click a different cell in the worksheet (in this case, C13). Notice that the active cell changes, as does the cell reference in the Name box.

End

TIP

Cell versus cell
No two cells have the same cell name, even if they are in two different worksheets in the same workbook. For example, Excel references cell B3 on Sheet1 as Sheet1!B3 and cell B3 on Sheet2 as Sheet2!B3. If they are the same cell name, sheet name, but different workbooks, the reference would be [filename.xls]Sheet1!B3.

Entering Data

Start

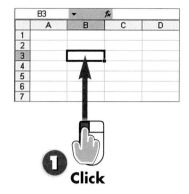

1 Click

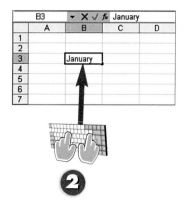

2

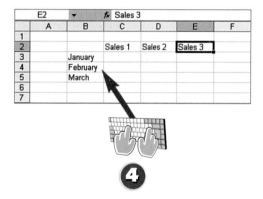

3

4

1 Click the cell to which you want to add data (for example, **B3**), making it the active cell.

2 Type some data (in this example, **January**) in the cell. As you type, the data also appears in the Edit bar because you are in Edit mode.

3 When you finish typing, press **Enter**. Excel makes the cell immediately below it (the one you typed in) the active cell.

4 Type some data into a few different cells and press the arrow keys to move to the next cell (for example, enter some row headers and column headers).

End

INTRODUCTION

Data is the technical term for the text and numbers you enter into an Excel worksheet. Data in each cell can contain text, numbers, or any combination of both; it can even be a graphic or some other type of object that you insert into the worksheet. You can enter data into a blank worksheet or add data to an existing worksheet.

TIP

Correcting Data
If you made a mistake when typing data into a cell, you can press the Backspace key to delete your entry and then simply type the correct data.

HINT

Editing Data
If you pressed Enter to accept a data entry, but that entry is incorrect, click the cell with the incorrect data to make it active and type the correct data over the old data. Turn to "Editing Data" in Part 3 for more information about editing your data.

Entering Repeat Cell Text

Start

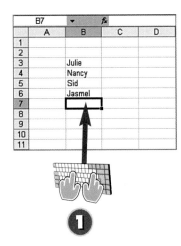

1

2

3

4

1 Type four different names into cells B3–B6 (for example, **Julie**, **Nancy**, **Sid**, and **Jasmel**) and press **Enter** to move to the next blank cell in the same column (B7).

2 In cell B7, type the first letter of one of the names—for example, **S**. The name Sid fills the cell. Press either the **Enter** or the **down arrow** key to enter the name.

3 In cell B8, type the first letter of another name—for example, **J**. Notice that no name automatically fills the cell because the inferred name could be either Julie or Jasmel.

4 Type the second letter of the name—for example, **u**. The name Julie appears. Press either the **Enter** or the **down arrow** key to enter the name into the cell.

End

TIP

Overriding Excel's entry
Suppose cell B3 contains the text **paper clips,** cell B4 contains **pencils,** and you want to type **paper** in cell B5. When you do, Excel will automatically enter **paper clips** in the cell. To ensure the cell holds only the data you want, simply continue to type the word **paper** and press the Delete key on the keyboard when you finish. The rest of the text will disappear; press the **Enter** key to move on to your next cell entry.

Selecting Cells

Start

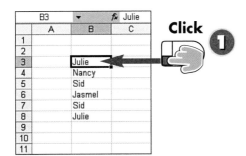

Click 1

Click 2

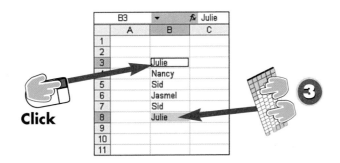

Click

3

1. Click the cell you want to make active (for example, **B3**). A thick black border around the cell indicates it is the active cell.

2. Click on another cell (for example, **B8**) to select it as the active cell. Notice that there is no longer a border around cell B3.

3. Press the **Ctrl** key on the keyboard while again clicking cell **B3**. The active cell is B3, but cell B8 now has a light blue background; this indicates that both cells are selected.

End

Selecting a Range of Cells

Start

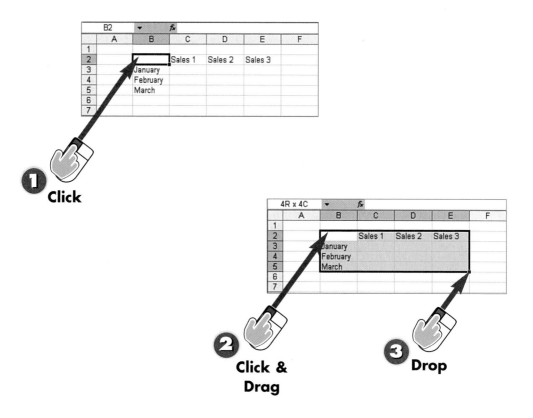

1 Click

2 Click & Drag

3 Drop

1 Click on the cell that you want to be the first cell in a range of cells (for example, **B2**).

2 Press and hold down the left mouse button as you drag the pointer to the last cell you want to include in the range (for example, **E5**).

3 When the range is selected, release the mouse button.

End

TIP

Range references
A range of cells is indicated with a *range reference*. This includes the upper-leftmost cell in the selection, a colon, and the lower-rightmost cell in the selection. For example, the range reference for cells B2 through E5 would be B2:E5.

TIP

Using Shift
Another way to select a range of cells is to click on a cell, press the Shift key, and then click on the cell at the other end of the desired range. All cells between the two clicked-on cells will be selected.

Automatically Filling a Series of Data

Start

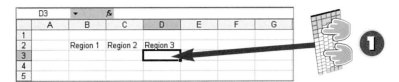

1

Click **2**

Click & Drag **3**

Drop **4**

1 Type the data for the first few cells in the series you want to fill. For example, type **Region 1**, **Region 2**, and **Region 3** into cells B2, C2, and D2, respectively.

2 Select cells **B2**, **C2**, and **D2** (B2:D2), and move the mouse pointer over the lower-right corner of the range until the pointer changes to a thin, black plus sign.

3 Press and hold down the mouse button and drag horizontally or vertically until all the cells you want to fill are selected.

4 Release the mouse button when you have filled the correct number of series data.

End

INTRODUCTION

If you have ever typed each and every cell of a series of data into a worksheet (for example, Monday, Tuesday, Wednesday, and so on), the information in this task will save you a lot of time. In a couple of quick steps, Excel completes all the time-consuming data-entry work for you. Be sure to check Excel's work.

TIP

More on series fills
You can fill a data series vertically in a column (down) as well as horizontally in rows (right). If you drag up or to the left, the data series will decrease instead of increasing.

TIP

Using intuitive series
Excel will automatically fill and repeat common series like days of the week, month names, and so on. To experiment, type **January** in a cell, and then click and drag to select the number cells you want to fill.

Working with Menus

Start

Click ❶

Click ❷ **Click** ❸

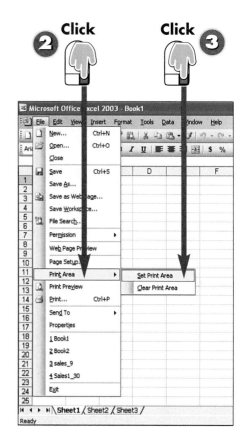

❶ Click the **File** menu and review the commands available to you.

❷ Move the mouse pointer down the File menu to the **Print Area** command. (Notice the small black arrow next to the command; this denotes the presence of a submenu.)

❸ To execute a command in the submenu, move the mouse pointer to the command you want (in this example, **Set Print Area**) and press the left mouse button.

End

The menu bar, just below the title bar, contains nine menus: File, Edit, View, Insert, Format, Tools, Data, Windows, and Help. You select commands on each menu to perform operations, such as saving a workbook, formatting data, printing a worksheet, checking spelling, and inserting charts.

TIP
Using your keyboard to issue commands
If you want to use your keyboard instead of your mouse to issue a menu command, press the **Alt** key, and then press the letter that's underlined in the menu name. For example, press Alt+F to view the File menu. Once the menu is displayed, press the underlined letter in the command you want to perform.

Using Shortcut Menus (the Right Mouse Button)

Start

Right Click ①

Right Click ②

Click ③

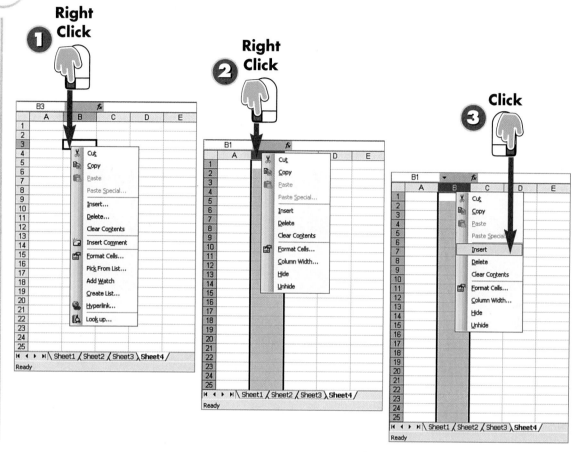

① Right-click a cell to see the shortcut menu.

② Right-click a column header to see a different shortcut menu. Notice that this shortcut menu contains slightly different command options.

③ Click a command, such as **Insert**, on the shortcut menu. The action is performed, and the shortcut menu disappears.

End

When you right-click an item in your workspace, a *short-cut menu* (also known as a *pop-up* or *context menu*) appears. The commands in a shortcut menu vary, depending on your selection; that is, shortcut menus include the commands used most often for whatever object is selected—text, cells, charts, graphics, and so on. If you open a shortcut menu that doesn't contain the command you want to use, exit the menu by pressing Esc or clicking elsewhere on the desktop.

TIP

Using traditional menus

The commands available on shortcut menus are also available on traditional menus (refer to the previous task, "Working with Menus," for more information). For example, instead of using the shortcut menu to insert a column, as you did in this task, you could open the **Insert** menu and choose the **Columns** command.

Working with Toolbars

Start

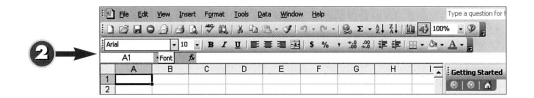

3 Click

1 Move the mouse pointer over each of the buttons on the **Standard** toolbar, pausing momentarily over each button to see a descriptive ScreenTip.

2 Move the mouse pointer over each of the buttons on the **Formatting** toolbar, again, pausing for a second over each button to see the descriptive ScreenTip.

3 Click on a button to perform the corresponding action. For example, click the down arrow next to the **Borders** button to choose from the border options.

End

INTRODUCTION

Excel provides two default toolbars, Standard and Formatting, that display the most commonly used commands as buttons. Some buttons feature a downward-pointing arrow (called a *drop-down menu*), which allows you to choose from multiple options for the same command. If multiple toolbars share the same row, one or more of the toolbars might feature a double-right arrow at its right-most end; click it to view any buttons that don't fit on the line. To move a toolbar to another location, move the mouse pointer over the left-most side of the toolbar; when the pointer changes to a four-pointed arrow, click and drag the toolbar to its new home.

TIP

ScreenTips
To display ScreenTips, open the **Tools** menu and choose **Options**; select the **Show ScreenTips on Toolbars** option, and click **Close**. When your mouse pointer hovers over a toolbar button, the Screentip will display.

Personalizing Menus and Toolbars

Start

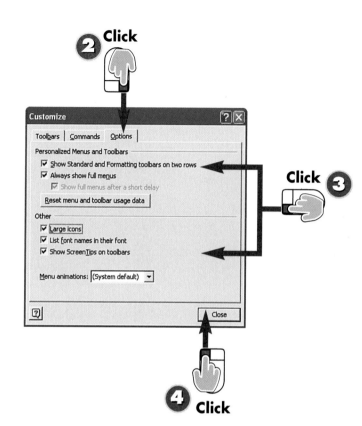

② **Click**

Click ③

④ **Click**

Click ①

---

① Open the **Tools** menu and choose **Customize** to open the Customize dialog box.

② Click the **Options** tab.

③ Check or uncheck the options in the Personalized Menus and Toolbars area as desired, as well as the options in the Other area.

④ Click the **Close** button.

End

INTRODUCTION

By default, Excel's menus are adaptive, which means they initially display only those commands that relate to what the program "thinks" you are trying to do in your worksheet. After a short delay, the full menu appears. To change this, and to specify whether the Standard and Formatting toolbars should be displayed all on the same row or on two separate rows, use the Customize dialog box.

TIP

Dialog box options
The settings in the Options tab's area are as follows: choose **Large icons** to view toolbar buttons at about four times their regular size; choose **List font names in their font** to configure the Font drop-down list on the Formatting toolbar to display font names in their own font; and choose **Show ScreenTips on toolbars** to configure Excel to display the name of a toolbar button when your mouse pointer hovers over it.

Using the Task Pane

Start

Click

1

Click

2

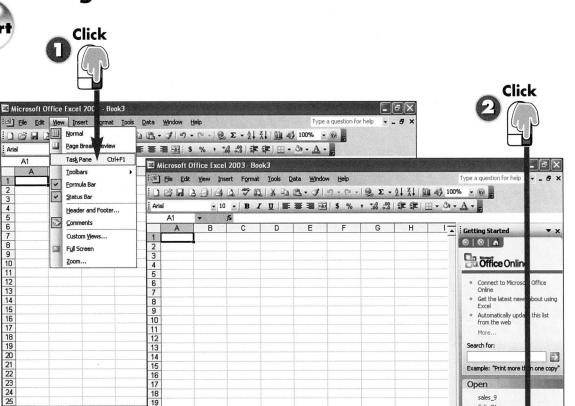

1 If the task pane isn't already visible, open the **View** menu and choose **Task Pane** to display it.

2 To open a new file, click the **Create a New Workbook** link in the task pane. You can also use the links in this area to access an online template from Microsoft.com.

INTRODUCTION

If you recently installed Excel, the task pane might be displayed when you start the application. The task pane simply offers additional ways to quickly perform common tasks in Excel, get help, find files, and much more. As you work in Excel, additional task panes become active depending on what tasks you are performing.

TIP

Resizing the task pane
If you find yourself frequently using the task pane and want constant access to it, you can slightly decrease its size so that it doesn't take up as much of your workbook area. Simply move the mouse pointer over the left-most edge of the task pane; when the pointer changes to a two-pointed arrow, click and drag the edge of the pane to the left (bigger) or to the right (smaller).

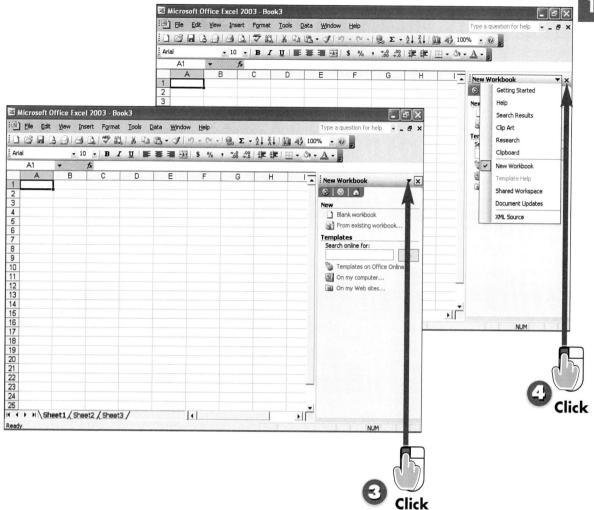

Click

Click

3️⃣ Click on the **down arrow** at the top of the task pane to view the other task panes available to you.

4️⃣ Click the Task pane's **Close** button, located at the top of the pane, to close it.

End

Getting Help

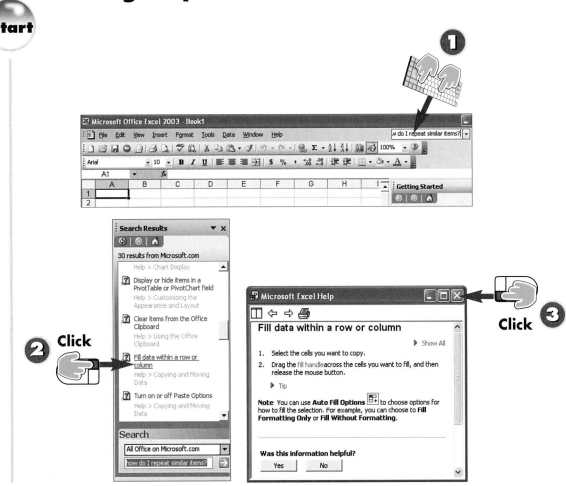

Start

Click ②

Click ③

① Type a question in the **Type a question for help** field. For example, in Excel, type **how do I repeat similar items?**.

② When you press **Enter**, the Search Results task pane opens, displaying a list of possible answers from Microsoft.com. Click the link that seems like the best match.

③ Read the information in the Help Window. Click additional links in the Search Results Task pane until your question is answered. Click **Close (x)** when finished.

INTRODUCTION

Microsoft makes it easy for you to get help in Excel—even if you don't know exactly what type of help you need. In addition to typing a question into the **Type a question for help** field in the Excel window, you can also use the Help task pane to find other Help resources to get on track.

TIP

Helping yourself
If none of the search results adequately answer your question, scroll to the bottom of the Search Results pane and click the **Tips for better search results** link for tips on conducting more effective searches.

TIP

Trying again
If the link you clicked in the Search Results pane doesn't answer your question, click the pane's **Back** button (similar to the Back button in a Web browser), and then type a new question or visit other help areas and try again.

Click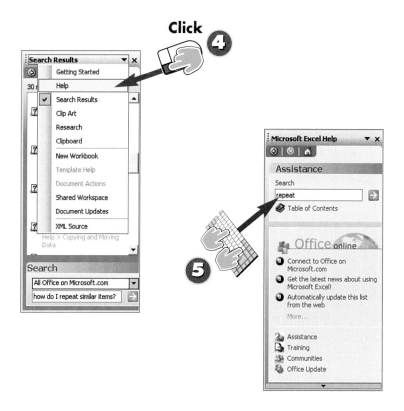

Click

4 To use the Help task pane to get help, click the **down arrow** at the top of the Search Results task pane and select **Help** from the list that appears.

5 In the **Search** field, type a key term relating to the task you need help with; then press **Enter** or click the **green arrow**.

6 Click the Search Results task pane's **Close** button   , located at the top of the pane, to close it.

End

Finding Files

Start

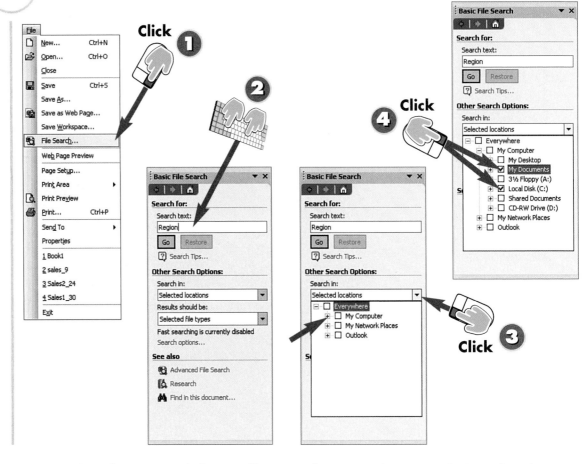

Click ①

Click ④

Click ③

① Open the **File** menu and choose **File Search** to open the Basic File Search task pane.

② Type all or part of the name of the file you are searching for (in this case, **Region**).

③ Click the **down arrow** next to the **Search in** field, and then click on the plus sign (**+**) next to **My Computer** to display a list of your computer's contents.

④ Click the check box next to the folders and drives you want to search, and uncheck any you want to bypass. When you're ready, click the down arrow to exit the list.

The more files you create and save in Excel, the harder it can be to locate them all. Fortunately, if you haven't kept all your files organized in folders according to project, date, or task, Excel can help you find your files.

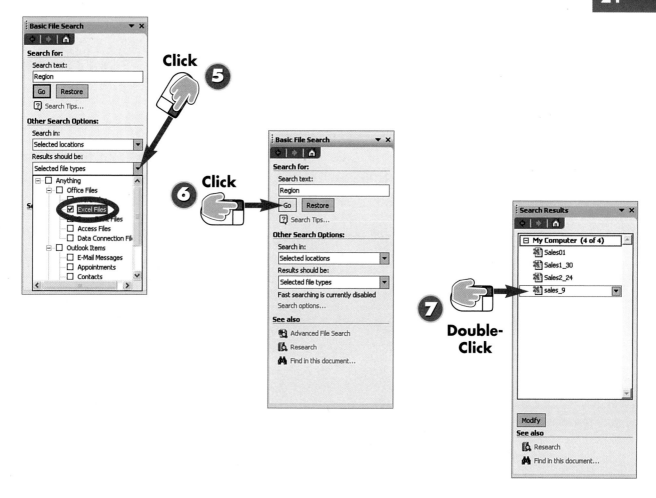

Click **5**

Click **6**

7 Double-Click

5 Click the **down arrow** next to the **Results should be** field. Click on the checked boxes in the list to uncheck all options except Excel Files; then click the **down arrow** to exit the list.

6 Click the **Go** button to initiate the search.

7 Double-click on the file once it is found to open it and begin working.

End

No matches found?

TIP

If your search yields no matches, you might need to modify your search criteria and perform these steps again. To do so, click the **Modify** button at the bottom of the task pane.

Using advanced file search options

TIP

If you've followed the steps in this task but still haven't found your file, use Excel's advanced file search options. To do so, click the **Advanced File Search** link at the bottom of the Basic File Search task pane. In the **Property** list box, select the criteria you want to look for; for example, File name or the Creation date. Then, in the **Value** box, type any information that you know about the file. Click the **Add** button to include the condition you've specified, and then click **Go** to locate the file (or files) that contains your criteria.

Managing and Viewing Workbooks

As you continue to work in Excel, you will learn how important it is to save your work and access workbook files. You should save often, and you also should spend some time keeping your documents organized.

In addition, using multiple worksheets can help you organize, manage, and consolidate your data. For example, you might want to create a sales forecast for the first quarter of the year. Sheet1, Sheet2, and Sheet3 could contain worksheet data for January, February, and March; Sheet4 a summary for the three months of sales data; and Sheet5 a chart showing sales over the three-month period.

Opening Excel Workbooks

Displays the current folder

Goes back to the previously viewed folder

Goes up one folder level

Displays recently saved files

Displays files on the desktop

Displays files in the My Documents folder

Displays folders and drives on your computer

Displays shared network folder and drives

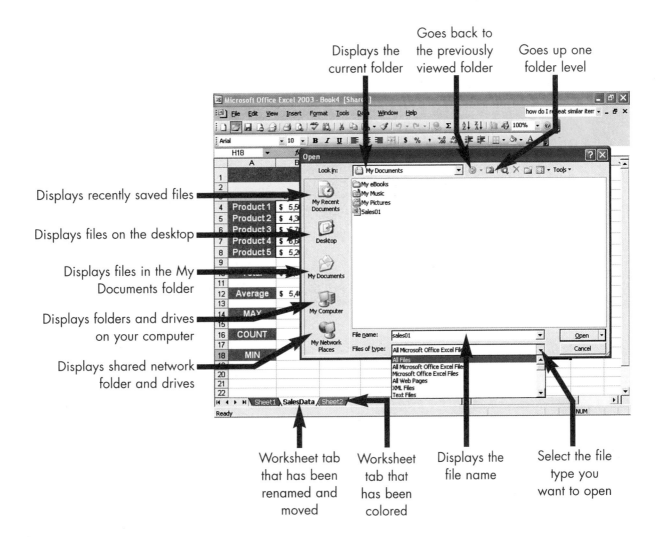

Worksheet tab that has been renamed and moved

Worksheet tab that has been colored

Displays the file name

Select the file type you want to open

Saving a Workbook

Start

Click
1

Click
2

3

Click

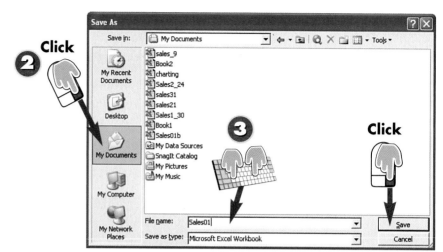

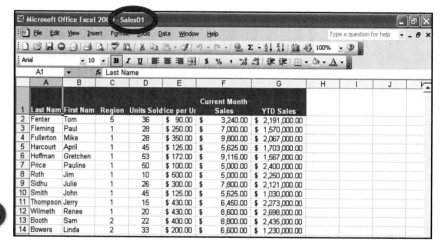

4

1 With the worksheet you want to save open in the Excel window, open the **File** menu and select **Save As** to open the Save As dialog box.

2 Click the **My Documents** icon or use the **Save In** drop-down list to move through the folder structure to save the file where you want.

3 In the **File Name** field, type a descriptive name for the file—for example, **Sales01**. Then click the **Save** button.

4 The Excel title bar now contains your workbook's name.

End

Until you save the workbook in which you are working, the data in the file is not stored on disk. You should regularly save your workbooks as you work in them so you don't lose your data. After you save a workbook, you can retrieve it later to work on. You can save a workbook as many times as you like, and you can even save it under another name if you want to keep track of multiple versions of your workbook.

TIP

Clicking the Save button
If you have already saved and named your file, you can resave it after making additional changes by clicking the **Save** button on the Standard toolbar.

Closing a Workbook

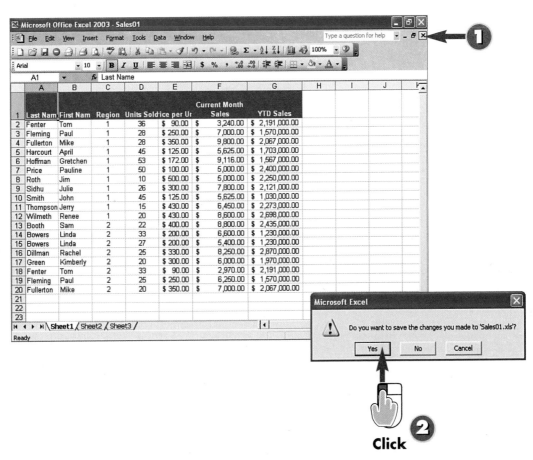

Click

1 Click the **Close** button in the document window.

2 If you have edited the workbook since saving it last, Excel prompts you to save your changes. Click **Yes** to save changes or **No** if you don't want to save your work. Excel closes the workbook.

INTRODUCTION

When you finish working on a workbook, you can close it—with or without saving changes—and continue to work in the application. If you have been working in a workbook and try to close it, Excel asks you whether you want to save the workbook before it closes.

TIP

Program window
Make sure you click the **Close** button in the document window, not the program window. Otherwise, you'll wind up closing all open workbooks in Excel.

TIP

Available buttons
When Excel has no workbooks open, only a few buttons are available on the Standard toolbar. Notice that as soon as you create a new workbook or open a workbook, the buttons are available again.

Exiting Excel

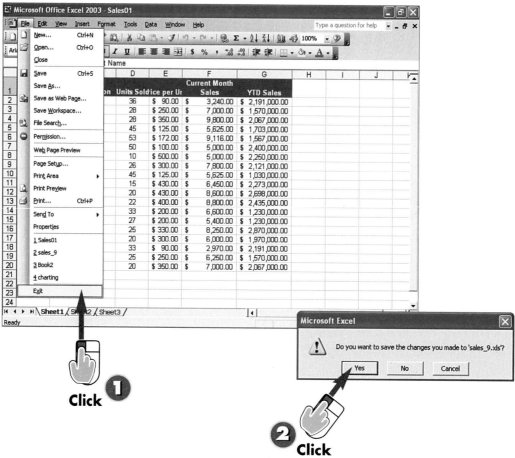

Click 1

Click 2

1 Open the **File** menu and choose **Exit**. If you have not edited any of your open workbooks since saving them, Excel will close.

2 If you have edited an open workbook since saving it last, Excel prompts you to save your changes. Click **Yes** to save changes or **No** if you don't want to save your work.

End

TIP

Quick exit
Another way to exit Excel is to simply click the Close (X) button in the upper-right corner of the Excel screen. If you haven't saved the spreadsheets you are currently working on, Excel will display the message box from step 2.

TIP

Closing a spreadsheet versus exiting Excel
Sometimes people get closing a workbook confused with exiting the entire Excel application. If all you want to do is close the workbook you are working in and work in a different one, refer to the preceding task.

Creating a New Workbook

Start

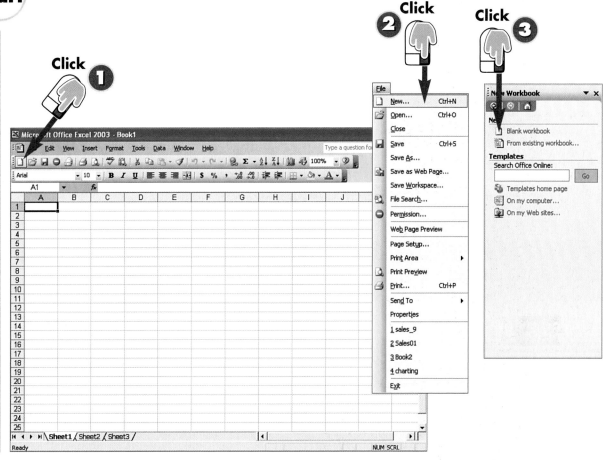

Click 1

Click 2

Click 3

① Click the **New** button on the Standard toolbar. Excel opens a new workbook, with A1 as the active cell.

② Another way to create a new workbook (with more options) is to open the **File** menu and choose **New**.

③ The New Workbook task pane opens. If you choose **Blank Workbook**, a new workbook will open as in step 1.

End

INTRODUCTION

Excel presents a new blank workbook each time you start the application. You can create another new workbook at any time, however. For example, when you save and close one workbook, you might want to begin a new one.

TIP

Saving a new workbook
When you go to save the new workbook you created based on a current workbook (in step 4), you will automatically be asked to save the workbook as a new filename in the Save As dialog box.

TIP

Understanding default filenames
The default filename for each new workbook (Book1, Book2, Book3, and so on) increases sequentially as you open new books. If you exit and restart Excel, the numbers begin at 1 again.

Opening a Workbook

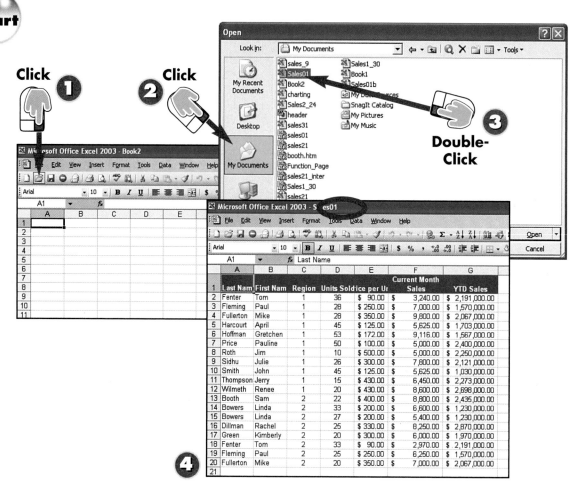

1 Click the **Open** button on the Standard toolbar.

2 In the Open dialog box, click the **My Documents** icon or use the **Look In** drop-down list to move through the folders to find the file you want.

3 Double-click the file you want to open in the Open dialog box (for example, **Sales01**).

4 Excel opens the workbook.

Switching Between Open Workbooks

Start

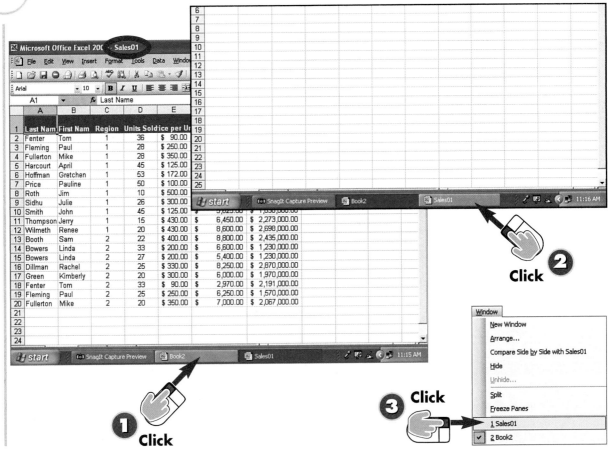

Click **1**

Click **2**

Click **3**

1 Click a workbook button (in this case, the **Book2** button) on the taskbar; this workbook becomes the active application and workbook.

2 Click a different workbook button (here, the **Sales01** button) on the taskbar; this workbook becomes the active application and workbook.

3 You can also select a workbook's filename from the **Window** menu to switch to that workbook.

End

Switching Between Worksheets

Start

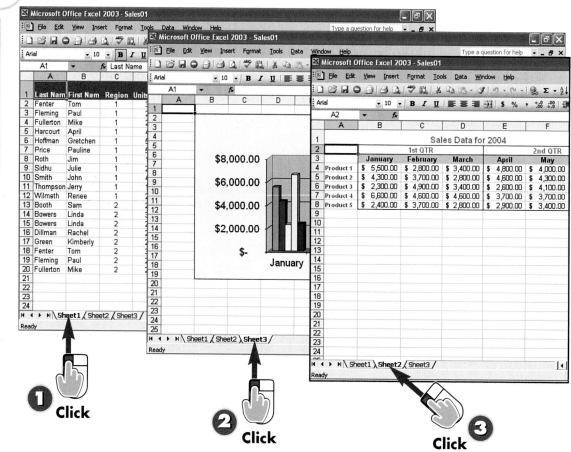

1 Click

2 Click

3 Click

① Click a worksheet tab (in this example, the **Sheet1** tab) to see the contents in that worksheet.

② Click a different worksheet tab (here, the **Sheet3** tab) to see the contents of that worksheet.

③ Click yet another worksheet tab (in this case, the **Sheet2** tab) to see the contents of that worksheet.

End

TIP

Scrolling through sheets
If your workbook contains more than the default three worksheets, you can scroll among the tabs using the scroll buttons in the far-left bottom corner of the worksheet.

Viewing Multiple Workbooks

Start

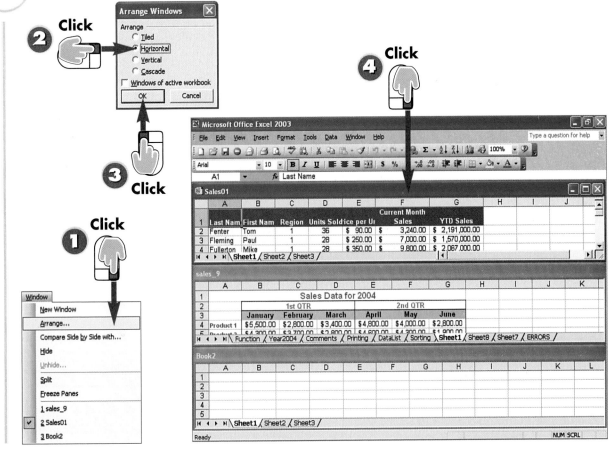

Click 2

Click 3

Click 1

Click 4

---

1 Open the **Window** menu and choose **Arrange** to open the Arrange Windows dialog box. (Note that you should have more than one workbook open in Excel.)

2 Select how you want the windows arranged (for example, **Horizontal**).

3 Click **OK**.

4 Multiple workbooks are displayed simultaneously. Click on the title bar or in the body of the workbook you want to work in to make it the active worksheet.

End

Comparing Workbooks

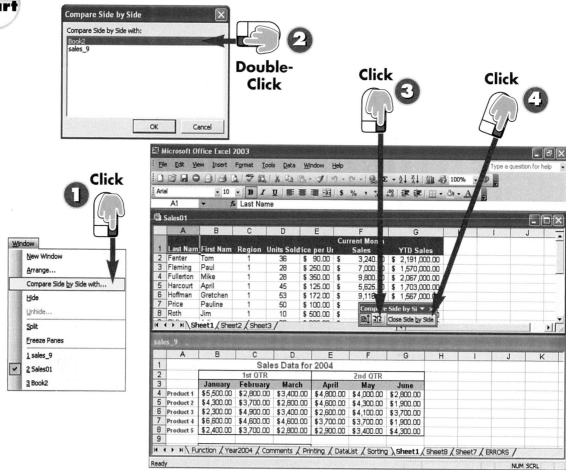

1 With two workbooks open, open the **Window** menu and choose **Compare Side by Side with [filename]**. Excel arranges the workbook windows.

2 If you have more than two workbooks open, the Compare Side by Side dialog box opens. Double-click the name of the file you want to compare with your current workbook.

3 If you don't already see both workbooks, you might need to click the **Reset Window Position** button on the Compare Side by Side toolbar.

4 Click the **Close Side by Side** button on the toolbar when finished; whichever document was last active will be full-size in the workbook window.

End

There might be times when you need to compare two worksheets, perhaps to see similarities or differences, or to simply verify data. Excel allows you to compare workbooks easily, and even lets you scroll through both worksheets simultaneously so you don't have to keep switching between the visible worksheets to scroll down.

TIP

Back to one workbook
To return to viewing only one workbook (maximizing the workbook), double-click on the title bar of the workbook in which you want to work. You can also open the **Window** menu and choose **Close Side by Side**.

TIP

Scrolling
The **Synchronous Scrolling** button on the Compare Side by Side toolbar allows you to scroll at the same rate in both documents.

Inserting and Deleting Worksheets

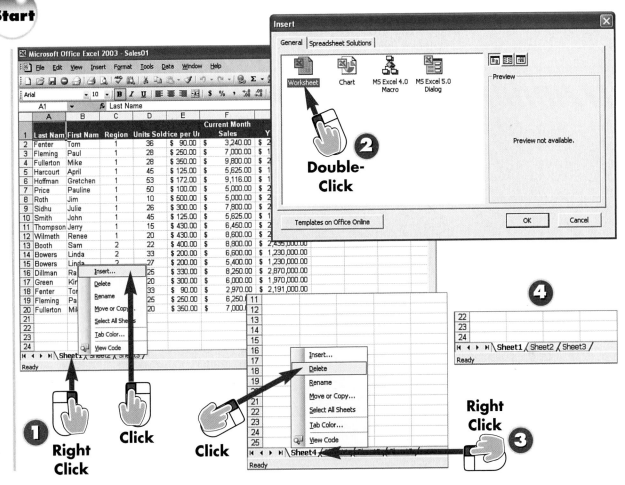

Start

Double-Click ②

Right Click ①

Click

Click

Right Click ③

④

Right Click

1. Right-click on the tab of the worksheet that you want a new worksheet placed *in front of* and select **Insert** from the shortcut menu to open the Insert dialog box.

2. Double-click on the type of worksheet you want to insert (for example, **Worksheet**); a new worksheet (the next sheet number in the sequence) will appear.

3. To delete a worksheet, right-click on the tab of the worksheet you want to delete and select **Delete** from the shortcut menu.

4. The worksheet (and the tab associated with it) is deleted.

End

INTRODUCTION

There might be times when the default three worksheets per workbook just aren't enough. You will likely need to insert additional worksheets and sometimes even delete ones you no longer use. Just be sure when you delete worksheets, that you definitely no longer need the information they contain.

TIP

Inserting worksheet
As an alternative, you can open the **Insert** menu and choose **Worksheet** to automatically insert a worksheet into your workbook *in front of* the currently selected worksheet. If you need to rearrange the worksheets, check out the task "Moving or Copying Worksheets."

Renaming Worksheets

Start

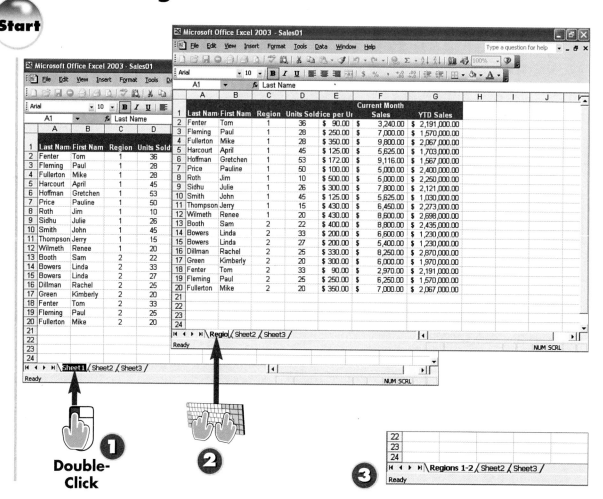

Double-Click

1   Double-click the sheet tab of the sheet you want to rename (for example, **Sheet1**). The current name is highlighted. Alternatively, right-click Sheet1 and select **Rename**.

2   Type the new name and press the **Enter** key.

3   Excel displays the new name on the worksheet tab.

End

The default worksheet names, Sheet1, Sheet2, and so on, aren't all that descriptive. If you use several sheets in a workbook, you should rename them so that you know what each sheet contains. Providing more descriptive names for your worksheets makes switching from one worksheet to another easier, too.

TIP

Saving workbook names
Don't confuse worksheet names with workbook (file) names. They aren't the same. You still need to name and save the workbook, as described in the task "Saving a Workbook" earlier in this part.

TIP

Scrolling through tabs
If you have several worksheets in a single workbook, you can scroll among the tabs using the scroll buttons in the bottom-left corner of the worksheet.

Adding Worksheet Tab Colors

Start

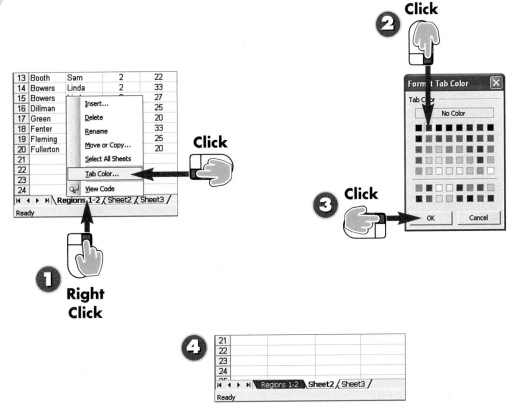

Click ②

Click

Click ③

Right Click ①

④

1 Right-click on the tab of the worksheet you want to color, and select **Tab Color** from the shortcut menu.

2 The Format Tab Color dialog box opens. Click on the desired color.

3 Click **OK**.

4 The tab color is applied.

End

INTRODUCTION

The more you work in Excel, the more you will need to organize and keep track of your worksheets and the data they contain. If you want to indicate something specific about a worksheet (for example, if a worksheet contains information on a particular sales region that is not doing well), you can assign it a tab color.

TIP

Renaming tabs
You can double-click on a worksheet tab to rename it. Simply type in the new name and continue working.

Moving or Copying Worksheets

Start

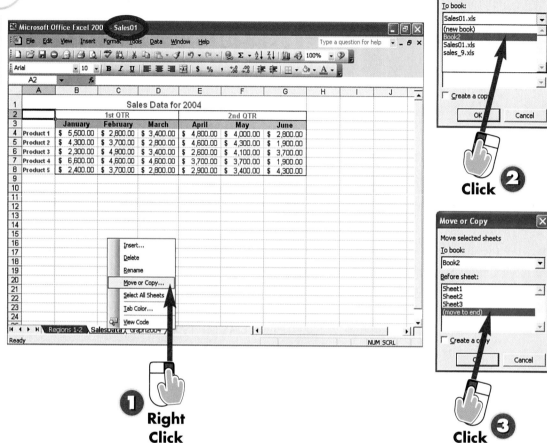

Click ②

Right Click

Click ③

① Right-click the worksheet tab that you want to move or copy, and select **Move or Copy** from the shortcut menu. The Move or Copy dialog box opens.

② Click the **down arrow** next to the **To book** field and choose from the open workbook to which you want to move or copy the selected worksheet.

③ In the **Before sheet** list, click the name of the worksheet in front of which you want the selected sheet to be placed, or choose **(move to end)**.

INTRODUCTION

When Excel inserts a new worksheet, it always places it *in front of* the currently selected worksheet. If you aren't in the correct worksheet tab before you insert the worksheet, however, you can simply move it. In addition, Excel understands that many times data in one worksheet can be used as a starting point in new worksheets and even other workbooks (or perhaps you need multiple sets of data), so you can copy a worksheet.

TIP

Drag move
You can also click on a worksheet tab and drag it in front of or after another worksheet tab to change its location. This is a lot faster if all you want to do is move around your worksheets.

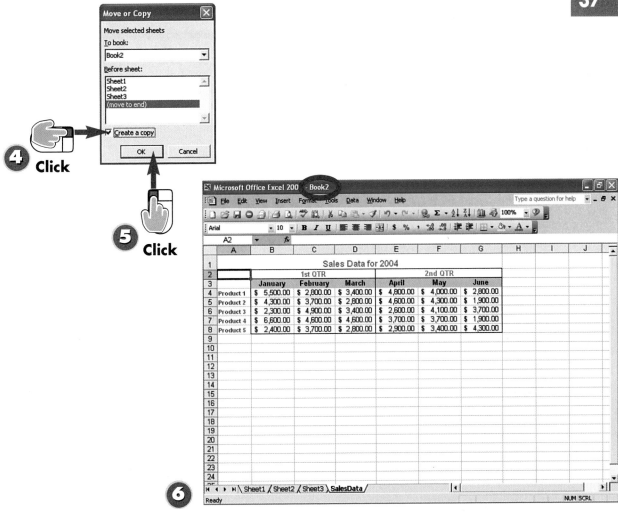

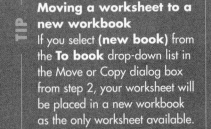
Click

Click

4. Click the **Create a copy** check box if you want to *copy* the worksheet (as shown here); if your intent is to *move* the worksheet, simply leave it unchecked.

5. Click **OK**.

6. The worksheet is copied to the new location.

End

TIP

Moving a worksheet to a new workbook
If you select **(new book)** from the **To book** drop-down list in the Move or Copy dialog box from step 2, your worksheet will be placed in a new workbook as the only worksheet available.

TIP

Moving a worksheet
If you choose to move a worksheet to another location instead of copying the worksheet, it will no longer be accessible in the current workbook. Make sure you really want to remove the worksheet.

Zooming a Worksheet

Start

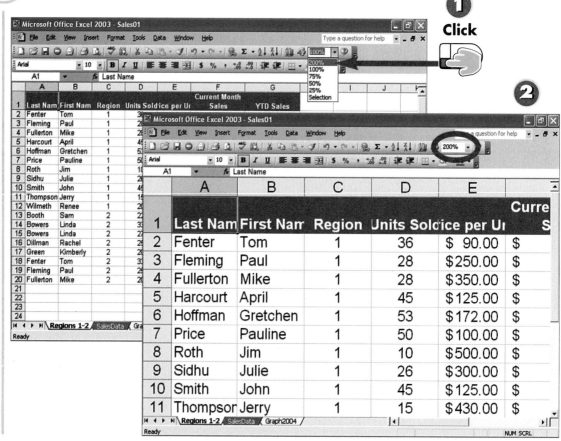

1 Click

2

① Click the **down arrow** next to the **Zoom** field in the Standard toolbar and select the zoom percentage you want from the list that appears—for example, **200%**.

② The worksheet appears with the Zoom setting you specified.

End

If you want to zoom in and get a closer look at data in your worksheet, you can select a higher percentage of magnification. On the other hand, if you want to zoom out so more of the worksheet shows on the screen at one glance, select a lower percentage of magnification.

TIP

Print Preview zoom
You also can zoom in Print Preview. To do so, simply click on the worksheet to zoom in; click again to zoom out. You also can click the **Zoom** button in the Print Preview toolbar.

TIP

Typing the percentage
Besides selecting one of the Zoom percentage options, you can click in the list box area and type the exact percentage.

Going to a Particular Cell

Start

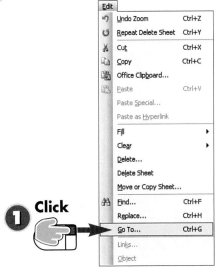

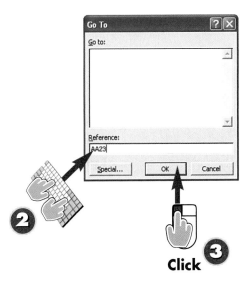

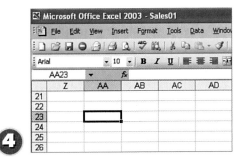

1 Open the **Edit** menu and choose **Go To** to open the Go To dialog box.

2 In the **Reference** field, type the cell reference for the cell you want to move to (for example, **AA23**).

3 Click **OK**.

4 Excel moves to the selected cell.

End

INTRODUCTION
Moving from cell to cell with the mouse or keyboard is fine when you want to move a short distance. If you want to move farther, however, you might want to investigate the Go To command. This command enables you to move quickly to any cell in the worksheet.

TIP
Quick Go To
Press the **Ctrl+G** shortcut key to quickly open the Go To dialog box.

TIP
Quick home
Press the **Ctrl+Home** shortcut key to quickly return to the beginning of the worksheet at cell A1.

Freezing Rows and Columns

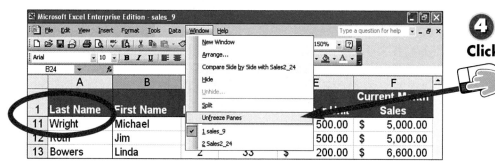

1. Click in the cell to the right of and below the area you want to freeze. (Typically this is cell **B2** if your main header row is Row 1 and your main column is Column A.

2. Click Freeze Panes.

3. Using the keyboard arrow keys, move through the worksheet. Notice the frozen rows and columns you selected enable you to reference data with the appropriate titles.

4. Open the **Window** menu and select **Unfreeze Panes** to unfreeze the columns and rows.

End

Splitting a Worksheet

Start

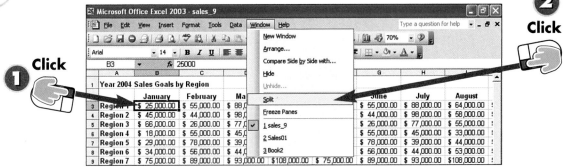

Click ①

Click ②

③

Click ④

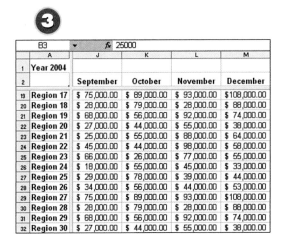

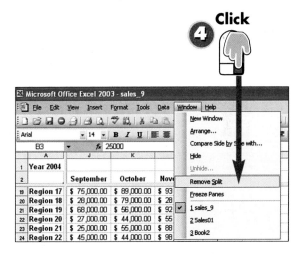

End

① Click in the cell to the right of and below the area you want to split.

② Open the **Window** menu and choose **Split** to insert the horizontal and vertical split bars (you can click on and drag them to other locations if necessary).

③ Move through the worksheet and see how easily you can view other parts of the worksheet simultaneously.

④ Open the **Window** menu and choose **Remove Split** to remove the horizontal and vertical split bars.

INTRODUCTION

By *splitting* a worksheet, you can scroll independently into different horizontal and vertical parts of a worksheet. This is useful if you want to view different parts of a worksheet or copy and paste between different areas of a large worksheet.

TIP

Moving the split bars

By moving the split bars, you can simultaneously view different portions of your workbook. For example, if you need to reference data in cells AA20 through AD30 and compare them with the data in cells A1 through D10, you can move the split between the locations and scroll until you see both sets of cells in the split areas. If you want to keep row and column labels visible as you work and scroll, see the task "Freezing Rows and Columns" earlier in this part for more information.

Protecting and Sharing Workbooks

Start

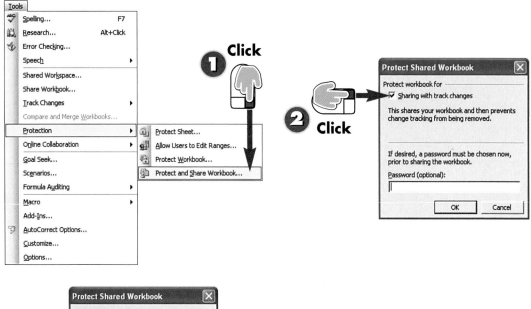

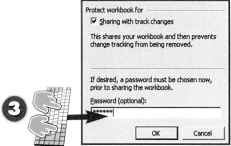

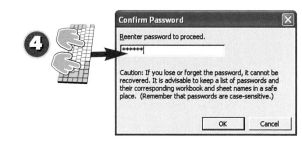

1 Open the **Tools** menu, choose **Protection**, and select **Protect and Share Workbook** to open the Protect Shared Workbook dialog box.

2 Click the **Sharing with Track Changes** check box, which activates the **Password (optional)** text box.

3 Type a password in the **Password (optional)** text box, and press the **Enter** key (or click **OK**). Users will be required to enter the password to access this workbook.

4 Type the same password in the Confirm Password dialog box, and press the **Enter** key.

INTRODUCTION

When you share files with other users, you might find it useful to protect your workbooks. You can protect your workbooks by restricting access to the workbook and preventing changes being made within each particular workbook. The three protection options are Protect Sheet, Protect Workbook, and Protect and Share Workbook. Don't forget any passwords you assign to your workbooks; otherwise, you are not able to access the workbook.

TIP

Alternative file-sharing options There are two other file-sharing options in Excel. **Protect Sheet** allows you to protect the contents, objects, and scenarios in a worksheet (and assign a password). **Protect Workbook** allows you to protect the structure and windows in a workbook (and assign a password).

Click

3

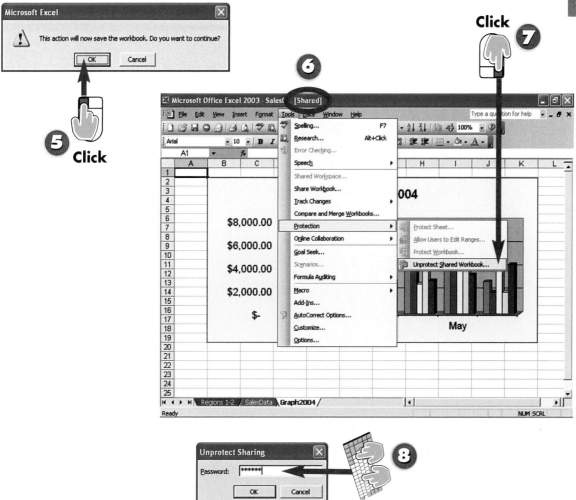

5 Excel notifies you that this action will save the workbook. Click **OK** when you receive this message.

6 **[Shared]** now appears to the right of the filename in the title bar.

7 Open the **Tools** menu, choose **Protection**, and select **Unprotect Shared Workbook** to open the Unprotect Sharing dialog box.

8 Type the workbook's password in the **Password** field and click **OK** to disable the password protection. **[Shared]** no longer appears in the Title bar.

End

Password protection

TIP

After you have protected your workbook with a password, send the file to someone else and have him try to open the file with and without the password. If he enters the correct password, the file opens; if he enters an incorrect password, he is denied the ability to open the file.

Editing Worksheets

The old paper-and-pencil method of calculating was a pain because if you made a mistake or forgot something, you had to do a lot of erasing—maybe even redo the whole thing. With an electronic worksheet, however, you can easily make changes. Forget something? You can insert a cell, row, or column. You also can delete entries. You can change a value, find and replace data, and even check for spelling errors. Besides editing the data in your worksheets, you can add comments to remind yourself of information and track when changes are made and by whom.

Inserting Comments and Changes

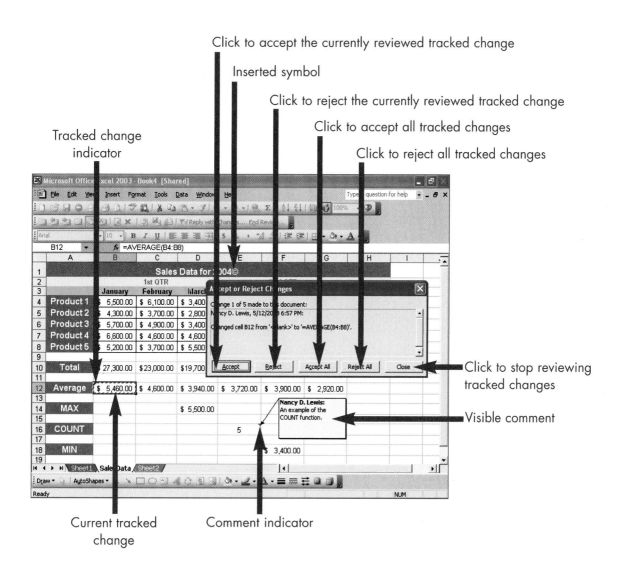

Click to accept the currently reviewed tracked change

Inserted symbol

Click to reject the currently reviewed tracked change

Click to accept all tracked changes

Click to reject all tracked changes

Tracked change indicator

Click to stop reviewing tracked changes

Visible comment

Current tracked change

Comment indicator

Editing Data

Start

Double-Click

1

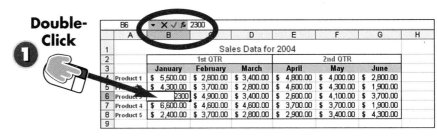

B6	▼ X √ *fx* 2300						
	A	B	C	D	E	F	G	H

1 Sales Data for 2004

	1st QTR			2nd QTR		
	January	February	March	April	May	June
Product 1	$ 5,500.00	$ 2,800.00	$ 3,400.00	$ 4,800.00	$ 4,000.00	$ 2,800.00
Product 2	$ 4,300.00	$ 3,700.00	$ 2,800.00	$ 4,600.00	$ 4,300.00	$ 1,900.00
Product 3	2300	$ 4,900.00	$ 3,400.00	$ 2,600.00	$ 4,100.00	$ 3,700.00
Product 4	$ 6,600.00	$ 4,600.00	$ 4,600.00	$ 3,700.00	$ 3,700.00	$ 1,900.00
Product 5	$ 2,400.00	$ 3,700.00	$ 2,800.00	$ 2,900.00	$ 3,400.00	$ 4,300.00

▼ X √ *fx* 2300

	A	B	C	D
1			Sales Data fo
2			1st QTR	
3		January	February	Mar
4	Product 1	$ 5,500.00	$ 2,800.00	$ 3,40
5	Product 2	$ 4,300.00	$ 3,700.00	$ 2,80
6	Product 3	230	$ 4,900.00	$ 3,40
7	Product 4	$ 6,600.00	$ 4,600.00	$ 4,60
8	Product 5	$ 2,700.00	$ 3,700.00	$ 2,80
9				

2

▼ X √ *fx* 5700

	A	B	C	D
1				Sales Data fo
2			1st QTR	
3		January	February	March
4	Product 1	$ 5,500.00	$ 2,800.00	$ 3,400.00
5	Product 2	$ 4,300.00	$ 3,700.00	$ 2,8
6	Product 3	570	$ 4,900.00	$ 3,4
7	Product 4	$ 6,600.00	$ 4,600.00	$ 4,6
8	Product 5	$ 2,400.00	$ 3,700.00	$ 2,8
9				

3

B7	▼	*fx* 6600	
	A	B	C	D
1				Sales Data fo
2			1st QTR	
3		January	February	March
4	Product 1	$ 5,500.00	$ 2,800.00	$ 3,400.00
5	Product 2	$ 4,300.00	$ 3,700.00	$ 2,800.00
6	Product 3	$ 5,700.00	$ 4,900.00	$ 3,400.00
7	Product 4	$ 6,600.00	$ 4,600.00	$ 4,600.00
8	Product 5	$ 2,400.00	$ 3,700.00	$ 2,800.00
9				

4

1 Double-click the cell you want to edit. The insertion point appears to the left of the data in the current cell (the entry also appears in the Formula bar).

2 Press the left and/or right arrow keys to move the insertion point where you want to make the change.

3 Type your changes (using the Backspace key if necessary).

4 Press the **Enter** key to accept your changes (the cell below becomes the active cell).

Being able to make changes to the values in your worksheet is what makes Excel such a valuable analysis tool. You can change any of your entries and see how that affects the formulas in your worksheet. To put the active cell in Edit mode, press F2 on the keyboard or click the mouse pointer on the data line of the Edit bar. You can then continue typing at the end of the current data, use the Backspace key to delete some data, use the left and right arrow keys to move through the data, or use the Home and End keys to move quickly to the beginning or the end of the data. Press Enter when you have finished editing the data.

Pressing the Enter key
You can't press an arrow key to confirm the entry and move to another cell. You must press **Enter**.

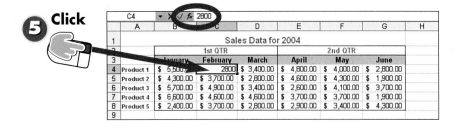

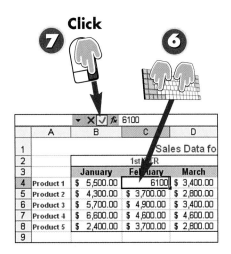

5 Click in the next cell you want to edit and press the **F2** key. The insertion point appears to the right of the data in the current cell (the entry also appears in the Formula bar).

6 Type your edits.

7 Click the green checkmark **Enter** button to accept the changes.

8 The changes are accepted and the edited cell remains the active cell.

End

Selecting characters
You can drag the mouse pointer across characters to select them. Press the **Delete** key to delete the selected characters.

Copying and moving
In addition to editing data, you might find it useful to copy and move data to a different location. See the tasks "Cutting, Copying, and Pasting Data" and "Moving Data" later in this part for more information on copying and moving data.

Overwriting and Deleting Data

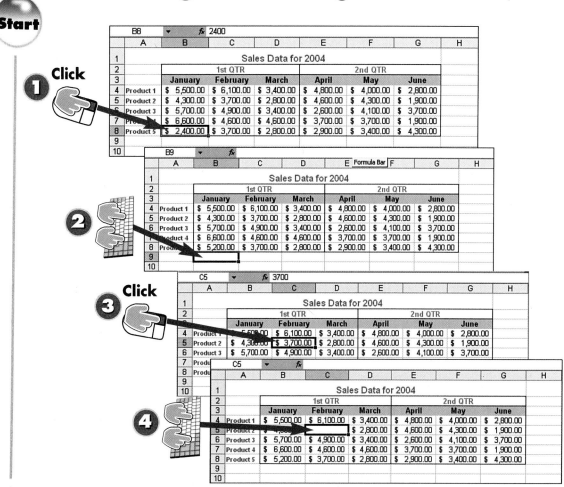

Start

Click ①

②

Click ③

④

1 Click the cell whose contents you want to overwrite, making it the active cell.

2 Type the correct data into the cell and press the **Enter** key.

3 Click the cell whose contents you want to delete, making it the active cell.

4 Press the **Delete** key to delete the data in a cell.

End

When you *overwrite* a cell, you replace the cell's contents with new data. Overwriting is handy when you want to correct typing errors or when a cell contains the wrong data. You can also easily erase the contents of a cell by using the Delete key. Erasing a cell is useful when you change your mind about the contents after you enter the data in the cell. You might find that a piece of data you initially typed into a cell is incorrect and needs to be changed.

Overwriting formulas

Be careful not to overwrite formulas if that is not what you intended. If you overwrite a formula with a constant value, Excel no longer updates the formula. If you accidentally overwrite a formula but you've saved your spreadsheet recently, you can reopen the spreadsheet to a version saved before you overwrote the formula.

Undoing and Redoing Changes

Start

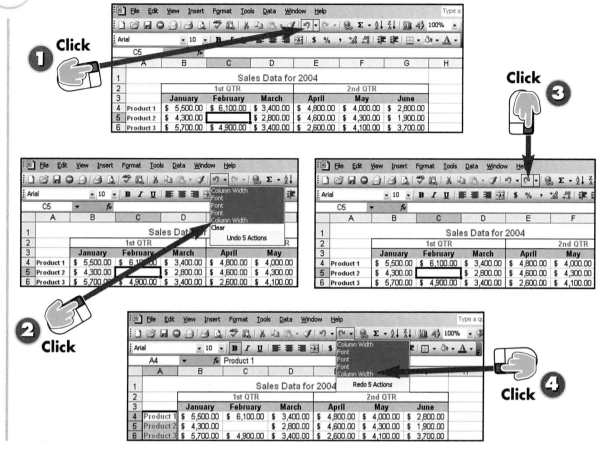

Click ①

Click ③

Click ②

Click ④

① To undo your most recent action, click the **Undo** button on the Standard toolbar. Continue clicking the **Undo** button to undo more of your recent actions.

② To undo multiple actions at the same time, click the **down arrow** next to the **Undo** button and select the action you want to undo.

③ If you undo an action in error, click the **Redo** button on the Standard toolbar to redo the action. Continue clicking the **Redo** button to redo more actions.

④ To redo multiple actions at the same time, click the **down arrow** next to the **Redo** button and select the actions.

End

INTRODUCTION

If you make a mistake while working on your spreadsheet, and you detect your error immediately, you can undo your action. In addition, if you undo an action by mistake, you can use Excel to quickly redo it.

Keyboard undo

A quick and easy way to undo an action is to use the **Ctrl+Z** shortcut key; you can redo an action using **Ctrl+Y**.

Undo not available?

When you save the worksheet, the available actions in the Undo/Redo lists are erased, so make sure you are happy with any changes before you perform a save operation.

Inserting Cells

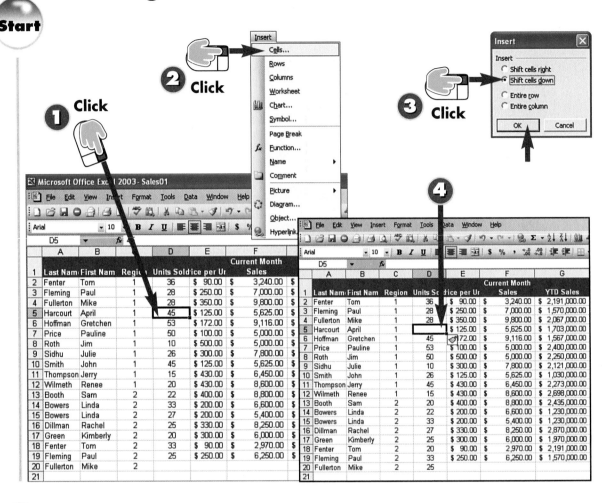

1. Click the spot in your worksheet where you want to insert a cell.

2. Open the **Insert** menu and choose **Cells** to open the Insert dialog box.

3. Select what you want to happen to the existing cells when the new cell is inserted; for example, **Shift cells down**, and click **OK**.

4. The existing cells shift and a new cell is inserted.

End

There might be times when you are entering data into your worksheet and notice that you typed the wrong information, so that you are off by one cell in a column or row. To avoid retyping all the data again, or copying and pasting, you can insert cells and shift the current cells to their correct locations.

Using the shortcut menu
Another way to insert a cell is to right-click the spot in your worksheet where you want the new cell to appear and choose **Insert** from the shortcut menu that appears. The Insert dialog box opens; proceed as normal.

Using the Insert Options Format Painter smart tag
When the new cell is inserted, click the Insert Options Format Painter smart tag to apply formatting to the inserted cell. Format the new cell like the cell above it or below it, or specify that no formatting be applied.

Deleting Cells

Start

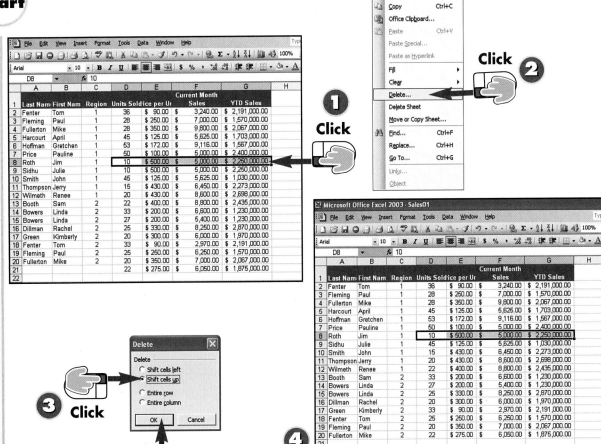

Click ①

Click ②

Click ③

Click

④

End

① Select the cell (or cells) you want to delete.

② Open the **Edit** menu and choose **Delete** to open the Delete dialog box.

③ Select what you want to happen to the rest of the cells when the selected cells are deleted; for example, **Shift cells up**, and click **OK**.

④ The selected cell(s) are deleted, and other cells are shifted.

As you work with worksheets, you might find that data needs to be eliminated to keep the worksheet up-to-date. Or you might accidentally add an extraneous cell of data in a row or column. To avoid typing all your data again to rectify the error, you can delete extraneous cells and shift other cells to their correct locations.

#REF! error

If the **#REF!** error appears in a cell after you delete a cell, it means you deleted a cell or cells that contained data that your worksheet needs to calculate a formula. To resolve the problem, undo the change (refer to the task "Undoing and Redoing Changes" earlier in this part to learn how).

Inserting and Deleting Rows

PART 3

Start

Click ①

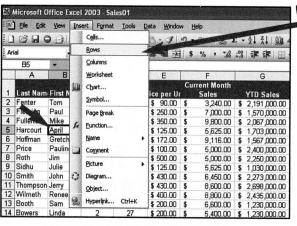

②

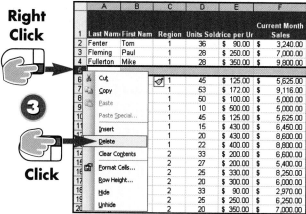

Right Click

③

Click

④

① ** After you click a cell above which you want to add a row, open the **Insert menu and choose **Rows**.

**② ** A new row is inserted (notice the Insert Options Format Painter smart tag, which allows you to format the row like the one above it, below it, or to apply no formatting).

③ ** To delete a row, right-click the row header for the row you want to delete, and choose **Delete from the shortcut menu that appears.

**④ ** The row is deleted.

End

You can insert extra rows into a worksheet to make more room for additional data or formulas. Adding more rows, which gives the appearance of adding space between rows, can also make the worksheet easier to read. Alternatively, you can delete rows from a worksheet to close up some empty space or remove unwanted information.

Automatic formula row updates

When you insert a new row, Excel automatically updates any formulas affected by the insertion (see Part 5 for more information).

#REF! error

If the **#REF!** error appears in a cell after you delete a row, it means you deleted a cell or cells that contained data that your worksheet needs to calculate a formula. To resolve the problem, undo the change (refer to the task "Undoing and Redoing Changes.")

Inserting and Deleting Columns

Start

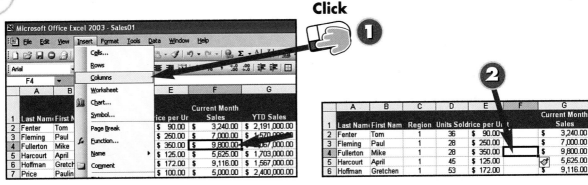

Click

①

②

Right Click **③** **Click**

④

---

① After you click a cell to the left of which you want to add a column, open the **Insert** menu and choose **Columns**.

② A new column is inserted (notice the Insert Options Format Painter smart tag, which allows you to format the column like the one to its left, to its right, or to apply no formatting).

③ To delete a column, right-click the column heading of the column you want to delete, and choose **Delete** from the shortcut menu that appears.

④ The column is deleted.

End

INTRODUCTION

You can insert extra columns into a worksheet to make room for more data or formulas. Adding more columns, which gives the appearance of adding space between columns, can also make the worksheet easier to read. Alternatively, you might want to delete columns from a worksheet to close up some empty space or remove unwanted information.

TIP

Automatic formula column updates
When you insert a new column, Excel automatically updates any formulas affected by the insertion (see Part 5 for more information).

TIP

#REF! error
If the **#REF!** error appears in a cell after you delete a column, it means you deleted a cell contained data that your worksheet needs to calculate a formula. To resolve the problem, undo the recent change.

Cutting, Copying, and Pasting Data

Start

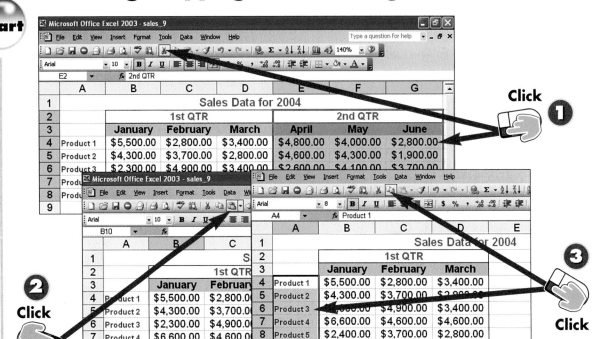

Click ❶

Click ❷

Click ❸

---

❶ Select the cells you want to cut and click the **Cut** button. These cells now display an active selection border.

❷ Click in the worksheet where you want to paste the cut data and click the **Paste** button.

❸ The cut cells appear in the new location. Select the cells you want to copy and click the **Copy** button. These cells now display an active selection border.

INTRODUCTION

You can save the time and trouble of retyping duplicate information in a worksheet by cutting or copying cell text and data and pasting it. In addition to the cut, copy, and paste commands, use the Office Clipboard task pane to work with multiple items known as "scraps." For example, if you need to copy two different selections of data from the beginning of a worksheet to two different locations toward the end of a worksheet, you can use the Clipboard to perform the procedure in fewer steps than if you were to copy and paste each separately.

TIP

Cutting versus copying
When you want to move (rather than copy) data from its current location to a new location, click the **Cut** button on the Standard toolbar. The Cut option removes the selected value from the old location.

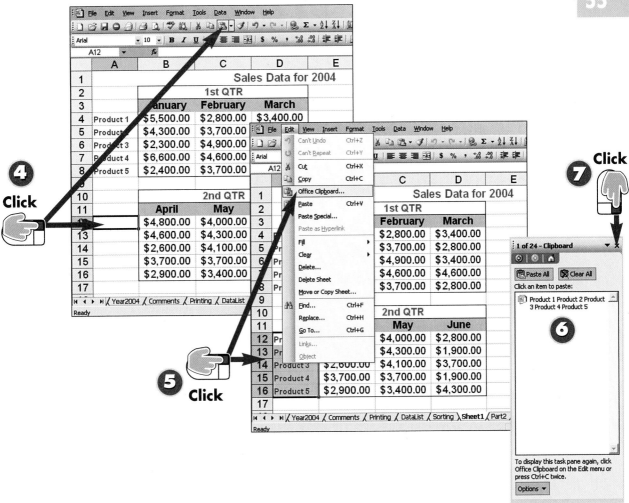

4 Click in the worksheet where you want to paste the copied data and click the **Paste** button.

5 The copied text is pasted in the new location. Unless the Clipboard task pane is already displayed, open the **Edit** menu and choose **Office Clipboard**.

6 Notice the copied data is displayed on the clipboard. Additional cut or copied items will display on the clipboard; click each "scrap" to paste them.

7 Click the **Close (x)** button on the Clipboard Task pane when finished.

End

Using the Paste button
You can still use the **Copy** or **Cut** and **Paste** buttons on the Standard toolbar when you want to perform a single cut/paste or copy/paste.

Using the Clipboard
If you want to clear all the items copied to the Clipboard, click the **Clear All** button in the Clipboard task pane. To paste all the items saved to the Clipboard in one location, click the **Paste All** button in the task pane.

Pasting formulas
If you paste cells using **Ctrl+V**, you can paste cell *formulas*. If you paste cells with formulas from the multi-element Clipboard, you paste the *values*, not the formulas.

Flipping Rows and Columns

Start

Click

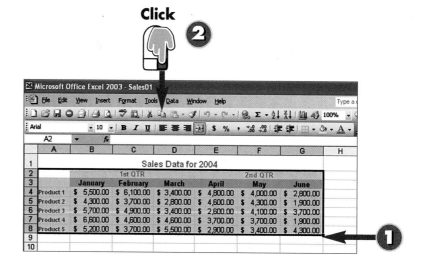

Click

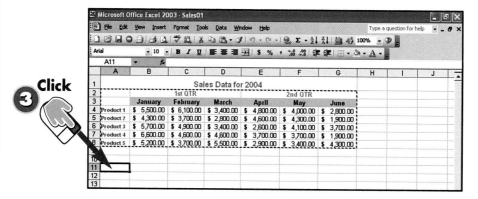

1 Select the range you want to transpose.

2 Click the **Copy** button on the Standard toolbar.

3 Click the first cell in which you want to paste the range.

INTRODUCTION

Transposing (flipping rows and columns) is a special copy feature you might need to use if you want to change the layout of your worksheet. For example, suppose your worksheet is set up with quarters in rows and divisions in columns, but that your boss prefers the opposite: quarters in columns and divisions in rows. In a case such as this one, you can flip the worksheet.

CAUTION

You cannot transpose a range of cells onto the original range selection. You must first transpose the range and then move the range.

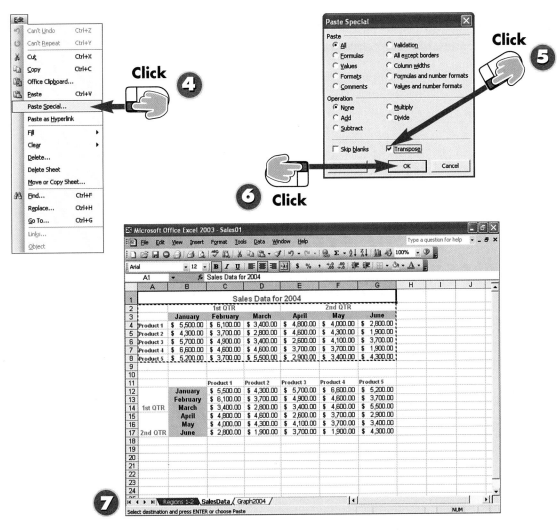

4. Open the **Edit** menu and choose **Paste Special** to open the Paste Special dialog box.

5. Click the **Transpose** check box to mark it.

6. Click **OK**.

7. The range is transposed (or flipped).

End

Using the Paste Special dialog box

Notice that the Paste Special dialog box enables you to paste all different types of formulas, values, formats, and so on. Practice using this dialog box and see the different types of results that you get.

Eliminating the original data

To eliminate the original data that you transposed, you must delete it. Refer to the task "Overwriting and Deleting Data" earlier in this part for more information.

Moving Data

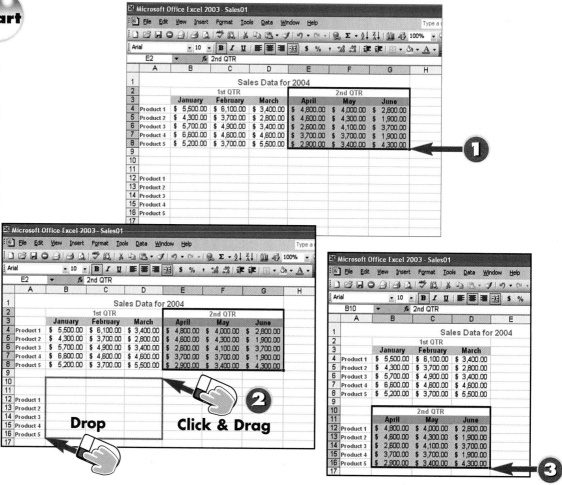

1 Select the cells you want to move.

2 Click the border of the selected cells and drag the cells to the location in the work-sheet where you want to paste the cell data.

3 Release the mouse button to drop the data in its new location.

Excel lets you move information from one cell into another cell, which means you do not have to type the data into the new cell and then erase the data in the old location. You might want to move data in a worksheet because the layout of the worksheet has changed.

Undoing a move

If you move the wrong data or move the data to the wrong loca-tion, click the **Undo** button on the Standard toolbar to undo the most recent move. Then start over. (See the task "Undoing and Redoing Changes" earlier in this part for more information.)

Finding Data

Start

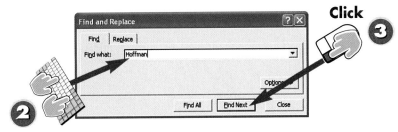
Click **3**

2

1 **Click**

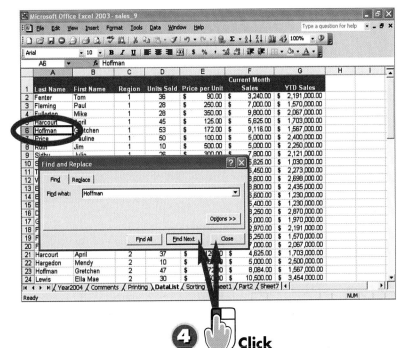

4 **Click**

1 Open the **Edit** menu and choose **Find**. The Find and Replace dialog box opens with the Find tab displayed.

2 In the **Find what** text box, type the data you want to find.

3 Click the **Find Next** button.

4 Excel finds the first instance of the data you typed and makes the cell that contains it the active cell. Click **Find Next** to search for the next instance, or **Close** to end.

End

There might be times when you'll need to find specific information in a large spreadsheet. For example, suppose you want to quickly find the row that deals with sales data in Region 5 of your company. Instead of scanning each row for the data you need, which can be time-consuming, you can use Excel's Find feature.

Finding all instances of data
Click the **Find All** button in the Find and Replace dialog box to view a list, complete with cell locations and worksheet tab names, of all the instances of the data you entered in the **Find what** text box.

INTRODUCTION

TIP

Replacing Data

Start

Click ③

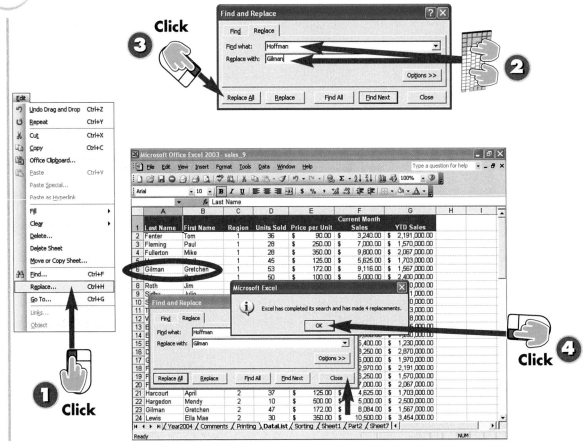

Click ①

Click ②

Click ④

① Open the **Edit** menu and choose **Replace**. The Find and Replace dialog box opens with the Replace tab displayed.

② In the **Find what** text box, type the data you would like to find. Press the **Tab** key to move the cursor to the **Replace with** text box, and type the replacement data.

③ Click **Replace All** to replace all instances of the data you typed. (Or, click **Find Next** to find the first instance of the data, and click **Replace** to replace it.)

④ Excel notifies you of the number of replacements it made; click **OK**. When you're done using the Find and Replace dialog box, click its **Close** button to close it.

End

Suppose you discover that you consistently misspelled a company's name in your worksheet, or that a person you reference in several cells has gotten married and changed her name. Fortunately, Excel enables you to search for instances of incorrect or outdated data and replace it with new data using its Find and Replace feature.

Narrowing search criteria

Click the **Options** button on the Find and Replace dialog box to make your search criteria more specific. To conduct a case-sensitive search (for example, finding all instances of **Hoffman** but not **hoffman**), choose the **Match case** option. Choose **Match entire cell contents** to limit your search to cells that contain no more and no less than the data you type (for example, to find all instances of **Hoffman**, but not **Hoffmann**. You can also specify where the search should be conducted (**Within Sheet** or **Within Workbook**), ways to search (**By Rows** or **By Columns**).

Adding and Viewing Cell Comments

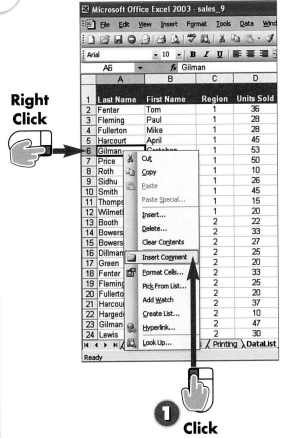

Right Click

Click

① Right-click the cell to which you want to add a comment, and choose **Insert Comment** from the shortcut menu that appears.

② Type the desired text into the comment area. When you're finished, click anywhere in the worksheet to accept the comment.

③ The cell's upper-right corner now contains a red triangle, indicating the presence of a comment. To view the comment, move the mouse pointer over the triangle.

④ The comment appears as a ScreenTip. To remove it from view, simply move the mouse pointer away from the triangle.

End

Editing and Deleting Cell Comments

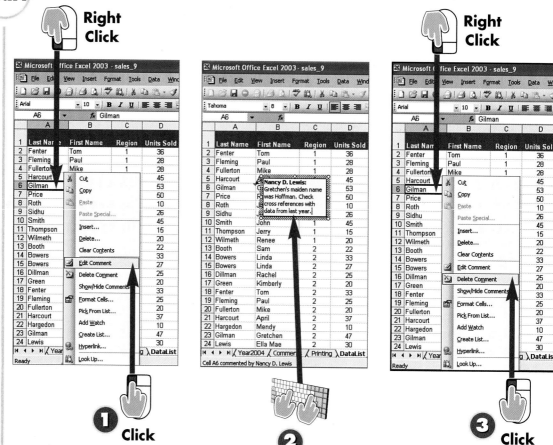

Right Click

Right Click

1 Click

2

3 Click

1 Right-click the cell that contains the comment you want to edit and choose **Edit Comment** from the shortcut menu that appears.

2 Type the edits into the comment area, and click anywhere in the worksheet area to accept the changes to the comment.

3 To delete a comment, right-click the cell that contains the comment and choose **Delete Comment** from the shortcut menu. The comment is deleted.

End

Excel lets you quickly edit or delete a comment. For example, if you no longer need the note to yourself or want to change the information about a cell.

Displaying comments

You can make it so that Excel automatically displays the full text of a cell's comments while you work in the worksheet. To do so, right-click the commented cell and choose **Show/Hide Comment** from the shortcut menu that appears. To re-hide the comment, right-click the commented cell and choose **Hide Comment**.

Inserting Symbols

Start

Click **1**

Double-Click **2**

Click **3**

Click

4

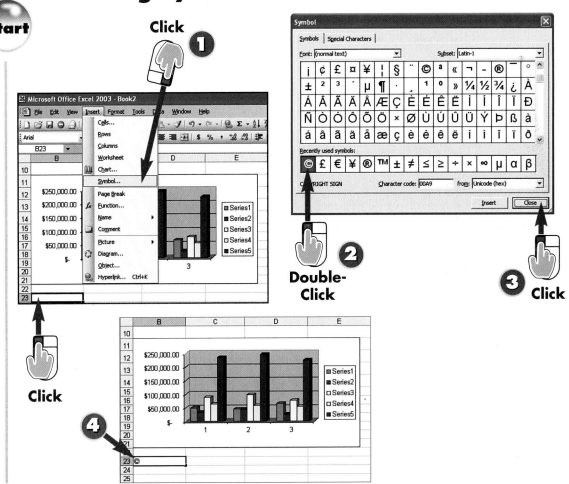

1 After you click the cell in which you want to add a symbol, open the **Insert** menu and choose **Symbol** to open the Symbol dialog box.

2 Double-click the symbol you want to insert into the cell—for example, the Copyright sign (©).

3 Click the **Close** button to close the Symbol dialog box.

4 The symbol is placed in the selected cell.

End

INTRODUCTION

The Symbol command enables you to insert special characters, international characters, and symbols such as the registered trademark (®) and trademark (™) symbols. You can easily add these and other special characters to your Excel worksheets. You delete symbols and special characters just as you delete any other text—by using the Backspace or Delete key.

Finding symbols
You can locate different types of symbols by clicking the **Font** drop-down arrow and selecting from the various fonts. Each font provides you with different symbols to choose from.

Adding foreign letters
Many foreign spellings (for example, Latin) include acute accent (´), grave accent (`), tilde (~), or other marks. To display those marks in the Symbol dialog box, open the **Font** drop-down list in the Symbol dialog box and select **(normal text)**.

Tracking Changes

Start

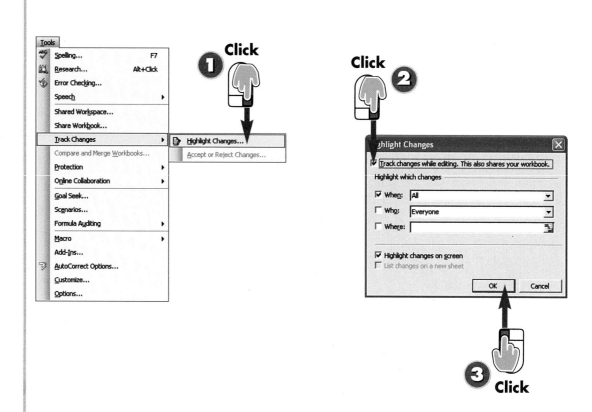

Click

Click

Click

---

1 Open the **Tools** menu, choose **Track Changes**, and select **Highlight Changes** to open the Highlight Changes dialog box.

2 Click the **Track Changes While Editing. This Also Shares Your Workbook** checkbox to select it.

3 The **Highlight Which Changes** options become available; click **OK** to accept the default change options.

Suppose you're working on a team project, and each member has access to the same workbook. To keep track of who makes what changes to the workbook, you can use Excel's Track Changes feature; that way, each person's edits appear in a different color. An edit can be changing the current information or adding completely new information to the workbook. (The only time the colors won't be different is when two people use the same computer or user information—such as login or password.)

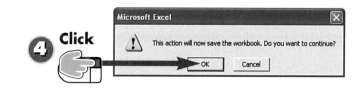

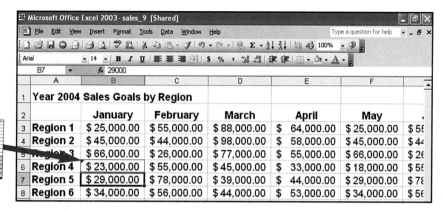

4 Excel notifies you that the workbook will be saved; click **OK**. The workbook is now shared, with Track Changes enabled.

5 Type a change in a cell and press **Enter**. The upper-left corner of the cell now contains a Track Changes marker, and a colored border.

6 Move the mouse pointer over the revised cell. A ScreenTip appears, showing the change that was made, who made the change, and when.

Rejecting changes
If a member of your team has changed the value in a cell in error, you can reject the change; see the next task to learn how.

Stopping sharing/tracking
The word **[Shared]** in the title bar of your workbook indicates that other people can use it. This is mostly useful in a network setting, where others can easily access your worksheet via the network. When you turn on Excel's Track Changes feature, you automatically share the workbook. To disable sharing and tracking, open the **Tools** menu, choose **Track Changes**, and select **Highlight Changes** to open the Highlight Changes dialog box. Then, deselect the **Track Changes While Editing...** check box and click **OK.**

Accepting or Rejecting Tracked Changes

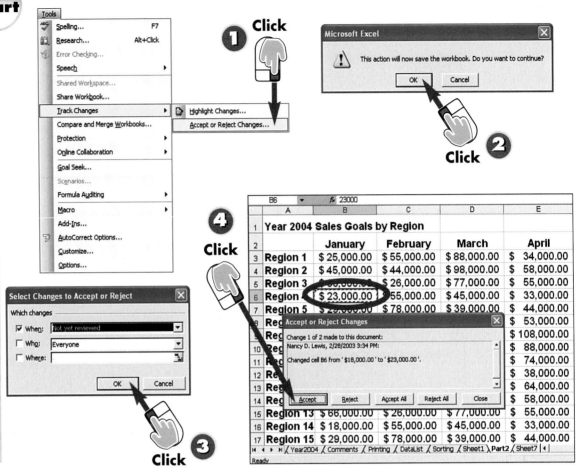

1. Open the **Tools** menu, choose **Track Changes**, and select **Accept or Reject Changes** to open the Select Changes to Accept or Reject dialog box.

2. Excel notifies you that the workbook will be saved; click **OK**. (If you have already saved your changes to the workbook, you won't get this message.)

3. Click **OK** to accept the default options in the **When**, **Who**, and **Where** fields.

4. Excel locates the first changed cell in your worksheet. To accept the change, click the **Accept** button.

When you are ready to finalize a worksheet containing tracked changes, you must determine which changes you want to keep, or *accept*, and which you want to reject. When you reject a change, Excel restores the cell to its previous value.

Accepting or rejecting all changes

Click **Accept All** if you want to accept all changes in the workbook; select **Reject All** if you want to reject all the changes in the workbook.

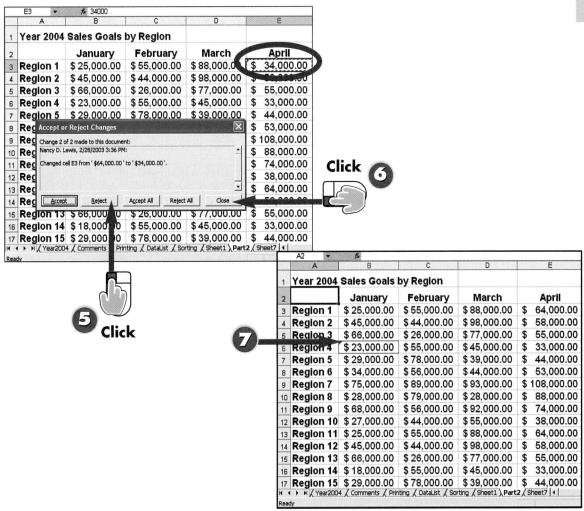

5 Excel locates the next changed cell in your workbook. To reject the change, click the **Reject** button.

6 When you're finished searching for tracked changes, click the **Close** button.

7 Notice that the Track Changes marker remains for your reference on cells in which you accepted changes, but is removed for rejected changes.

End

Viewing descriptions of changes
Any changes made to your workbook while the Track Changes feature is on will be displayed in the Accept or Reject Changes dialog box.

Checking Spelling

Start

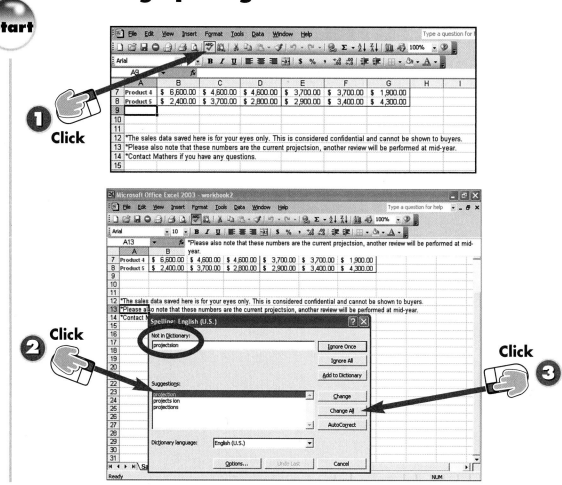

① **Click**

② **Click**

③ **Click**

① Click the **Spelling** button on the Standard toolbar. The Spelling dialog box opens, displaying the first spelling error it finds.

② If the correct spelling of the word appears in the **Suggestions** list, click the word. If the correct spelling isn't listed, type the correction directly in the **Not in Dictionary** box.

③ Click **Change** to change only this instance of the word, or **Change All** to correct all instances in the workbook. Excel makes the change, and flags the next word.

If your worksheet is for your eyes only, you might not think that mis-spellings are a big deal. But if you plan to turn over your worksheet to your manager, she might not think the mistakes are so minor. Fortunately, you can use Excel to check your spelling quickly and easily.

Adding words to your dictionary

If you notice that Excel incorrectly flags a word as a misspelling, you can add that word to the Office dictionary that Excel uses to check spelling. To do so, click the **Add to Dictionary** button in the Spelling dialog box.

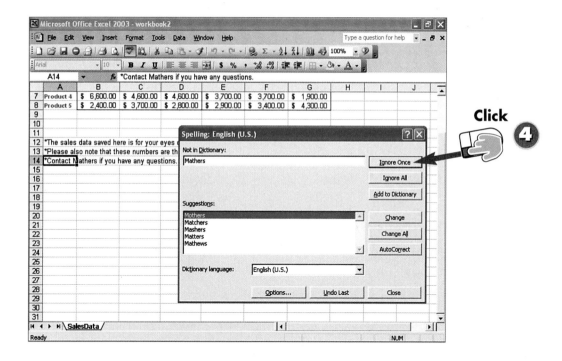

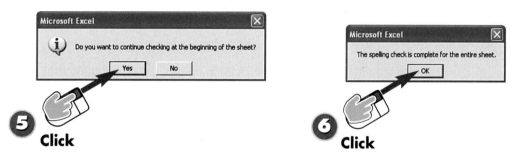

Click

Click

If the word flagged by Excel is not misspelled (for example, it's a proper name), click **Ignore Once** to ignore this instance or **Ignore All** to ignore it throughout.

If you started the spelling check in the middle of the workbook, Excel checks until it reaches the end. If you want to continue checking from the beginning, click **Yes**.

As Excel continues locating spelling errors, change or ignore them as needed. Excel notifies you when all inaccuracies have been reviewed; click **OK**.

End

Checking from the beginning

You don't have to be at the beginning of a workbook when you check for spelling errors. If you start in the middle of a workbook, Excel checks until it reaches the end and then asks you whether you want to continue checking from the beginning of your workbook.

Formatting Worksheet Data

When you *format* a worksheet, you can change the appearance of the data in it. With Excel's formatting tools, you can make your worksheet more attractive and readable. For example, you can increase and decrease the width of columns and height of rows, as well as change the color of your data or the cell background.

One of the most common ways to format your worksheet data is by changing the display of the numbers or text in your cells. Numeric values in Excel are typically more than just numbers—they can represent a dollar value ($2.00), a date (January 1, 2005), a percent (100%), or some other value. Each of these can be applied to your data.

In addition to changing the look of your cell data, you can change how it is displayed in your worksheet. For example, you can merge and center a title or header information. You can change the placement of the data in a cell so that it is at the top, bottom, left, right, justified, centered, or even displayed vertically.

After you add different types of formatting to your data, you can always clear it and return to the regular default data format. Or, perhaps after applying all the different types of formatting to your data, you want to save it as a specific style so you can apply it to future worksheets. Perhaps you would rather choose one of Excel's default formats, known as an AutoFormat. Excel even lets you apply formatting based on a set of conditions you establish.

Formatting Numbers and Text

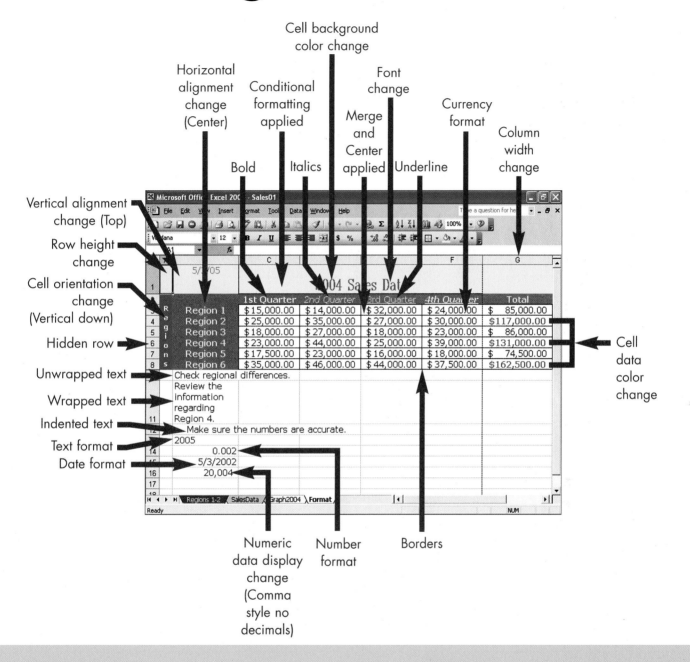

Changing the Font and Font Size

Start

Click 1   **Click** 2   **Click** 3

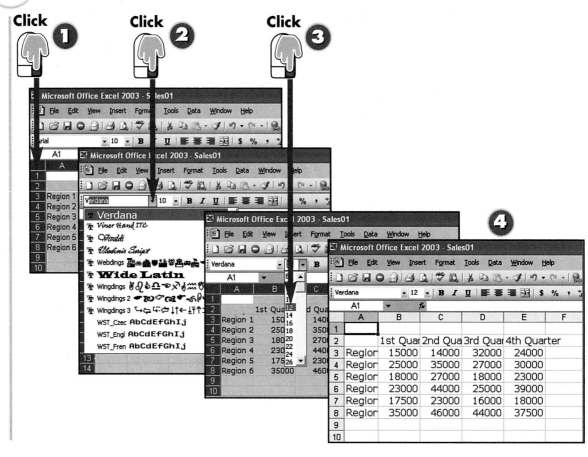

1 Select the cells whose font and font size you want to change, or click the **All Cells** button (to the left of column A and above row 1) to format all the cells in the worksheet.

2 Click the **Font** field **down arrow** in the Standard toolbar and scroll through the available fonts. When you find the one you want to use, click it to select it.

3 Click the **Font Size** field **down arrow** and scroll through the available sizes (in points). When you find the size you want to use, click it to select it.

4 The font and font size you selected are applied.

End

INTRODUCTION

One way to format data in your worksheet is to change the font used to display it. This gives data a different look and feel, which can help differentiate the type of data a cell contains. You can also change the font's size for added emphasis.

TIP

Finding font names
If you know the name of the font you want to apply, select the down arrow next to the **Font** field and type the first letter of the font name. You will immediately be moved to the portion of the list that starts with the typed letter.

TIP

Formatting options
To format only a portion of a cell's data, select only that portion and then change the font. You can also select a font (or other options) *before* you begin typing. Then all the data in a cell will be that font.

Changing Column Width

Start

1 Click & Drag

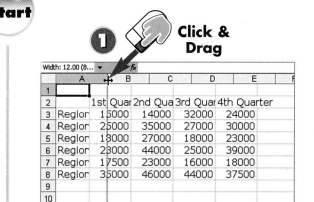

2

Click & Drag **3**

4

1 Move the mouse pointer over one side of the column header; click and drag the column edge to the desired width (the column size displays in the Name Box).

2 Release the mouse pointer and the column is resized. To resize multiple columns simultaneously, select the columns that you want to alter.

3 Click and drag one of the selected columns' header edges to the desired width, and release it.

4 All the selected columns are resized to the same width.

End

INTRODUCTION

There might be times when data is too wide to be displayed within a cell, particularly if you just applied formatting to it. Excel provides several alternatives for remedying this problem. You can select columns and specify a width, or force Excel to automatically adjust the width of a cell to exactly fit its contents.

TIP

Specific widths
To resize a column to an exact width, open the **Format** menu, choose **Column**, and select **Width**. Enter the exact width in the dialog box that appears and click **OK**. To automatically make an entire column the width of the widest cell in that column, open the **Format** menu, choose **Column**, and select **AutoFit Selection**. Or, move the cursor over the right side of the column header and double-click when the cursor changes to a two-headed arrow.

Changing the Color of the Cell Background and Cell Text

Start

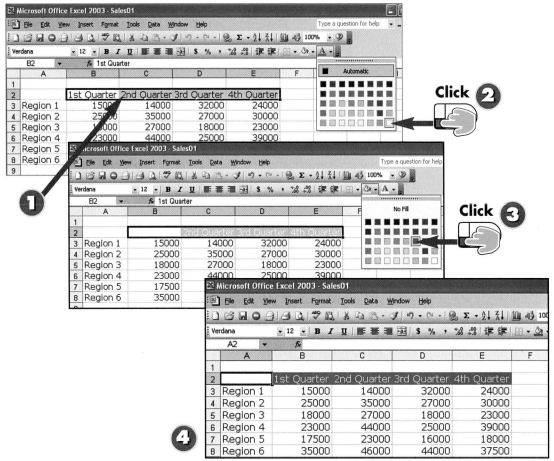

Click 2

Click 3

1 Select the cells whose background color and/or font color you want to change.

2 To change the color of the text in the selected cells, click the **Font Color down arrow** on the Formatting toolbar and choose a color from the list (here, **white**).

3 To change the color of the selected cells' background, click the **Fill Color down arrow** and choose a color from the list (here, **blue**).

4 Excel applies the colors you chose.

End

Generally, cells present a white background for displaying data, but you can apply other colors or shading to the background. You can even combine these colors with various patterns for a more attractive effect. In addition, you can change the color of the data contained within your worksheet's cells.

Choosing colors

Be sure a shading or color pattern doesn't interfere with the readability of your data. To improve readability, you might need to make the text bold or select a text color that goes well with your cells' background color. Also, be aware that if you print the worksheet to a noncolor printer, the color you select prints gray—and the darker the gray, the less readable the data. Yellows generally print as a pleasing light gray that doesn't compete with the data.

Formatting the Display of Numeric Data

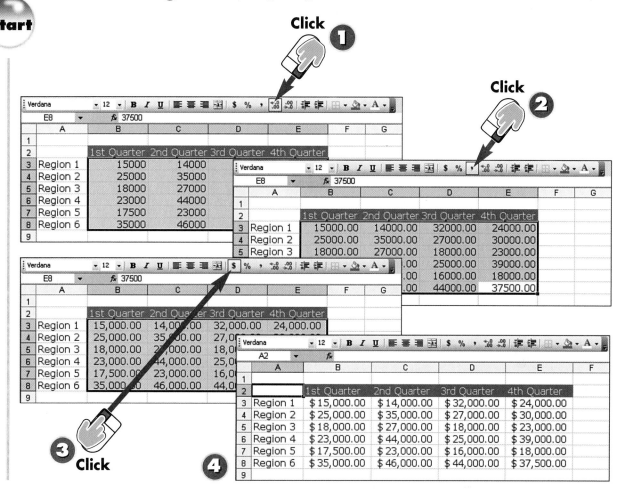

1 After you select the cells you want to format, click twice (once for each decimal place you want displayed) on the **Increase Decimal** button on the Formatting toolbar.

2 The decimal places are added. Click the **Comma Style** button on the Formatting toolbar to add a comma to the numeric data.

3 Click the **Currency Style** button on the Formatting toolbar to format numbers in the selected cells with a dollar sign ($), commas, a decimal point, and two decimal places.

4 The Currency style is applied.

End

INTRODUCTION

You can alter the display of different numbers depending on the type of data the cells contain. By formatting numeric data, you can display data in a familiar format to make it easier to read. For example, sales numbers can be displayed in a currency format, and scientific data can displayed with commas and decimals.

Percent style
If you click the **Percent Style** button on the Formatting toolbar, your numbers will be converted to a percentage, displayed with a % symbol.

Handling the #### error
If, after you apply a style to cells, any cells display the error ########, it simply means that the data in the cell exceeds the current cell width. Refer to the task "Changing Column Width" to fix the problem.

Using a General Format

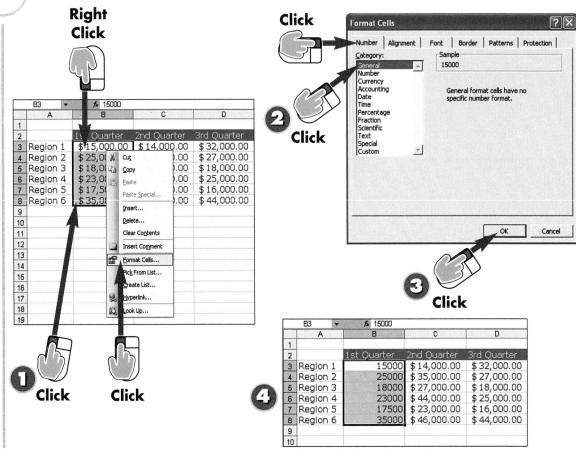

Start

Right Click

Click

Click

Click

Click

Click

Click

Click

① After you select the cells you want to format, right-click the selection and choose **Format Cells** from the shortcut menu that appears.

② The Format Cells dialog box opens (click the **Number** tab if it's not displayed already). Click the **General** option in the **Category** list.

③ Click **OK**.

④ Excel changes the format.

End

Quickly applying the General format
Another way to quickly format numbers in the General format is to open the **Edit** menu, choose **Clear**, and select **Formats**. Excel clears all the formatting and returns the numbers to the General format (unless you originally entered them in a different format).

Using a Number Format

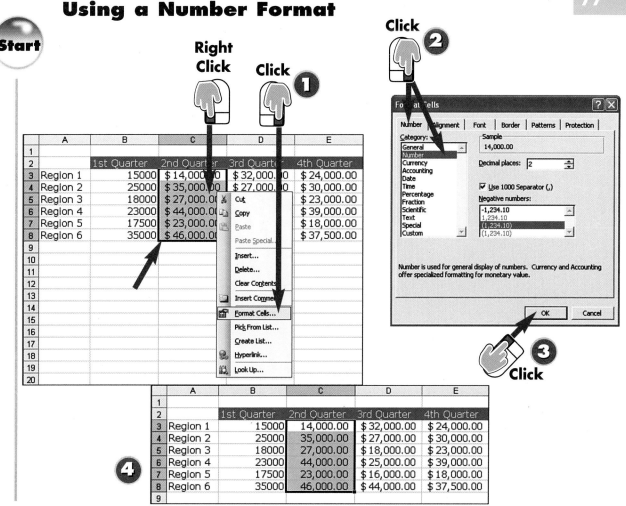

1. After you select the cells you want to format, right-click the selection and choose **Format Cells** from the shortcut menu that appears.

2. The Format Cells dialog box opens (click the **Number** tab if it's not displayed already). Click the **Number** option in the **Category** list.

3. Click **OK**.

4. Excel changes the format.

When you apply the Number format in Excel, it uses two decimal places by default. You have the option to alter the number of decimal places, use a comma separator, and even determine the way you want negative numbers to appear (for example, with a minus sign, in red, in parentheses, or some combination of the three).

Number format options
Use the **Decimal places** field in the Number tab of the Format Cells dialog box to change the number of decimal places used. To specify how negative numbers should appear, choose an option from the **Negative numbers** list.

Displaying fractions
Excel offers other number-related formats. For example, the Fraction format enables you to determine the type of fraction you want to appear and the number of digits that are displayed.

Using a Currency Format

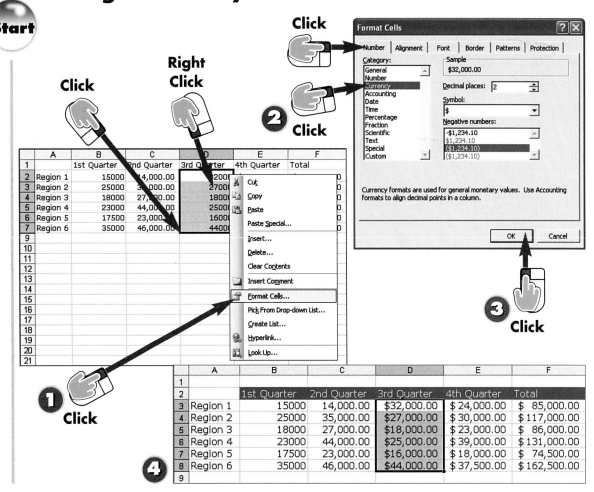

Start

Click

Right Click

Click

2 Click

Format Cells dialog

| Number | Alignment | Font | Border | Patterns | Protection |

Category:
- General
- Number
- Currency
- Accounting
- Date
- Time
- Percentage
- Fraction
- Scientific
- Text
- Special
- Custom

Sample: $32,000.00

Decimal places: 2

Symbol: $

Negative numbers:
- -$1,234.10
- $1,234.10
- ($1,234.10)
- ($1,234.10)

Currency formats are used for general monetary values. Use Accounting formats to align decimal points in a column.

OK   Cancel

3 Click

	A	B	C	D	E	F
1		1st Quarter	2nd Quarter	3rd Quarter	4th Quarter	Total
2	Region 1	15000	14,000.00	2000		
3	Region 2	25000	35,000.00	27000		
4	Region 3	18000	27,000.00	1800		
5	Region 4	23000	44,000.00	25000		
6	Region 5	17500	23,000.00	16000		
7	Region 6	35000	46,000.00	44000		

Shortcut menu:
- Cut
- Copy
- Paste
- Paste Special...
- Insert...
- Delete...
- Clear Contents
- Insert Comment
- Format Cells...
- Pick From Drop-down List...
- Create List...
- Hyperlink...
- Look Up...

1 Click

	A	B	C	D	E	F
2		1st Quarter	2nd Quarter	3rd Quarter	4th Quarter	Total
3	Region 1	15000	14,000.00	$32,000.00	$ 24,000.00	$ 85,000.00
4	Region 2	25000	35,000.00	$27,000.00	$ 30,000.00	$ 117,000.00
5	Region 3	18000	27,000.00	$18,000.00	$ 23,000.00	$ 86,000.00
6	Region 4	23000	44,000.00	$25,000.00	$ 39,000.00	$ 131,000.00
7	Region 5	17500	23,000.00	$16,000.00	$ 18,000.00	$ 74,500.00
8	Region 6	35000	46,000.00	$44,000.00	$ 37,500.00	$ 162,500.00

4

1 After you select the cells you want to format, right-click the selection and choose **Format Cells** from the shortcut menu that appears.

2 The Format Cells dialog box opens (click the **Number** tab if it's not displayed already). Click the **Currency** option in the **Category** list.

3 Click **OK**.

4 Excel changes the format.

End

When you apply the Currency format in Excel, it uses two decimal places and a dollar sign by default. You have the option to alter the number of decimal places, display a symbol for a different currency, and even determine the way you want negative numbers to appear.

Currency format options
Use the **Decimal places** field in the Number tab of the Format Cells dialog box to change the number of decimal places used. To choose a different currency symbol, select it from the **Symbol** drop-down list.

Currency-related formats
The Accounting format automatically lines up the currency symbols and decimal points for the cells in a column. The Percentage format multiplies the cell value by 100 and displays the result with a percent symbol.

Using a Date Format

Start

Click **Right Click** **Click** **Click** ①

Click ②

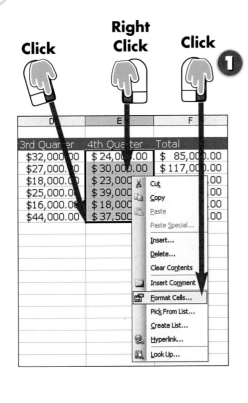

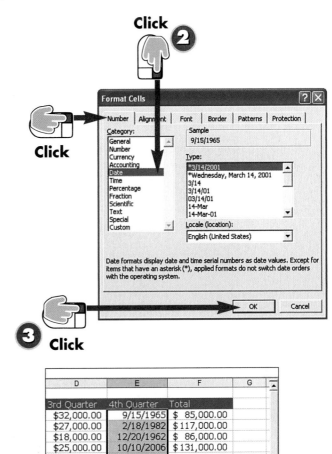

③ **Click**

④

---

① After you select the cells you want to format, right-click the selection and choose **Format Cells** from the shortcut menu that appears.

② The Format Cells dialog box opens (click the **Number** tab if it's not displayed already). Click the **Date** option in the **Category** list.

③ Click **OK**.

④ Excel changes the format.

End

When you apply the Date format in Excel, it displays the date and time serial numbers as date values. There are numerous different date types you can assign to your dates. For example, you might find it easier to skim through dates as numbers with or without the assigned year visible. Or, perhaps you would rather use the actual name of the month (as opposed to a numeral) for reference.

Using Time and Custom formats

You can use the Time format if you want to display just the time (not the date) in your spreadsheet. In addition, you can use the Custom format option to create a Date and Time format all your own.

Using a Text Format

Start

Click

Right Click

Click

1

	A	B	C	D	E	F	G
1							
2		1st Quarter	2nd Quarter	3rd Quarter	4th Quarter	Total	
3	Region 1	15000	14,000.00	$32,000.00	9/15/1965	$ 85,000.00	
4	Region 2	25000	35,000.00	$27,000.00	2/18/1982	117,000.00	
5		18000	27,000.00	$18,000.00	12/20/1962	$	
		23000	44,000.00	$25,000.00	10/10/2006	$1	
		17500	23,000.00	$16,000.00	4/12/1949	$	
		35000	46,000.00	$44,000.00	9/1/2002	$1	

Format ...ls ? X

Number | Alignment | Font | Border | Patterns | Protection

Category:
General
Number
Currency
Accounting
Date
Time
Percentage
Fraction
Scientific
Text
Special
Custom

Sample
85000

Text format cells are treated as text even when a number is in the cell. The cell is displayed exactly as entered.

Cut
Copy
Paste
Paste Special...
Insert...
Delete...
Clear Contents
Insert Comment
Format Cells...
Pick From List...
Create List...
Hyperlink...
Look Up...

OK

Click 3

Click

2 Click

F3	▼	fx =SUM(B3:E3)					
	A	B	C	D	E	F	G
1							
2		1st Quarter	2nd Quarter	3rd Quarter	4th Quarter	Total	
3	Region 1	15000	14,000.00	$32,000.00	9/15/1965	85000	
4	Region 2	25000	35,000.00	$27,000.00	2/18/1982	117000	
5	Region 3	18000	27,000.00	$18,000.00	12/20/1962	86000	
6	Region 4	23000	44,000.00	$25,000.00	10/10/2006	131000	
7	Region 5	17500	23,000.00	$16,000.00	4/12/1949	74500	
8	Region 6	35000	46,000.00	$44,000.00	9/1/2002	162500	
9							

4

1 After you select the cells you want to format, right-click the selection and choose **Format Cells** from the shortcut menu that appears.

2 The Format Cells dialog box opens (click the **Number** tab if it's not displayed already). Click the **Text** option in the **Category** list.

3 Click **OK**.

4 Excel changes the format. Notice that numbers automatically align to the right (column B), and text-based numbers automatically align to the left (column F).

End

When you type numeric data into a cell, the display defaults to a Number format. When you apply the Text format in Excel, it displays numbers as text regardless of whether the data in the cell is numeric or text-based. This can be convenient when you want to enter a number, but want to make sure Excel warns you with a Smart Tag if you try to use it in any type of formula or function.

Immediate number text
Another way to immediately make a number a textual cell entry is to type an apostrophe (') before you type the number. This tells Excel that the number is to be treated as text.

Applying Bold, Italic, and Underline

Start

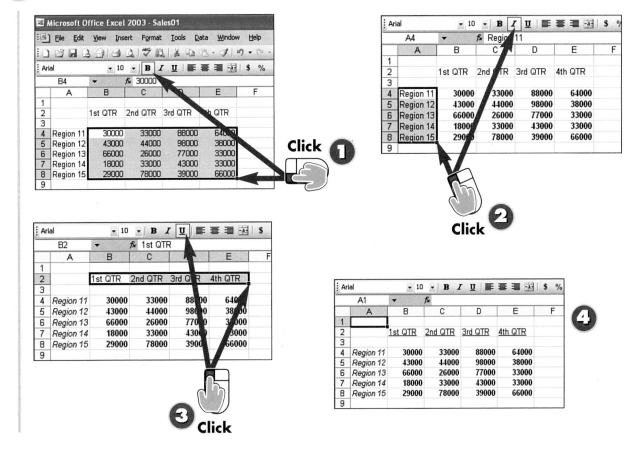

Click ❶

Click ❷

Click ❸

❹

❶ Select the cells in which you want to apply bold formatting and click the **Bold** button.

❷ Select the cells in which you want to apply italic formatting and click the **Italic** button.

❸ Select the cells in which you want to apply underline formatting and click the **Underline** button.

❹ The bold, italics, and underlining are applied to the selected cells.

End

INTRODUCTION

You can format the data contained in one or more cells as bold, italic, or underlined (or some combination of the three) to draw attention to it or make it easier to find. Indicating summary values, questionable data, or any other cells is easy with this type of formatting.

TIP

Combination formatting
You can use several formatting techniques in combination, such as applying bold, italic, and underlining all at the same time. Simply select the text you want to format and click each of the buttons on the toolbar.

Using Merge and Center on Cells

Start

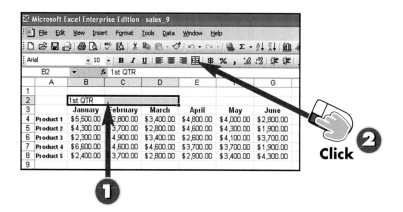

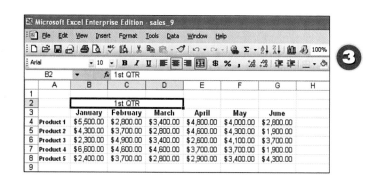

1. Select the cells you want to merge together, including the cells that don't contain any data.

2. Click the **Merge and Center** button on the Formatting toolbar.

3. The cells in the group header are merged, and the data is centered. Repeat the steps in this task as needed to group additional columns in your worksheet.

End

Using Excel's Merge and Center feature, you can group similar data under one heading. Columns of data usually have column headers, but they can also have group header information representing multiple columns.

Inserting a row
If no blank row exists above the row of cells you want to Merge and Center (from step 1), click the row you want the new row to be placed above, open the **Insert** menu and select **Row**.

Undoing Merged and Centered Cells
Select the cells to separate, open the **Format** menu, select **Cells**, click the **Alignment** tab, deselect the **Merge Cells** check box, and click **OK**.

Changing Horizontal Data Alignment

Start

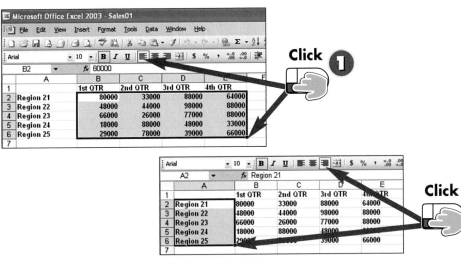

Click **1**

Click **2**

Click **3**

4

1 Select the cells in which you want to align the data to the left and click the **Align Left** button on the Formatting toolbar.

2 Select the cells in which you want to align the data to the right and click the **Align Right** button.

3 Select the cells in which you want to center the data and click the **Center** button.

4 The alignments are applied to the selected cells.

End

Excel provides several ways to format data. One way is to align data. The most common alignment changes you make are probably to center data in a cell, align data with a cell's right edge (right-aligned), or align data with a cell's left edge (left-aligned). The default alignment for numbers is right-aligned; the default alignment for text is left-aligned.

More alignment options

If you want more alignment options than are readily available on the Formatting toolbar, open the **Format** menu, choose **Cells**, and click the **Alignment** tab in the dialog box that appears. In the **Horizontal** drop-down list, scroll through the additional options available to you.

Changing Row Height

Start

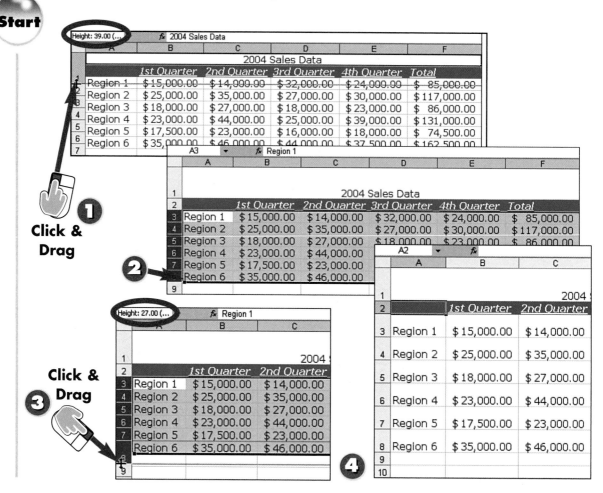

Click & Drag ①

② ➤

Click & Drag ③

④

1. Move the mouse pointer over the bottom edge of the row header. Click and drag the row to the desired height; the row size is displayed in the Name Box.

2. Release the mouse pointer and the row is resized. To resize *multiple* rows simultaneously, select the rows you want to alter.

3. Click and drag one of the selected row's bottom edges to the desired height, then release it.

4. All the selected rows are resized to the same height.

End

Depending on the formatting changes you make to a cell, data might not display properly. Increasing the font size or forcing data to wrap within a cell might prevent data from being entirely displayed or cause it to run over into other cells. You can frequently avoid these problems by resizing rows.

Specific heights

To resize a row to an exact height, open the **Format** menu, choose **Row**, and select **Height**. Enter the exact height in the dialog box that appears and click **OK**; the exact row height will be set.

AutoFitting rows

To automatically make an entire row fit the height of the tallest cell, open the **Format** menu, choose **Row**, and select **AutoFit Selection**.

Changing Vertical Data Alignment

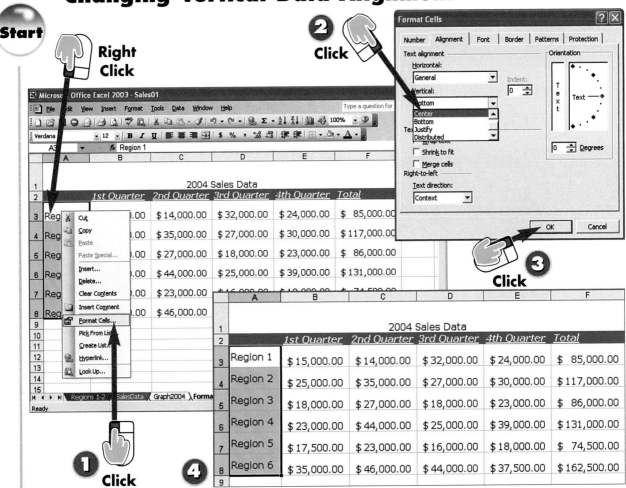

1 After you select the cell or cells whose contents you want to vertically align, right-click the selection and choose **Format Cells** from the shortcut menu that appears.

2 On the **Alignment** tab of the Format Cells dialog box, click the **down arrow** next to the **Vertical** field and scroll through the available options.

3 After you make your selection (here, **Center**), click **OK**.

4 The data is vertically aligned within the cell.

End

INTRODUCTION

In addition to aligning the data in your cells horizontally, you can align your cell data in a vertical format. Perhaps you want the data in your cells to align to the top of the cell, the bottom of the cell, or the center of the cell, or to justify within the cell. Cell data defaults to the bottom of the cell, but you can change this according to the look you are going for.

Justifying cell text

TIP
If you choose the Justify option in step 3, you must have enough text in the cell to fill from the top to the bottom of the cell—for example, a sentence. The text will automatically wrap to fit the cell.

Changing Cell Orientation

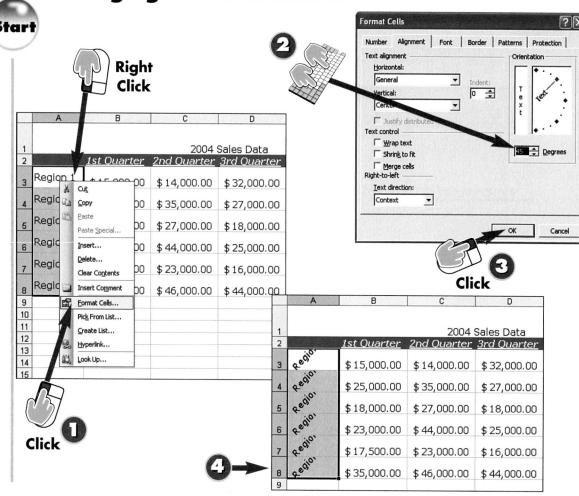

1 After you select the cell or cells whose orientation you want to change, right-click the selection and choose **Format Cells** from the shortcut menu that appears.

2 On the **Alignment** tab of the Format Cells dialog box, type the desired angle in the **Degrees** field in the **Orientation** area (here, **45**).

3 Click **OK**.

4 The data reorients within the cell. (You might need to increase or decrease the height and width of the cells.)

Excel lets you alter the orientation of cells—that is, the angle at which a cell displays information. The main reason for doing this is to help draw attention to important or special text. This feature can be convenient when you have a lot of columns in a worksheet and you don't want your column headers to take up much horizontal space, or if you simply want the information to stand out.

Rotating data
Click the half circle in the **Orientation** section of the **Alignment** tab to quickly change the angle at which data is rotated within the selected cell(s).

Wrapping Data in a Cell

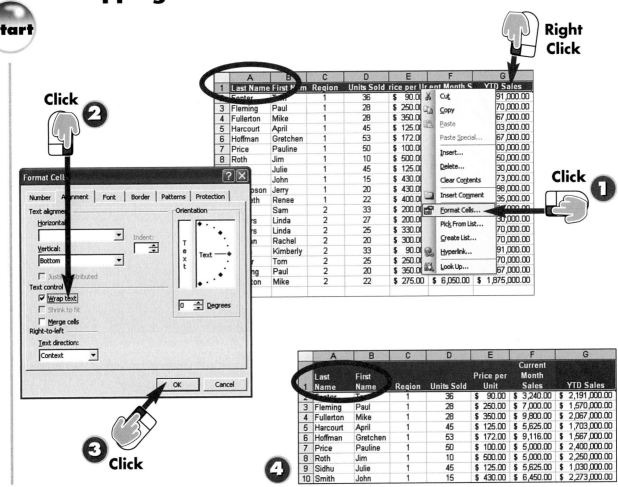

Start

Click ②

Right Click

Click ①

Click ③

④

End

① After you select the cell or cells whose text you want to wrap, right-click the selection and choose **Format Cells** from the shortcut menu that appears.

② On the **Alignment** tab of the Format Cells dialog box, mark the **Wrap text** check box in the **Text control** area.

③ Click **OK**.

④ The data in the selected cells is automatically wrapped.

Excel provides several ways to format data. One way is to allow text to wrap in a cell. For example, suppose a heading (row or column, for example) is longer than the width of the cell holding the data. If you are trying to make your worksheet organized and readable, it is a good idea to wrap the text in the heading so it is completely visible in a cell.

TIP

Aligning wrapped text
You might need to alter the column width to have the data wrap at the location you desire. Note, too, that you can align data that has been wrapped, which can give your text a cleaner look. Refer to the tasks "Changing Horizontal Data Alignment" and "Changing Vertical Data Alignment" earlier in this part to learn how to align data in cells.

Changing Borders

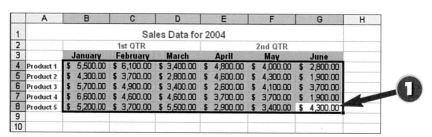

Click

1. Select the cells to which you want to add some type of border.

2. Click the **down arrow** next to the **Borders** button on the Formatting toolbar and choose an option from the list that appears—for example, **All Borders**.

3. The border is applied.

End

Each side of a cell is considered a *border*. These borders provide a visual cue as to where a cell begins and ends. You can customize borders to indicate other beginnings and endings, such as grouping similar data or separating headings from data. For example, a double line is often used to separate a summary value from the data being totaled. Changing the bottom of the border for the last number before the total accomplishes this effect.

TIP

Removing borders
To remove a border, select the bordered cells, click the **down arrow** next to the **Borders** button on the Formatting toolbar, and choose the **No Border** option from the list that appears. Be careful, though; you might eliminate an intended border in a nearby cell. That's why there are all kinds of border options on the drop-down list.

Indenting Entries in a Cell

Start

Click 1

Click 3

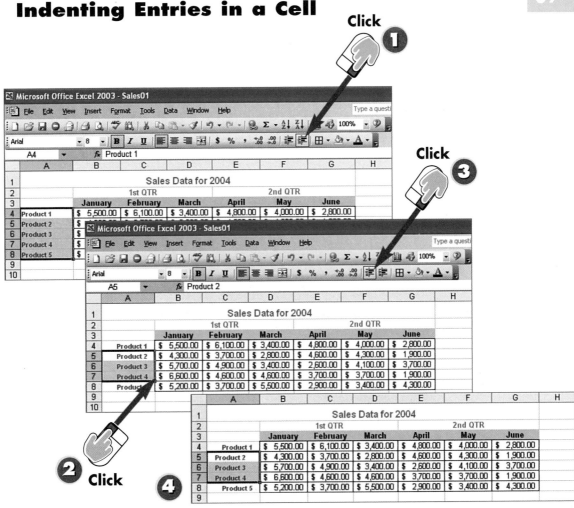

2 **Click**

4

1 After you select the cell or range whose data you want to indent, click the **Increase Indent** button the number of times you want the entries indented.

2 The data in the selected cells is indented. To decrease the indent, select the cell or range whose indent you want to decrease.

3 Click the **Decrease Indent** button to decrease the number of indents.

4 The indent is decreased.

End

Clearing Formatting

Start

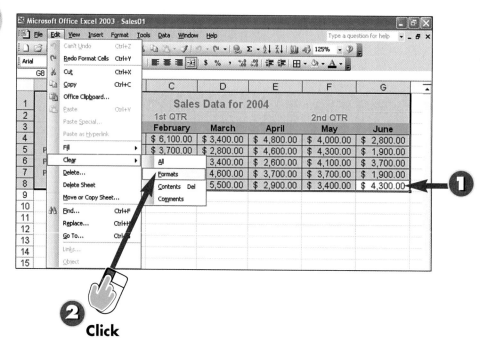

Click

1 Select the cells whose formatting you want to clear.

2 Open the **Edit** menu, choose **Clear**, and select **Formats**.

3 The cell data remains, but all the formatting is gone.

End

More clear options

If you open the **Edit** menu, choose **Clear**, and select **Contents**, the formatting will remain intact, but the text and data (contents) will be deleted (just as if you simply pressed the Delete key on the keyboard). If you open the **Edit** menu, select **Clear**, and choose **All**, all the formatting and contents (and comments) will be removed from the cell.

Hiding and Unhiding Rows

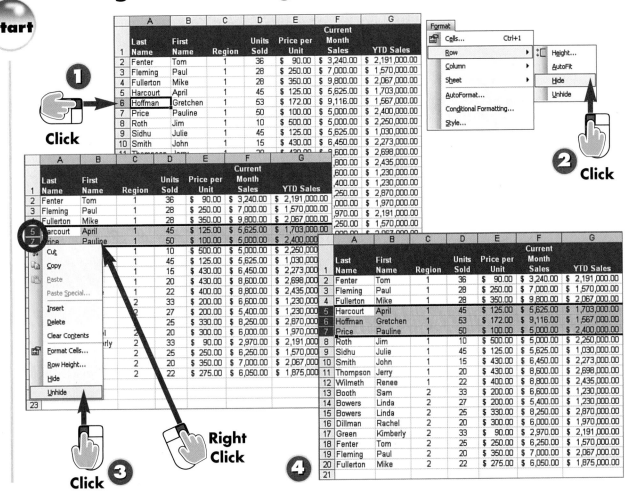

1. Click any cell in the row you want to hide.

2. Open the **Format** menu, choose **Row**, and select **Hide**. Excel hides the row. (You can tell that row 6 is hidden by the jump in the row-header numbering.)

3. To unhide the row, select the rows on both sides of the hidden row(s), right-click the selection, and choose **Unhide** from the shortcut menu that appears.

4. The row is unhidden.

End

INTRODUCTION
Hiding rows is a good way to hide calculations that aren't really critical for your audience to see. You also can hide other rows that you want to include in the worksheet, but don't want to display. It's kind of tricky to unhide a row, because you need a way of selecting the hidden row; you'll learn how here.

Caution
Hidden elements don't print when you print the worksheet.

Dragging to hide rows
You also can hide a row by dragging its bottom border past the top border of the row you want to hide.

Hiding and Unhiding Columns

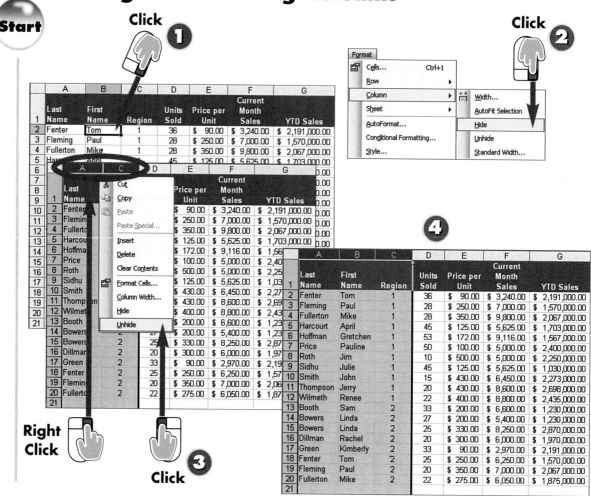

1. Click any cell in the column you want to hide.

2. Open the **Format** menu, choose **Column**, and select **Hide**. Excel hides the column. (You can tell that column B is hidden by the jump in the column-header lettering.)

3. To unhide a column, select the columns on both sides of the hidden column(s), right-click the selection, and choose **Unhide** from the shortcut menu that appears.

4. The column is unhidden.

End

Hiding columns is a good way to hide calculations that aren't really critical for your audience to see. You also can hide columns that you want to include in the worksheet, but don't want to display. It's kind of tricky to unhide a column because you need a way of selecting the hidden column; you'll learn how here.

Caution
Hidden elements don't print when you print the worksheet.

Dragging to hide columns
You also can hide a column by dragging its right border past the left border of the column you want to hide.

Hiding and Unhiding a Worksheet

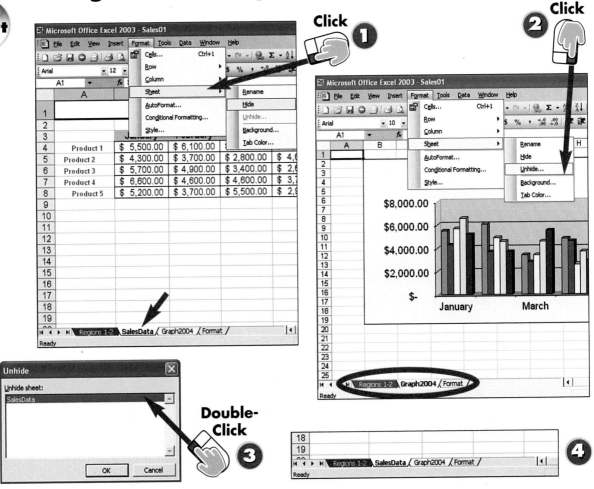

Start

Click 1

Click 2

Double-Click 3

4

End

1. After you select the tab of any sheet you want to hide, open the **Format** menu, choose **Sheet**, and select **Hide**. Excel hides the sheet.

2. To unhide the sheet, open the **Format** menu, choose **Sheet**, and select **Unhide**.

3. The Unhide dialog box opens, listing sheets that are hidden in your workbook. Double-click the worksheet name you want to unhide.

4. The sheet is unhidden.

Hiding worksheets is a good way to hide data and information that aren't really critical for your audience to see.

Caution
Hidden elements don't print when you print the worksheet.

Using AutoFormat

Start

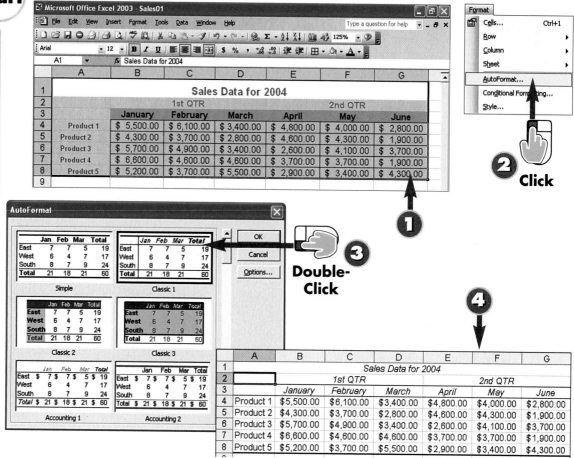

Click

Double-Click

1. Select the cells to which you want to apply an AutoFormat.

2. Open the **Format** menu and choose **AutoFormat** to open the AutoFormat dialog box.

3. Scroll through the available AutoFormats and double-click the one you want to apply to your data.

4. The AutoFormat is applied.

End

INTRODUCTION

Using all the formatting capabilities discussed to this point, you could format your worksheets in a very effective and professional manner—but it might take a while to get good at it. In the meantime, you can use Excel's AutoFormat feature, which can format selected cells using predefined formats. This feature is a quick way to format large amounts of data and provides ideas on how to format data manually.

TIP

Modifying AutoFormats
If you find a format in the AutoFormat dialog box that almost—but doesn't quite—meet your requirements, you can apply that format, but then make any necessary changes directly in the worksheet.

Copying Formatting

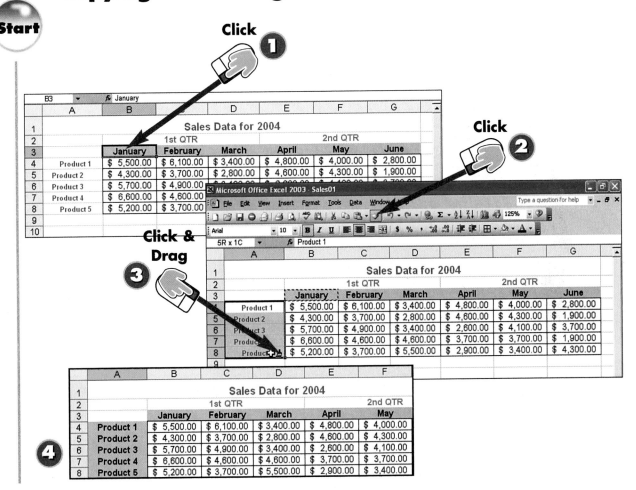

Start

Click 1

Click 2

Click & Drag 3

4

1. Click the cell with the formatting that you want to copy and apply to other cells.

2. Click the **Format Painter** button on the Standard toolbar; the mouse pointer changes to a Format Painter pointer (paintbrush symbol).

3. Click and drag the mouse pointer to select the cells to which you want to apply the copied formatting.

4. Release the mouse button. The formatting is applied to the data in the selected cells.

End

INTRODUCTION

If you have taken the time to format a specific cell just so, you might decide you want to apply those same formatting options to other cells. Instead of repeating each step in the format process over and over again, you can simply use the Format Painter button.

TIP

Removing cell formatting
To quickly remove any cell formatting, select the cells you want to return to their default settings; then open the **Edit** menu, choose **Clear**, and select **Formats**.

Creating and Applying a Formatting Style

Start

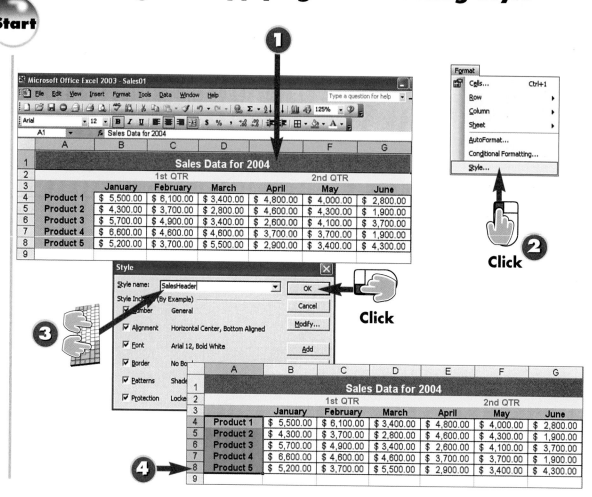

1. Apply any specific cell formatting that you want the style to use in your worksheet (here, Arial, Bold, 12 pt, White text, Red fill color).

2. With the cell that contains the desired formatting selected, open the **Format** menu and choose **Style** to open the Style dialog box.

3. Type a descriptive name for the new style in the **Style name** field (for example, Sales Header) and click **OK**.

4. Select the cell(s) to which you want to apply your newly created style.

Instead of assigning your data an existing Excel style (for example, Normal, Currency, Percent, and so forth), you can create your own style and apply it to cells. You begin by applying the specific formatting (for example, font, font style, font size, font color, and cell color) that you want the style to have, and then give the style a specific name.

Saving the style
The next time you exit Excel, you will be notified that you made a change to your global template and asked if you want to save the changes. If you want to keep the style you just created, click the **Yes** button; otherwise, click the **No** button.

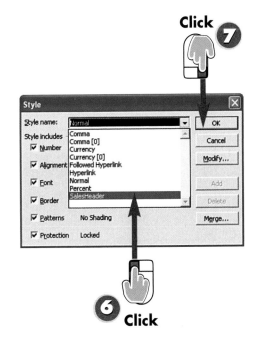

Click **7**

Click **6**

5

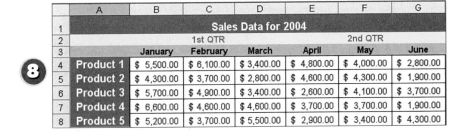

	A	B	C	D	E	F	G
1	Sales Data for 2004						
2		1st QTR			2nd QTR		
3		January	February	March	April	May	June
4	Product 1	$ 5,500.00	$ 6,100.00	$ 3,400.00	$ 4,800.00	$ 4,000.00	$ 2,800.00
5	Product 2	$ 4,300.00	$ 3,700.00	$ 2,800.00	$ 4,600.00	$ 4,300.00	$ 1,900.00
6	Product 3	$ 5,700.00	$ 4,900.00	$ 3,400.00	$ 2,600.00	$ 4,100.00	$ 3,700.00
7	Product 4	$ 6,600.00	$ 4,600.00	$ 4,600.00	$ 3,700.00	$ 3,700.00	$ 1,900.00
8	Product 5	$ 5,200.00	$ 3,700.00	$ 5,500.00	$ 2,900.00	$ 3,400.00	$ 4,300.00

8

5 Open the **Format** menu and choose **Style** to open the Style dialog box.

6 Click the **down arrow** next to the **Style name** field and select the style you just created from the list that appears.

7 Click **OK**.

8 The style is applied to the cells you selected.

End

Default styles

TIP

Notice that there are also default styles—including Hyperlink, Normal, Percent, and so on—that Office provides for Excel workbooks.

Using Conditional Formatting

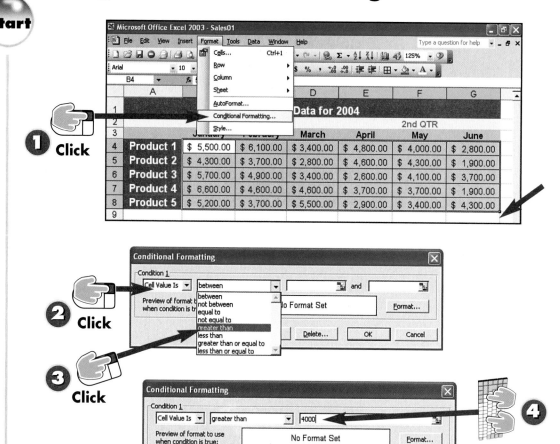

Start

1 Click

2 Click

3 Click

4

① Select the cells to which you want to apply conditional formatting, then open the **Format** menu and choose **Conditional Formatting**.

② In the conditional Formatting dialog box, keep **Condition** as the default **Cell Value Is**; the other option, Formula Is, is for indicating a specific formula.

③ Display the second drop-down list to select the type of condition (for example, **greater than**).

④ Type the value of the condition (the number that the cells must be "greater than").

There might be times when you want the formatting of a cell to depend on the value it contains. For this, use *conditional formatting*, which lets you specify conditions that, when met, cause the cell to be formatted in the manner defined for that condition. If none of the conditions are met, the cell keeps its original formatting. For example, you can set a conditional format such that if sales for a particular month were above $4,000, the data in the cell is bold and red.

Painting a format onto other cells
You can copy the conditional formatting from one cell to another. To do so, click the cell whose formatting you want to copy. Then click the **Format Painter** button. Finally, drag over the cells to which you want to copy the formatting.

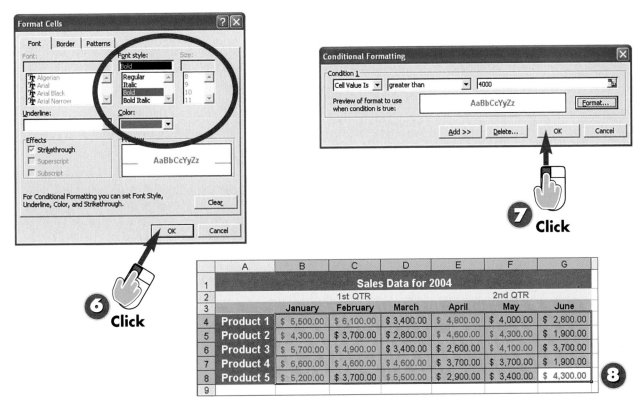

5 Click the **Format** button to set the format to use when the condition is met.

6 Click the options you want to set in the Format Cells dialog box (for example, **Pink** in the **Color** field and **Bold** in the **Font style** list), and click **OK**.

7 Click **OK** in the Conditional Formatting dialog box.

8 Excel applies the formatting to any cells that meet the condition you specified.

End

When to use conditional formatting

Use conditional formatting to draw attention to values that have different meanings, depending on whether they are positive or negative, such as profit and loss values.

Working with Formulas and Functions

In Excel, a *formula* calculates a value based on the values in other cells of the workbook. Excel displays the result of a formula in a cell as a numeric value.

Functions are abbreviated formulas that perform a specific operation on a group of values. Excel provides more than 250 functions that can help you with tasks ranging from determining loan payments to calculating investment returns. For example, the SUM function automatically adds entries in a range. To use it, you first type =SUM(in either lower- or uppercase letters. Then you select the range. You end the function by typing), which tells Excel you are finished selecting the range.

The way you refer to a cell in a formula determines how the formula is affected when you copy it into a different cell. You can use three types of cell references: relative, absolute, and mixed. The formulas you create in this part contain *relative cell references*. When you copy a formula from one cell to another, the relative cell references in the formula change to reflect the new location of the formula.

An *absolute cell reference* does not change when you copy the formula to a new cell. In certain formulas, you might want an entry to always refer to one specific cell value. For example, you might want to calculate the interest on several different principal amounts. The interest percentage remains unchanged, or *absolute*, so you designate the entry in the formula that refers to the interest percentage as an absolute cell reference. The principal amounts do change, so they have relative cell reference entries in the formula. When you copy this formula, the interest cell reference always refers to the one cell that contains the interest percentage.

A *mixed cell reference* is a single cell entry in a formula that contains both a relative and an absolute cell reference. A mixed cell reference is helpful when you need a formula that always refers to the values in a specific column but the values in the rows must change, and vice versa.

Functions and Correcting Errors

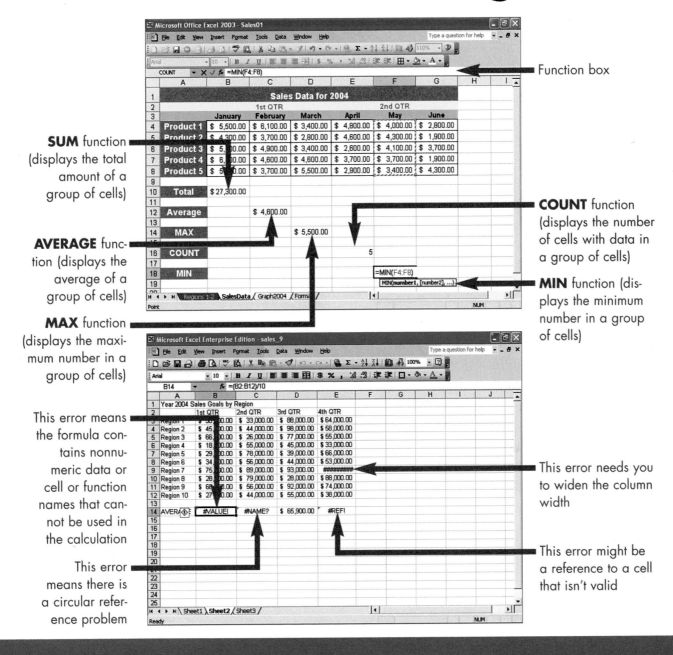

SUM function (displays the total amount of a group of cells)

AVERAGE function (displays the average of a group of cells)

MAX function (displays the maximum number in a group of cells)

Function box

COUNT function (displays the number of cells with data in a group of cells)

MIN function (displays the minimum number in a group of cells)

This error means the formula contains nonnumeric data or cell or function names that cannot be used in the calculation

This error means there is a circular reference problem

This error needs you to widen the column width

This error might be a reference to a cell that isn't valid

Using AutoSum (SUM)

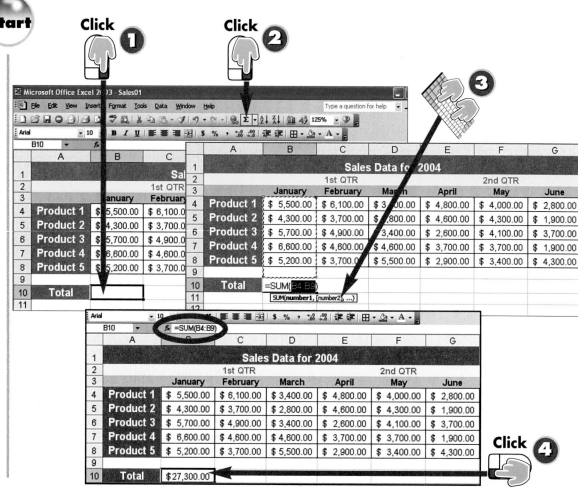

1 Click in the cell in which you want the result of the AutoSum operation to appear (this is called the *resultant cell*).

2 Click the **AutoSum** button on the Standard toolbar.

3 Excel selects the most obvious range of numbers and puts a dotted line around the cells. Press **Enter** to accept the range or use the mouse to select alternative cells.

4 Click the resultant cell to make it the active cell. Notice that the formula is displayed in the Formula bar.

End

Excel can use formulas to perform calculations for you. Because a formula refers to cells rather than to the values those cells contain, Excel updates the sum whenever you change the values in the cells. You'll probably use the AutoSum formula a lot—it adds numbers in a range of cells.

Selecting specific AutoSum cells

If you don't want to use the range of cells that Excel selects for you, click on the first cell you want, hold down the **Ctrl** key, and click on each additional cell you would like to include in the calculation. When you finish selecting the cells you want to calculate, press **Enter** to see the result. Alternatively, if you let Excel select the cells for you but Excel doesn't select exactly the right set of cells, you can resize the selection by clicking the first cell to include, holding down the **Shift** key, and clicking the last cell to include.

Finding a Cell Average (AVERAGE)

Click ❶   **Click** ❷   ❸

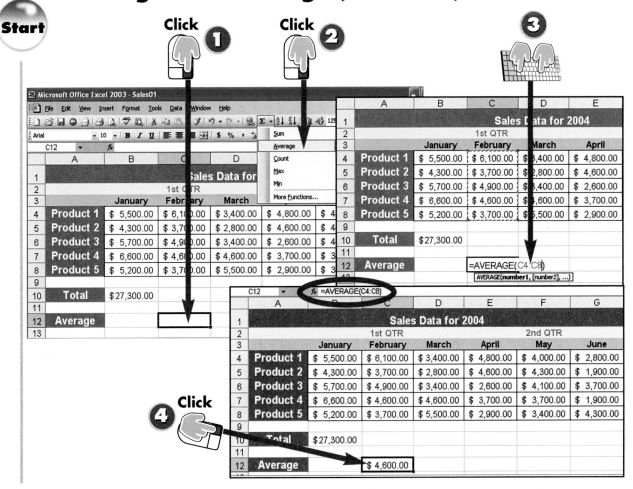

Click ❹

❶ Click the cell in which you want the result of the **AVERAGE** function to appear (this is called the *resultant cell*).

❷ Click the **down arrow** next to the **AutoSum** button on the Standard toolbar and choose **Average** from the list that appears.

❸ Excel selects the most obvious range of numbers and puts a dotted line around the cells. Press **Enter** to accept the range or use the mouse to select alternative cells.

❹ Click the resultant cell to make it the active cell. Notice that the formula is displayed in the Formula bar.

End

INTRODUCTION

A *function* is one of Excel's many built-in formulas for performing a specialized calculation on the data in your worksheet. For example, instead of totaling your sales data, you can use Excel's AVERAGE function to determine the average of each quarter per region.

TIP

Selecting specific AutoSum cells

If you don't want to use the range of cells that Excel selects for you, click on the first cell you want, hold down the **Ctrl** key, and click on each additional cell you would like to include in the calculation. When you finish selecting the cells you want to calculate, press **Enter** to see the result. Alternatively, if you let Excel select the cells for you but Excel doesn't select exactly the right set of cells, you can resize the selection by clicking the first cell to include, holding down the **Shift** key, and clicking the last cell to include.

Finding the Largest Cell Amount (MAX)

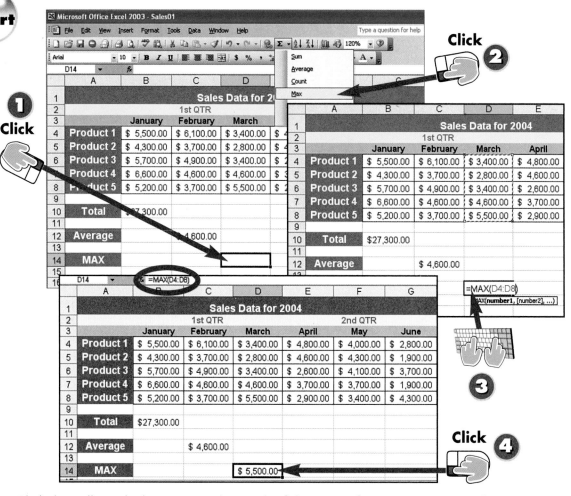

① Click the cell in which you want the result of the **MAX** function to appear (this is called the *resultant cell*).

② Click the **down arrow** next to the **AutoSum** button on the Standard toolbar and choose **Max** from the list that appears.

③ Excel selects the most obvious range of numbers and puts a dotted line around the cells. Press **Enter** to accept the range or use the mouse to select alternative cells.

④ Click the resultant cell to make it the active cell. Notice that the formula is displayed in the Formula bar.

End

INTRODUCTION

You can use Excel's MAX function to, for example, determine the quarter in which you had the most sales.

TIP

Finding the minimum cell amount

In addition to enabling you to find the largest cell amount, you can also find the smallest cell amount. See the task "Finding the Smallest Cell Amount (**MIN**)" later in this part for more information.

Counting the Number of Cells (COUNT)

Start

1 Click

Click 2

=COUNT(E4:E8)

=COUNT(E4:E8)
COUNT(**value1**, [value2], ...)

3

Click 4

End

1. Click the cell in which you want the result of the **COUNT** function to appear (this is called the *resultant cell*).

2. Click the **down arrow** next to the **AutoSum** button on the Standard toolbar and choose **Count** from the list that appears.

3. Excel selects the most obvious range of numbers and puts a dotted line around the cells. Press **Enter** to accept the range or use the mouse to select alternative cells.

4. Click the resultant cell to make it the active cell. Notice that the formula is displayed in the Formula bar.

INTRODUCTION

Suppose you want to know how many sales reps are associated with a specific region. In that case, you could use Excel's COUNT function to count the number of cells in a selected range.

TIP

COUNTIF

You can use the **COUNTIF** function to count the number of cells in a range that meet specific criteria. For example, instead of totaling your sales data, maybe you want to know how many regional quarters were under $20,000.

	A	B	C	D	E	F	G
1			Sales Data for 2004				
2			1st QTR			2nd QTR	
3		January	February	March	April	May	June
4	Product 1	$ 5,500.00	$ 6,100.00	$ 3,400.00	$ 4,800.00	$ 4,000.00	$ 2,800.00
5	Product 2	$ 4,300.00	$ 3,700.00	$ 2,800.00	$ 4,600.00	$ 4,300.00	$ 1,900.00
6	Product 3	$ 5,700.00	$ 4,900.00	$ 3,400.00	$ 2,600.00	$ 4,100.00	$ 3,700.00
7	Product 4	$ 6,600.00	$ 4,600.00	$ 4,600.00	$ 3,700.00	$ 3,700.00	$ 1,900.00
8	Product 5	$ 5,200.00	$ 3,700.00	$ 5,500.00	$ 2,900.00	$ 3,400.00	$ 4,300.00
9							
10	Total	$ 27,300.00					
11							
12	Average		$ 4,600.00				
13							
14	MAX			$ 5,500.00			
15							
16	COUNT				5		

Finding the Smallest Cell Amount (MIN)

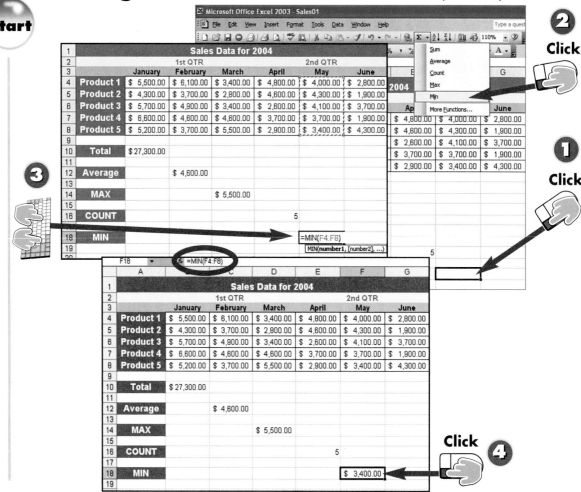

1. Click the cell in which you want the result of the function to appear (this is called the *resultant cell*).

2. Click the **down arrow** next to the **AutoSum** button on the Standard toolbar and choose Min from the list that appears.

3. Excel selects the most obvious range of numbers and puts a dotted line around the cells. Press **Enter** to accept the range or use the mouse to select alternative cells.

4. Click the resultant cell to make it the active cell. Notice that the formula is displayed in the Formula bar.

End

TIP

Finding the maximum cell amount
In addition to enabling you to find the smallest cell amount, you can also find the largest cell amount. Refer to the task "Finding the Largest Cell Amount (**MAX**)" earlier in this part for more information.

Entering a Formula

Start

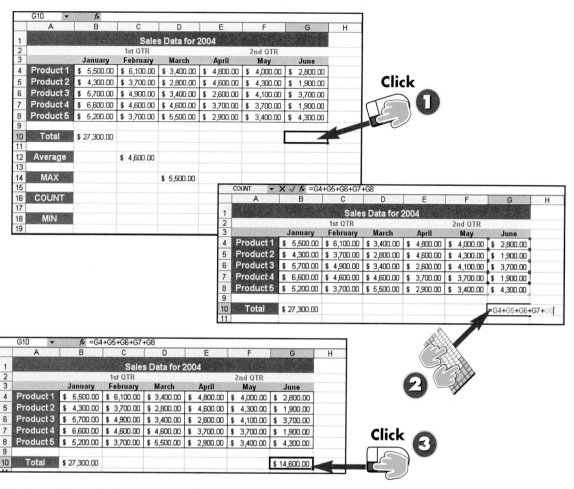

Click ❶

Click ❸

❶ Click the cell in which you want the result of the formula to appear (this is called the *resultant cell*).

❷ Type = (the equal sign) followed by the references of the cells containing the data you want to total (for example, **G4+G5+G6+G7+G8**), and then press **Enter**.

❸ Click the resultant cell to make it the active cell; the values in the specified cells are added together.

End

INTRODUCTION

Another way to use a formula is to type it directly into the cell. You can include any cells in your formula; they do not have to be next to each other. Also, you can combine mathematic operations—for example, C3+C4–D5.

TIP

Canceling a formula
If you start to enter a formula and then decide you don't want to use it, you can cancel it by pressing the **Esc** key.

TIP

Order of operation
Excel first performs calculations within parentheses. Then it performs multiplication or division calculations from left to right. Finally, it performs any addition or subtraction from left to right.

Editing a Formula or Function

Start

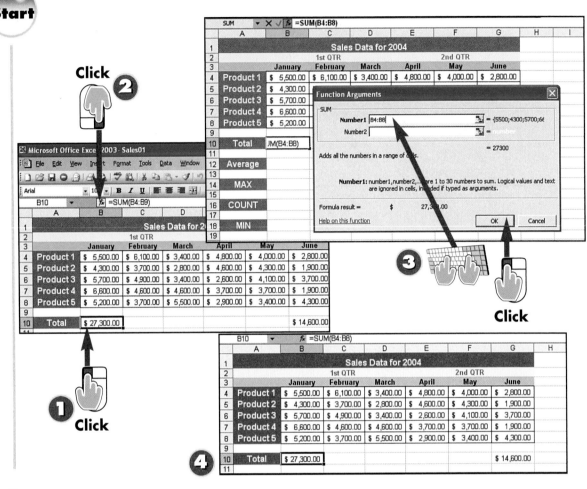

Click **②**

Click **①**

Click **③**

Click

④

---

① Click the cell you want to edit; the function is displayed in the Formula bar.

② Click the **Insert Function** button on the Formula bar to open the Function Arguments dialog box. (If a formula, the Insert Function dialog box will appear.)

③ Type the changes to your function. For example, change the cells being summed to B4–B8 instead of B4–B9. Then click **OK**.

④ The changes are made and the result appears in the cell.

End

INTRODUCTION

After you enter a formula or function, you can change the values in the referenced cells, and Excel automatically recalculates the value based on the changes. You can include any cells in a formula or function; they do not have to be next to each other. Also, you can combine mathematical operations— for example, C3+C4–D5.

TIP

Pressing F2
Instead of using the Function Arguments dialog box to edit your formulas, you can press the F2 key and edit your formula just like you would regular text or data on the Formula bar.

Copying a Formula

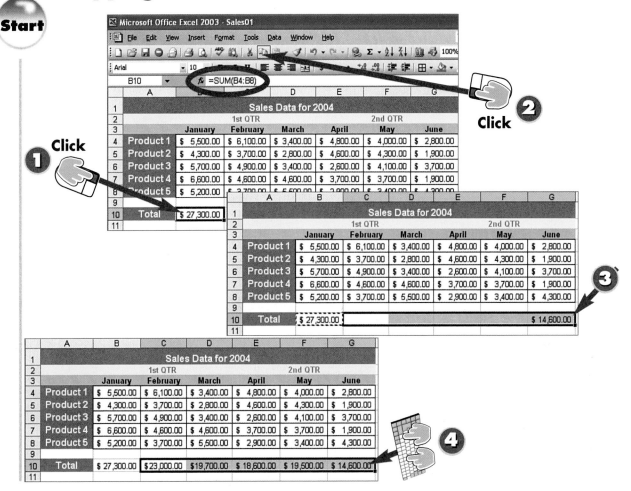

1. Click the cell that contains the function you want to copy.

2. Click the **Copy** button on the Standard toolbar; a line surrounds the cell you are copying.

3. Click the cell or cells into which you want to paste the formula.

4. Press **Enter** to paste the formula into each of the selected cells.

INTRODUCTION

When you build your worksheet, you might want to use the same data and formulas in more than one cell. With Excel's Copy command, you can create the initial data or formula once and then place copies in the appropriate cells. For example, suppose you want to find the average sales per quarter in other sales regions. To do so, create the formula for the first region, and copy it to cells for the other regions.

TIP

Increasing cell width

If you paste a copied formula, you might need to alter the size of your columns to accommodate the new size of the data in the cell. To automatically make an entire column (or multiple columns) fit the width of the widest cell in that column (or columns), move the cursor over the right side of the column header and double-click when the cursor changes to a two-headed arrow.

Assigning Names to a Cell or Range

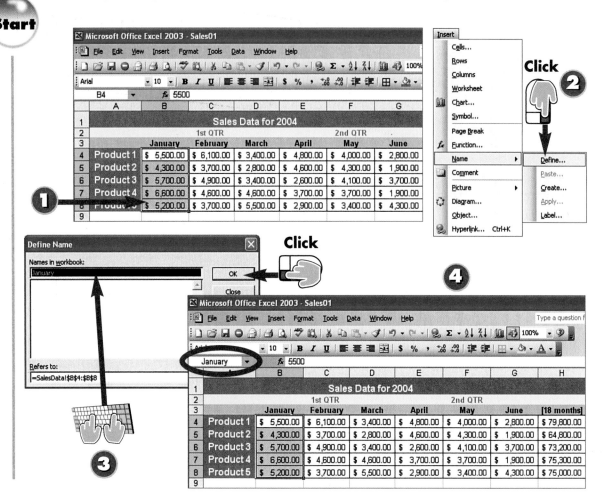

1. Select the cell or range you want to name.

2. Open the **Insert** menu, choose **Name**, and select **Define** to open the Define Name dialog box, which displays the range coordinates and suggests a name.

3. If you do not like the name Excel suggests, type a new name. When you are satisfied with the name, click **OK**.

4. Excel names the range. When the range is selected, the name appears in the Name box.

Referencing Names in a Function

Start

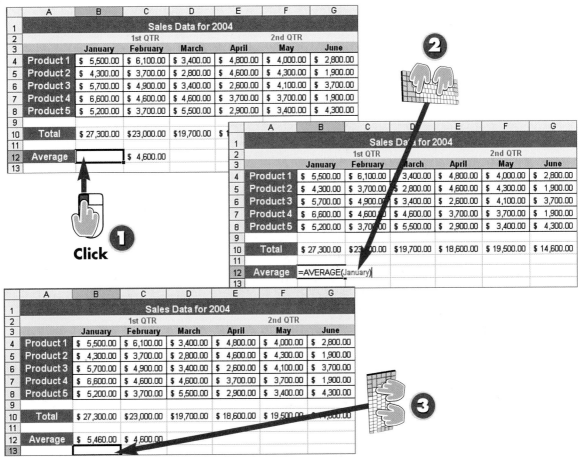

Click

1 Click in the cell in which you want the result of the formula to appear (this is called the *resultant cell*).

2 Type the function in the cell using a named cell or range—for example, **=AVERAGE(January)**. The name appears in the same color as the border.

3 Press the **Enter** key.

End

INTRODUCTION

One of the reasons you create a name for a cell or group of cells is so that you can easily refer to that cell or range in a function. That way, rather than typing or selecting a range or cell, you can type the name or select it from the Paste Name dialog box.

TIP

Pasting the name
If you forget the name of a range while you are typing a formula, open the **Insert** menu, choose **Name**, select **Paste**, choose the correct range name, and click **OK**. The range name is automatically placed in the formula.

TIP

Deleting a name
To delete a name, open the **Insert** menu, choose **Name**, and select **Define**. In the Define Name dialog box, select the range you want to delete, and then click the **Delete** button. Click **OK** to confirm the deletion.

Using Functions Across Worksheets

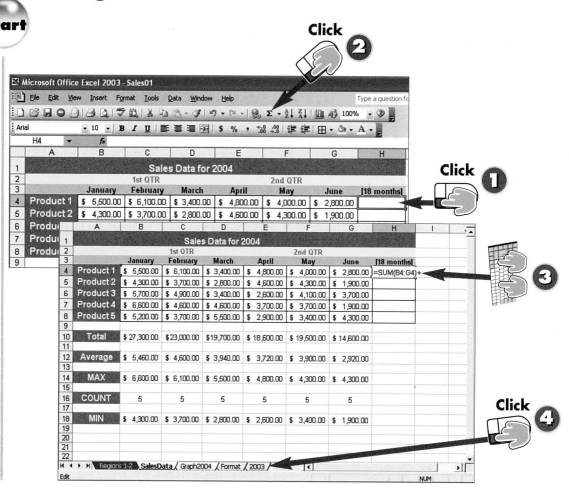

1. Click in the cell in which you want the result of the formula to appear (this is called the *resultant cell*).

2. Click the **AutoSum** button on the Standard toolbar. Excel selects the logical cells to sum.

3. In this example, we are going to add the sum of this operation to last year's data in another worksheet (2003), so type a **+** outside the right bracket.

4. Click the tab of the worksheet that contains the cell you want to reference in the calculation.

INTRODUCTION

You can use cell references from other worksheets in your calculations. For example, suppose you have two worksheets that contain the calculations for the total sales by region for a particular year. In a third worksheet, you want to calculate the total sales by region for the last two years. You can reference the cells in the first two worksheets that contain the totals and perform calculations on them in the third worksheet.

TIP

Worksheet name references
Instead of switching back and forth between worksheets, you can reference the worksheet name in your calculations. The location of a cell in a particular worksheet is the cell row and column location in addition to the sheet name—for example, **Sheet1!A1**.

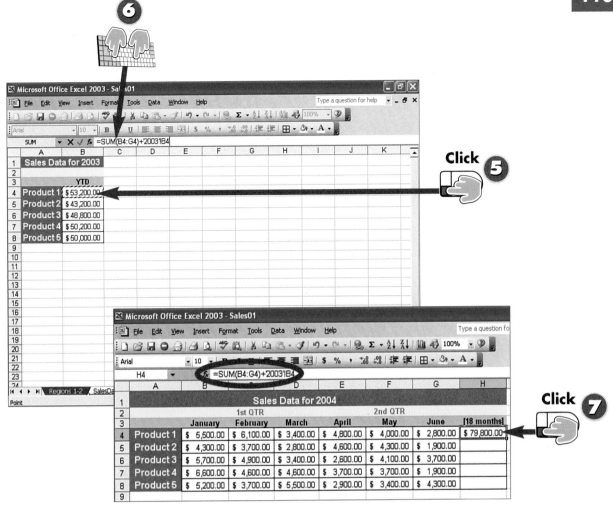

5 Click the cell that you want to use in your calculation; it appears next to the worksheet name in the Formula bar.

6 Press the **Enter** key. Excel performs the calculation and returns you to the original worksheet.

7 Click the resultant cell to make it the active cell. Notice that the function is displayed in the Formula bar.

End

CAUTION

If you only reference one worksheet name in a formula, the cells referenced in the formula will all apply to the one referenced worksheet. For example, if you have the formula **=SUM(Sheet1!A1+B1)** in cell C3 of Sheet2, this will reference cell A1 from Sheet1 and B1 from Sheet1. If you need to reference a cell in another worksheet, you must include the worksheet name in the formula, like so: **=SUM(Sheet1!A1+Sheet2!B1)**.

Using AutoCalculate

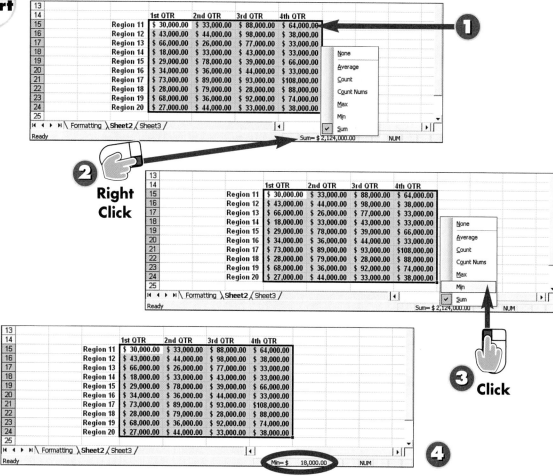

1 Select the cells that you want to AutoCalculate.

2 Right-click the Status bar and review the AutoCalculate options.

3 To find the lowest number in the selection, click **Min** in the shortcut menu that appears. (Notice that the default AutoCalculate operation is to sum the numbers.)

4 The Status bar displays the lowest number in the selection (in this case, **$18,000.00**).

INTRODUCTION

Suppose you want to see a function performed on some of your data—in this example, to determine the lowest quarterly sales goal of any region in 2004—but you don't want to add the function directly into the worksheet. Excel's AutoCalculate feature can help.

TIP

Turning off AutoCalculate
You can turn off the AutoCalculate feature by selecting **None** from the AutoCalculate shortcut menu. Otherwise, it continues to display when you select cells.

TIP

AutoCalculate options
In addition to using AutoCalculate to find a minimum number, you can also select cells to be averaged (Average), count the total number of cells containing data (Count), count the total number of cells containing numeric data (Count Nums), find the largest number (Max), and sum a total (Sum).

Finding Functions

Click

1

2

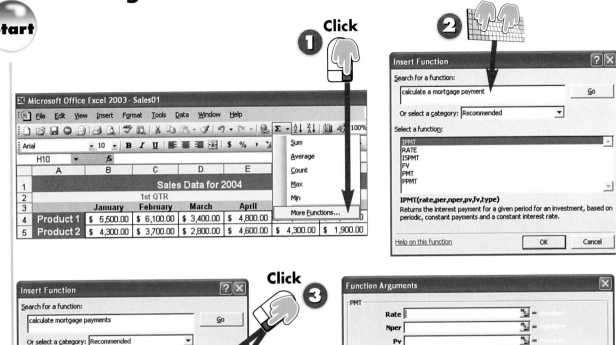

Click

3

4

1 Click the **down arrow** next to the **AutoSum** button on the Standard toolbar and choose **More Functions** from the list that appears.

2 Type a description of the function you are looking for in the **Search for a function** text box and press **Enter** (or click the **Go** button).

3 Scroll through the list in the **Select a function** box and click a function to read a description of it. When you find the function you are looking for, click **OK**.

4 Excel walks you through the process of inputting the function's arguments in the Function Arguments dialog box.

End

INTRODUCTION

In the old days, you had to know the name of the function you wanted to use. Now, however, Excel makes it easy to find the function you need—all you have to know is what you want the function to do.

TIP

Function arguments help
If you need help while you are inputting your function arguments, click the **Help on this function** link in the bottom-left corner of the Function Arguments dialog box.

Calculating a Loan Payment (PMT)

Start

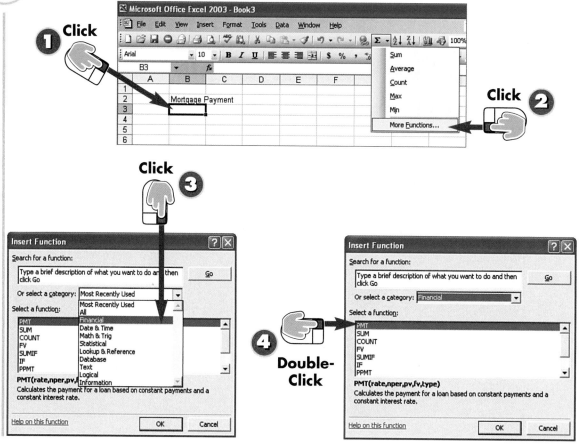

Click ①

Click ②

Click ③

Double-Click ④

① Click in the cell in which you want the result of the function to appear (this is called the *resultant cell*).

② Click the **down arrow** next to the **AutoSum** button on the Standard toolbar and choose **More Functions** from the list that appears.

③ The Insert Function dialog box opens. Click the **down arrow** next to the **Or select a category** field and choose **Financial** from the list that appears.

④ A list of financial-related functions appears in the **Select a function** list. Scroll through the list to locate the **PMT** function, and double-click it.

INTRODUCTION

Using Excel, you can determine a monthly loan payment based on a constant interest rate, a specific number of pay periods, and the current loan amount.

TIP

Function arguments help
If you need help while you are inputting your function arguments, click the **Help on this function** link in the bottom-left corner of the Function Arguments dialog box.

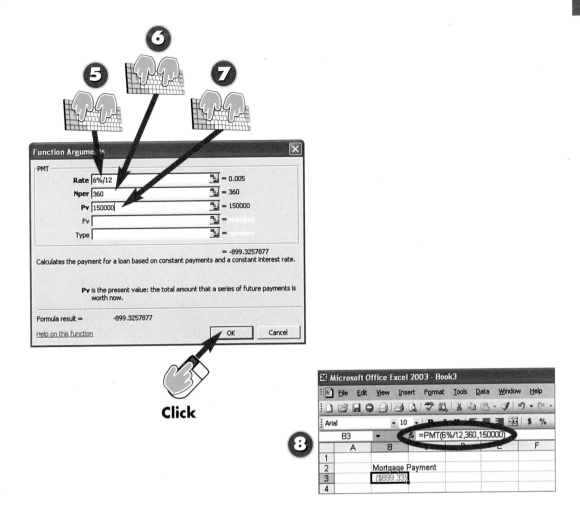

Click

5 In the **Rate** field, type the interest rate per period. For example, type **6%/12** for monthly payments on a 6% annual percentage rate (APR).

6 In the **Nper** field, type the total number of loan payments. For example, type **360** if you'll be making 12 payments per year on a 30-year loan.

7 In the **Pv** field, type the present value of the loan—for example, **150,000**. Click **OK**.

8 Excel calculates the payment and inserts it in the resultant cell.

Negative payment
Your resulting payment is a negative number because payments are considered a debit.

Type argument
If you don't enter a number in the **Type** argument, it defaults to 0, which means that the last payment will pay off the mortgage loan (this is because mortgages are paid in arrears—at the end of the payment period). If you are calculating a car payment, you might put a 1 in the Type argument because you make your payments at the beginning of the payment period. A 1 versus a 0 makes a slight difference in the calculation because of the interest accrued.

Performing a Logical Test Function (IF)

Start

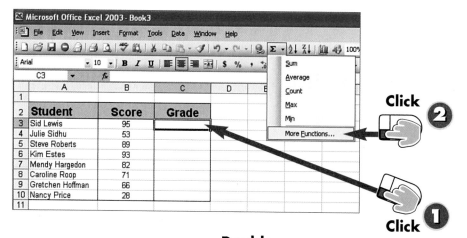

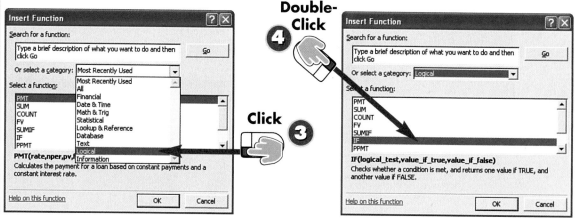

1. Click in the cell in which you want the result of the function to appear (this is called the *resultant cell*).

2. Click the **down arrow** next to the **AutoSum** button on the Standard toolbar and choose **More Functions** from the list that appears.

3. The Insert Function dialog box opens. Click the **down arrow** next to the **Or select a category** field and choose **Logical** from the list that appears.

4. A list of logical functions appears in the **Select a function** list. Scroll through the list to locate the **IF** function, and double-click it.

Using Excel, you can perform a logical test function—for example, to indicate whether scores equal a passing or failing grade based on an established set of criteria.

TIP

Embedded IFs
You can set up embedded IF statements to use in your logical test. For example, suppose scores between 90–100 are an A, 80–89 are a B, 70–79 are a C, 60–69 are a D, and below 59 are an F. Your formula might look like this: **=IF(B3>89, "A", IF(B3>79, "B", IF(B3>69, "C", IF(B3>59, "D", "F").**

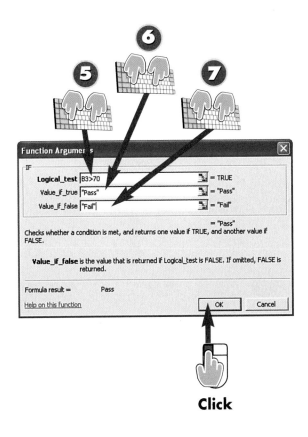

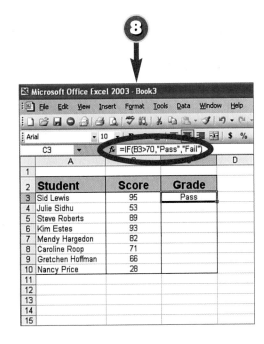

Click

5 In the **Logical_test** field, type the condition to determine whether a grade is above 70. The logical test is if the cell is greater than 70, for example, **B3>70**.

6 In the **Value_if_true** field, type the value you want to use if the grade is above 70 (that is, a passing grade)—for example, **"Pass"**.

7 In the **Value_if_false** field, type the value you want to use if the grade is below 70 (that is, a failing grade)—for example, **"Fail"**. Click **OK**.

8 Excel performs the logical test and inserts the result in the resultant cell.

Copying a logical test
You can copy a logical test function in a cell and paste it so that you have the same function performed on all cells in a list—for example, if you need this pass/fail test performed on a set of student grades.

Function arguments help
If you need help while you are inputting your function arguments, click the **Help on this function** link in the bottom-left corner of the Function Arguments dialog box.

Adding a Range Given Criteria (SUMIF)

Start

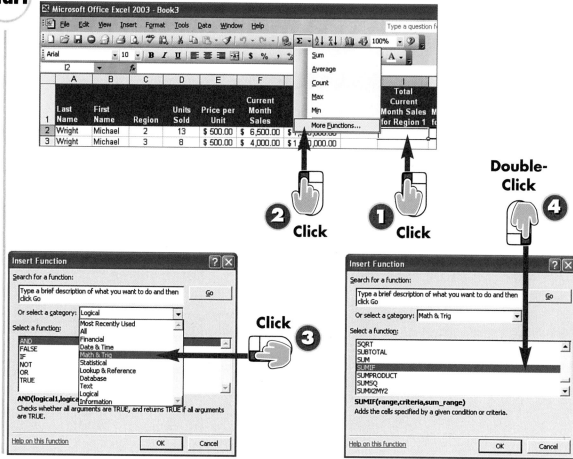

Double-
Click

Click

Click

Click

1. Click in the cell in which you want the result of the function to appear (this is called the *resultant cell*).

2. Click the **down arrow** next to the **AutoSum** button on the Standard toolbar and choose **More Functions** from the list that appears.

3. The Insert Function dialog box opens. Click the **down arrow** next to the **Or select a category** field and choose **Math & Trig** from the list that appears.

4. A list of math and trig functions appears in the **Select a function** list. Scroll through the list to locate the **SUMIF** function, and double-click it.

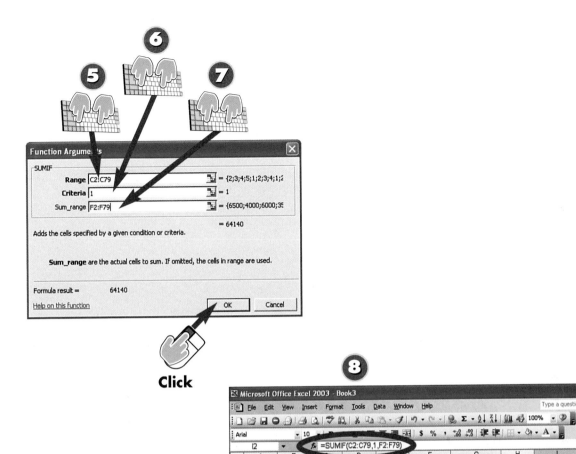

Click

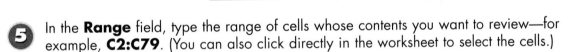

5 — In the **Range** field, type the range of cells whose contents you want to review—for example, **C2:C79**. (You can also click directly in the worksheet to select the cells.)

6 — In the **Criteria** field, type the criterion you want to check in the range—in this case, type **"1"** because you want to add sales data from Region 1 only.

7 — In the **Sum_range** field, type the range of cells that match your criterion—in this case, **F2:F79**, which contains the current month sales data. Click **OK**.

8 — Excel adds the range given your criteria and inserts the result in the resultant cell.

End

Range selection

In addition to typing specific Range and Sum_range arguments, you can click in the worksheet and select each range of cells using the mouse.

COUNTIF

Instead of totaling cells that meet a criterion with **SUMIF**, you can use **COUNTIF** to count the number of cells in a range that meet a specific criterion. For example, instead of totaling your sales data, maybe you want to know how many regional quarters were under $20,000.

Finding the Future Value of an Investment (FV)

Start

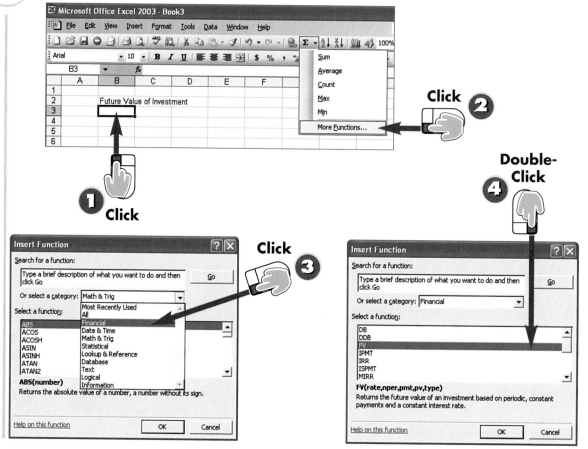

Click ②

Double-Click ④

① Click

Click ③

① Click in the cell in which you want the result of the function to appear (this is called the *resultant cell*).

② Click the **down arrow** next to the **AutoSum** button on the Standard toolbar and choose **More Functions** from the list that appears.

③ The Insert Function dialog box opens. Click the **down arrow** next to the **Or select a category** field and choose **Financial** from the list that appears.

④ A list of financial-related functions appears in the **Select a function** list. Scroll through the list to locate the **FV** function, and double-click it.

INTRODUCTION

If you open a 3% interest-bearing money market account with $100 in January, and make deposits of $100 each month, how much money will you have at the end of the year? Excel can help you calculate the future value of an amount of money, based on a constant interest rate, over a specific number of periods, in which you make a constant payment.

TIP

Function arguments help
If you need help while you are inputting your function arguments, click the **Help on this function** link in the bottom-left corner of the Function Arguments dialog box.

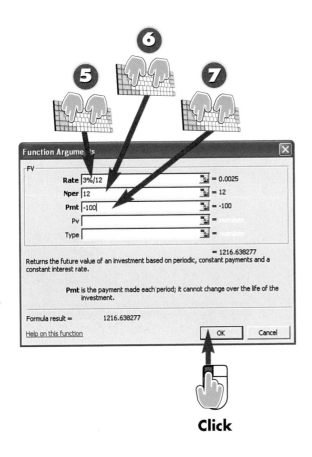

Click

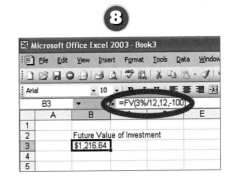

In the **Rate** field, type the interest rate per period. For example, type **3%/12** for monthly accrual on a 3% interest-bearing account.

In the **Nper** field, type the total number of payments for the investment (in this example, **12** deposits).

In the **Pmt** field, type the amount to be paid in each deposit—in this case, **-100**. Click **OK**.

Excel calculates the future investment value and inserts it in the resultant cell.

End

Negative payments

TIP

Because you are making a payment with each deposit, you need to make sure the **Pmt** argument is a negative value.

Fixing the #### Error

Start

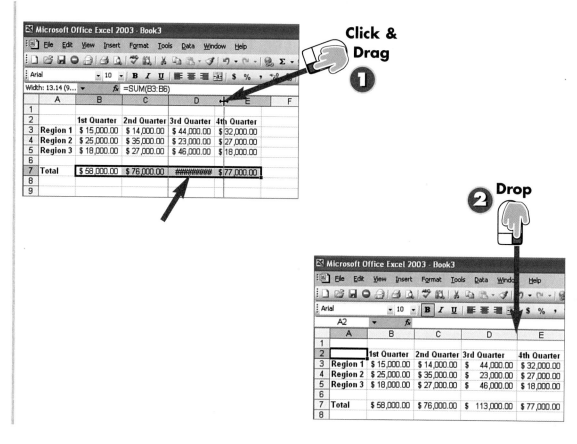

Click & Drag
1

Drop
2

1 If one of the cells in your worksheet contains the #### error, click on the cell's column border and drag it to increase the column width.

2 Drop the column border and the error disappears, and the cell's actual data is displayed.

End

Fixing the #DIV/0! Error

Start

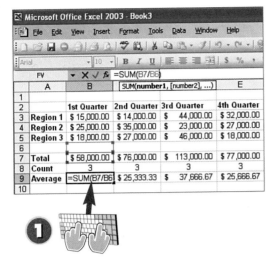

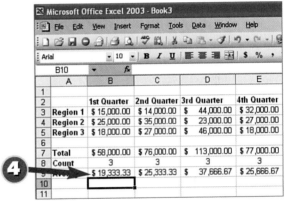

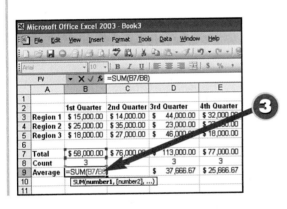

1 In the cell you want to use as the resultant cell, type a formula to obtain an average, for example, type **=SUM(B7/B6)** in cell B9 and press **Enter**.

2 If one of the cells in your worksheet now contains the **#DIV/0!** error, locate the empty cell referenced by the formula (in this case, cell **B6**).

3 Click on the resultant cell (here, **B9**), press **F2** on the keyboard, and retype the formula to omit the empty cell—in this case, **=(B7/B8)**—and press **Enter**.

4 The error disappears because it is no longer trying to divide a number by an empty cell.

End

Fixing the #NAME? Error

Start

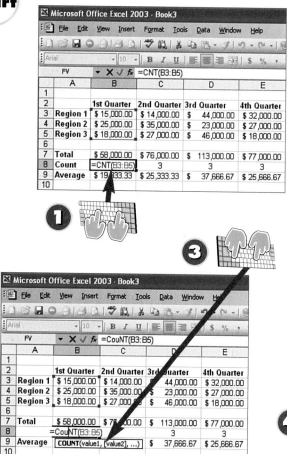

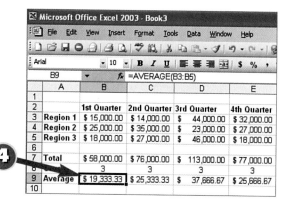

1 In the cell you want to use as the resultant cell, type the formula you want to use in your calculation. For example, type **=CNT(B3:B5)** in cell B8 and press **Enter**.

2 In this case, you get the **#NAME?** error because **CNT** is not the correct spelling for the referenced function; it is **COUNT**.

3 Click on the resultant cell (here, **B8**), press **F2** on the keyboard, and retype the formula—in this case, **=COUNT(B3:B5)**—and press **Enter**.

4 The error disappears because the function is spelled correctly.

End

TIP

Using the Paste Function dialog box
The Paste Function dialog box offers many functions. Practice using different functions and see the results you get from your calculations. As you experiment, you can move the Paste Function dialog box around or collapse it to see your cells.

Fixing the #VALUE! Error

Start

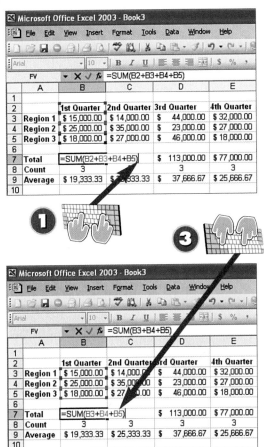

① In the cell you want to use as the resultant cell, type the formula you want to use in your calculation. For example, type **=SUM(B2+B3+B4+B5)** in cell **B7**, and press **Enter**.

② In this case, you get the **#VALUE!** error because the value in cell B2 is textual, not numeric. You won't get the error if you enter **=SUM(B2:B5)** instead of the plus signs.

③ Click on the resultant cell (here, **B7**), press **F2** on the keyboard, and retype the formula—in this case, **=SUM(B3+B4+B5)**—and press **Enter**.

④ The error disappears because all cells are numeric.

End

INTRODUCTION

Excel notifies you when there are errors in your data by displaying different error descriptions in the cell that contains the error. For example, when a cell contains a #VALUE? value, it means the formula contains nonnumeric data or cell or function names that cannot be used in the calculation.

TIP

Overwriting cells
See the task "Overwriting and Deleting Data" in Part 3 to make sure you are overwriting data in cells correctly.

Recognizing the #REF! Error

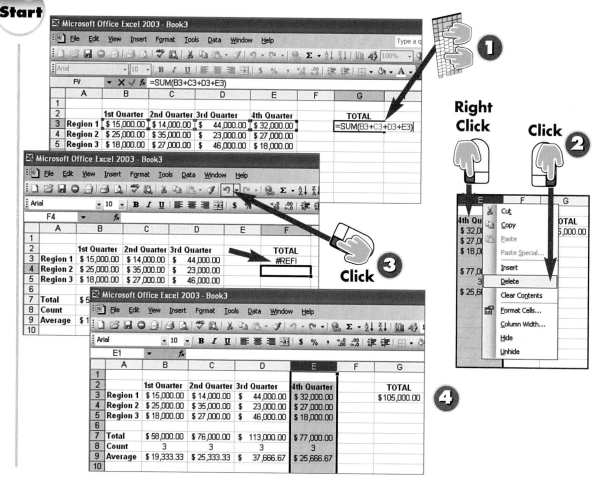

① In the cell you want to use as the resultant cell, type the formula you want to use in your calculation. For example, type **=SUM(B3+C3+D3+E3)** and press **Enter**.

② Right-click one of the columns that contains a cell referenced in the formula you just typed (here, column **E**), and choose **Delete** from the shortcut menu that appears.

③ In this case, the **#REF!** error appears because the values in cells referenced in column E are no longer available in the formula. Click the **Undo** button to correct it.

④ The error disappears because the formula values are restored.

INTRODUCTION

Excel notifies you when there are errors in your data by displaying different error descriptions in the cell that contains the error. For example, when a cell contains a #REF! error, it means the formula contains a reference to a cell that isn't valid. Frequently, this means you deleted a referenced cell. The best solution is to undo your action and review the cells involved in the formula.

TIP

Checking references
If after you undo what caused the **#REF!** error you want to find out what caused it, see the tasks "Checking for Formula References (Precedents)" and "Checking for Cell References (Dependents)" later in this part for more information on checking formula and cell references.

Recognizing Circular References

Start

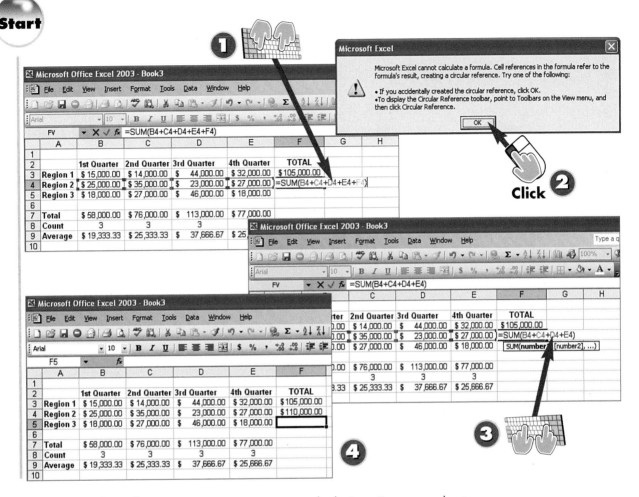

Click

1. Type the formula you want to use in your calculation. For example, type **=SUM(B4+C4+D4+E4+F4)** and press **Enter**.

2. Excel displays an error message, notifying you that the formula contains a circular reference. Click **OK**.

3. Click on the resultant cell, press **F2** on the keyboard, and retype your formula—in this case, **=SUM(B4+C4+D4+E4)**—and press **Enter**.

4. The error is fixed because the result cell no longer is in the calculation.

End

INTRODUCTION

Excel notifies you when there are errors in your data by displaying different error descriptions in the cell that contains the error. For example, you receive a circular reference error message when one of the cells you are referencing in your calculation is the cell in which you want the calculation to appear.

TIP

Circular reference toolbar
If you didn't intend to create a circular reference and you chose **OK** in the message box, the Circular Reference toolbar and Help will appear to assist you in correcting your actions.

Checking for Formula References (Precedents)

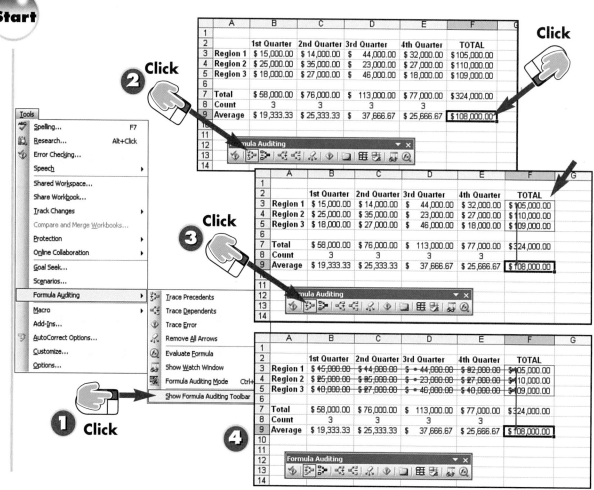

1. Open the **Tools** menu, choose **Formula Auditing**, and select **Show Formula Auditing Toolbar**.

2. Click the cell you want to trace (this cell must contain a formula) and click the **Trace Precedents** button. Excel draws tracer arrows to the appropriate cells.

3. Click the **Trace Precedents** button again to see if there are any precedents for these calculations.

4. If additional precedents are present, Excel draws additional tracer arrows to the appropriate cells.

End

INTRODUCTION

One way to check a formula to see if it is referencing the correct cells is to select that formula and then trace all cells that are referenced in that formula. Cells that are referenced are called *precedents*.

TIP — Moving references
You can double-click the arrows to move from one reference to another. Click the **Remove Precedents Arrows** button on the Auditing toolbar to remove the arrows.

TIP — Closing the toolbar
Close the Auditing toolbar by clicking the **Close** button (×) in the upper-right corner of the toolbar.

Checking for Cell References (Dependents)

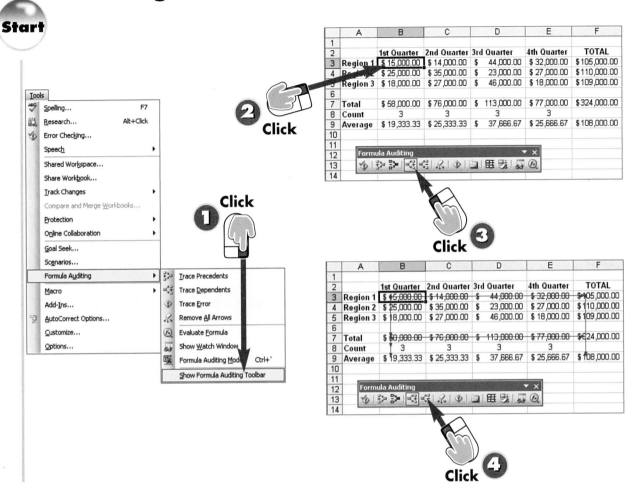

1. Open the **Tools** menu, choose **Formula Auditing**, and select **Show Formula Auditing Toolbar**.

2. Click the cell you want to trace. This cell must *not* contain a formula.

3. Click the **Trace Dependents** button until the tracer arrows stop adding on to the appropriate cells.

4. Click the **Remove Dependents Arrows** button enough times to remove all the arrows (or click the **Remove All Arrows** button).

End

Closing the toolbar
Close the Auditing toolbar by clicking the **Close** button (×) in the upper-right corner of the toolbar.

Using Trace Errors
If the cell contains an error message, use the Trace Errors button to have Excel trace possible reasons for the error.

Working with Charts

You've already learned the fundamentals of creating a worksheet. Now you can concentrate on some of the other features that add to a data presentation. For example, you can create a chart based on data in a worksheet. Charts are very useful for interpreting data; however, different people look at data in different ways. To account for this, you can quickly change the appearance of charts in Excel by clicking directly on the chart. You can change titles, legend information, axis points, category names, and more.

The *axes* are the grid on which the data is plotted. On a 2D chart, the y-axis is the vertical axis on a chart (*value axis*), and the x-axis is the horizontal axis (*category axis*). A 3D chart has three axes (add a z-axis). You can control all the aspects of the axes—the appearance of the line, the tick marks, the number format used, and more.

Using the Chart Toolbar

Chart toolbar

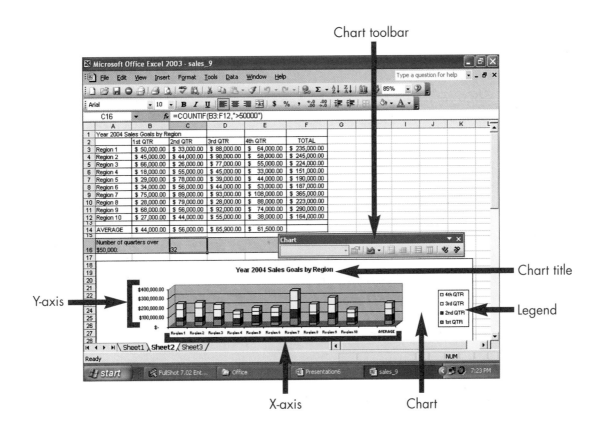

Chart title

Y-axis

Legend

X-axis

Chart

Creating a Chart

Start

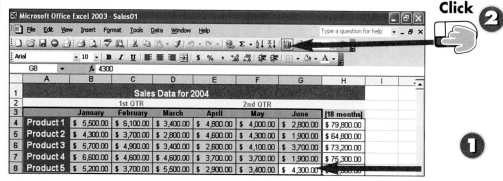

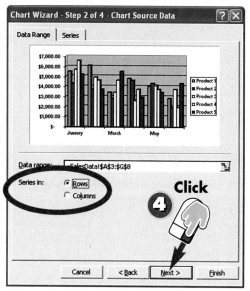

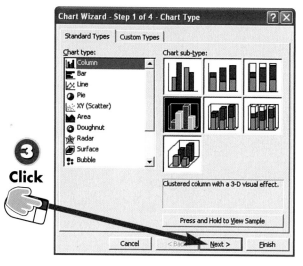

1. Select the cells you want to include in your chart.

2. Click the **Chart Wizard** button on the Standard toolbar.

3. The first page of the Chart Wizard opens. Select the desired **Chart Type** and **Chart Sub-type**; then click **Next**.

4. Depending on how you want your chart information to appear, click **Rows** or **Columns** in the **Series in** area.

INTRODUCTION

Interpreting numeric data by looking at numbers in a table can be diffi-cult. Using data to create charts can help people visualize the data's significance. For example, you might not have noticed in a spreadsheet that the same month of every year has low sales figures, but it becomes obvious when you make a chart from the data in that spreadsheet. The chart's visual nature also helps others review your data without the need to review every single number.

TIP

Using Back and Cancel
At any time while using the Chart wizard, you can click the **Back** button to return to previ-ous screens or the **Cancel** but-ton to start over. In addition, you can click the **Finish** button any time and add information to your chart afterward.

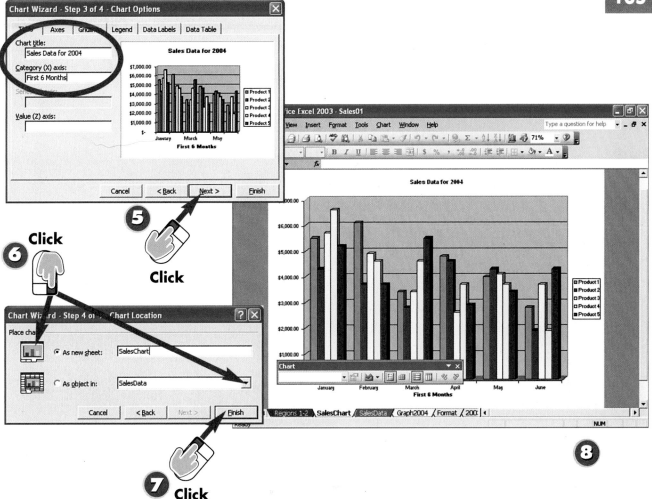

Click (6)

Click (5)

Click (7)

(8)

(5) Type a name for the chart in the **Chart title** field, a value for the x-axis in the **Category (X) axis** field, and any other values you want; then click **Next**.

(6) Click the **As New Sheet** option to enter the chart as a new sheet (and type a sheet name), or the **As Object in** option to enter the chart in the sheet you select.

(7) Click **Finish**.

(8) Excel creates the chart, displaying it along with a Chart toolbar.

End

Changing the Chart Type

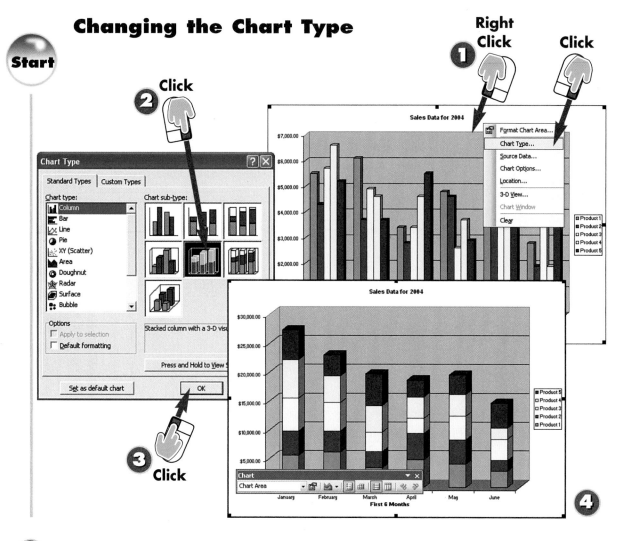

1 Right-click the plot area and select **Chart Type** from the shortcut menu.

2 Select a new chart type and chart subtype in the Chart Type dialog box.

3 Click **OK**.

4 The updated chart type appears in your chart.

INTRODUCTION

Charting is one of those skills you learn by doing. At first, you might not even know the type of chart you want to create until you *see* it. You can always select a different chart type for a chart so that it better represents the data.

TIP

Using the default chart type

The default chart type is a column chart. To make another chart type the default, select it in the Chart Type dialog box and then click the **Set as default chart** button.

Altering the Source Data Range

Start

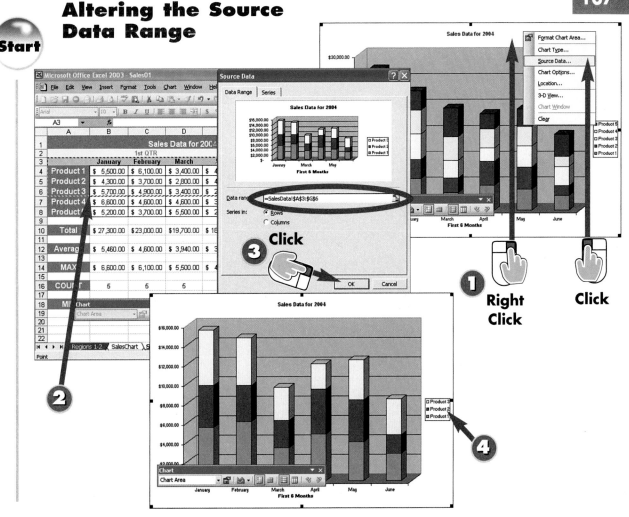

Click

Right Click

Click

Start

1 Right-click the plot area of your chart and select **Source Data** from the shortcut menu.

2 Click directly in your worksheet and select the new data range. The **Data range** area in the Source Data dialog box automatically updates.

3 Click **OK**.

4 The updated data range appears in your chart.

End

INTRODUCTION

There might be times when you create a chart and then decide that you want that chart to include additional information. You can easily add data series to your chart by altering the source data you select in your original worksheet.

TIP

Locating incorrect data
If you notice that one of the data points in your chart is way off scale, this is a good sign that you might have entered data into your worksheet incorrectly. If this is the case, edit the worksheet data, and the chart will update automatically. (Also see the task "Changing the Chart Source Data" later in this part for help altering the original data.

Altering Chart Options

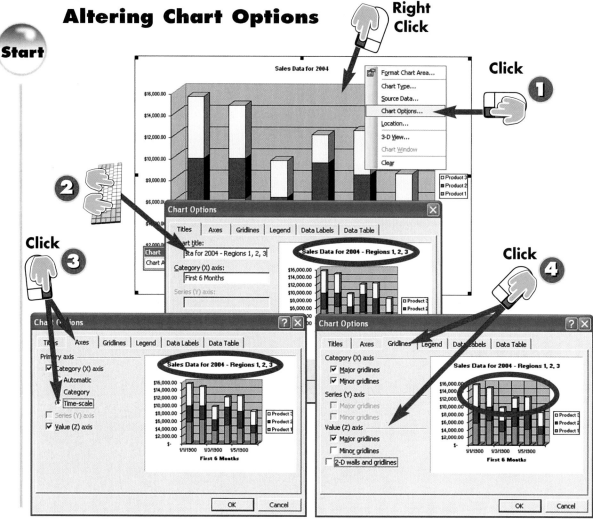

1. Right-click the plot area and select **Chart Options** from the shortcut menu that appears.

2. The Chart Options dialog box opens. Type any changes to the chart titles on the **Titles** tab.

3. Click the **Axes** tab and select from the **Primary axis** options to see how altering these settings affects your chart.

4. Click the **Gridlines** tab and select from the various major gridlines and minor gridlines for each of the Category, Series, and Value axes.

Double-clicking the chart
One of the fastest ways to edit charting options is to double-click directly on the element in the chart you want to alter. The appropriate dialog box opens, enabling you to make the changes you need.

Formatting the axes gridlines
To change the pattern and scale of the gridlines, double-click the gridline itself. Then use the Format Gridlines dialog box to make your selections. Click **OK**.

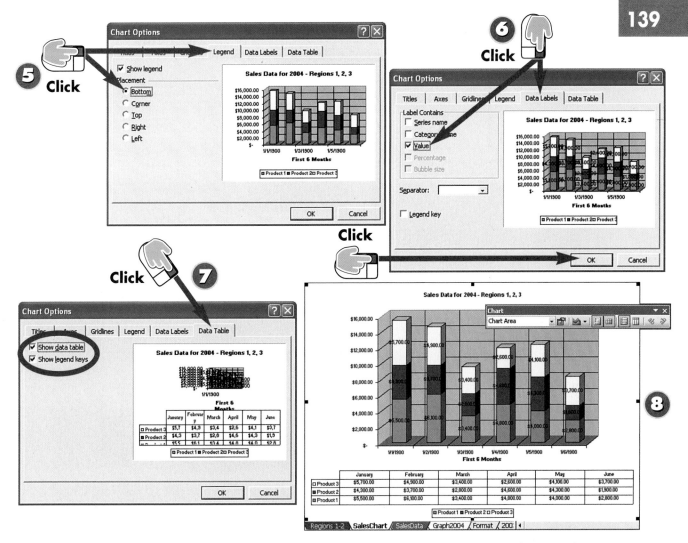

5. Click the **Legend** tab, select whether you want to show a legend, and review how altering the **Placement** options affects your chart.

6. Click the **Data Labels** tab and see how the addition of label descriptions affects your chart.

7. Click the **Data Table** tab and select whether you want to show the data table (with or without the legend keys). When you're finished, click **OK**.

8. Review how your chart has changed.

End

Adding data tables
TIP
If you want to show a data table along with the chart, click the **Data Table** tab in the Chart Options dialog box. Then click the **Show data table** check box and click **OK**.

Printing charts
TIP
You can print a chart, just like you print anything else in Excel. If you select the chart in a worksheet, you can choose the **Selection** option when printing to print only the chart you have selected. If you are in a chart sheet (no data, only the chart on a worksheet), you can print it like a regular worksheet.

Formatting the Plot Area

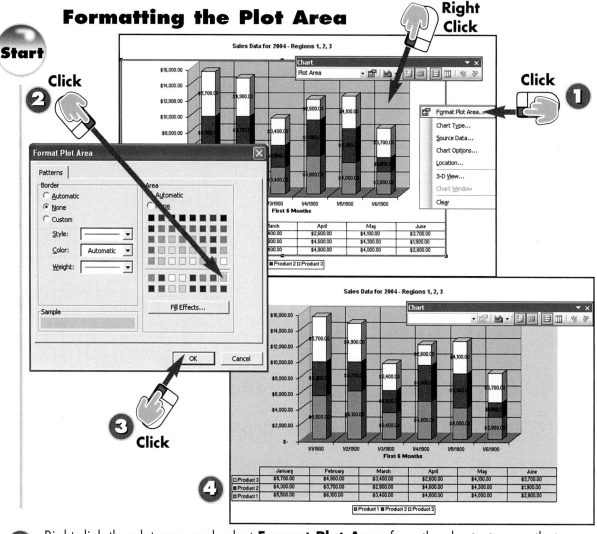

1 Right-click the plot area and select **Format Plot Area** from the shortcut menu that appears.

2 Click a color in the Area section of the Patterns tab of the Format Plot Area dialog box.

3 Click **OK**.

4 Review how your chart has changed.

The *plot area* consists of a border and the location of the data points in your chart. You can alter the style, color, and weight of the border. You can also alter the color of the plot area.

Areas

If you are unsure whether you are in the chart area or the plot area, click directly on the chart. A ScreenTip appears telling you what area you are in. Alternatively, you can refer to the Name Box.

Changing the border

Right-click the chart and select Format Chart Area from the shortcut menu; you can alter the Border options from the Patterns tab. Be careful not to overpower the chart with lines that are too thick—it can take the attention away from the data.

Formatting the Chart Area

Start

Click

Right Click

1

Click

2

3

Click

Click

4

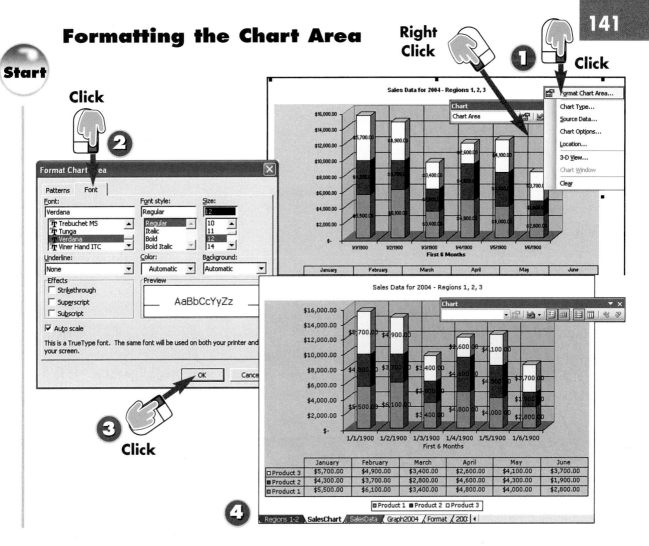

1 Right-click the chart area and select **Format Chart Area** from the shortcut menu that appears.

2 Click the **Font** tab of the Format Chart Area dialog box and select the Font options you prefer.

3 Click **OK**.

4 Review how your chart has changed.

End

Areas

TIP
If you are unsure whether you are in the chart area or the plot area, click directly on the chart. A ScreenTip appears telling you what area you are in. Alternatively, you can refer to the Name Box.

Using the Patterns tab

TIP
You can alter the background color of your chart just like you did in the preceding task, when you changed your plot area color. Refer to that task for more information.

Formatting the Axis Scale

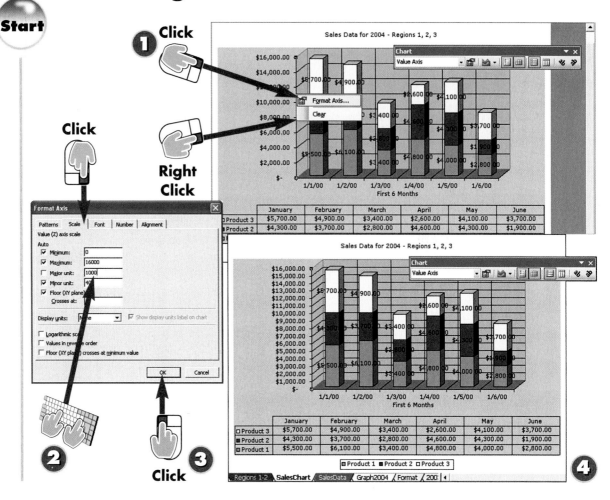

1. Right-click the **Value** axis (left axis) and select **Format Axis** from the shortcut menu that appears.

2. Click the **Scale** tab of the Format Axis dialog box and type changes to the axis scale increments—for example, decrease the value in the **Major unit** field.

3. Click **OK**.

4. Review how your chart has changed.

End

INTRODUCTION

Excel automatically establishes the axis increments according to the maximum amount on the chart. Usually this will suffice, but if you want to show more detail about actual numbers, it can be convenient to alter your value axis.

TIP

Number and alignment
To change the number format, click the **Number** tab and select the numeric format you want to use. To change the alignment, click the **Alignment** tab and select a rotation for the axes.

Altering the Original Data

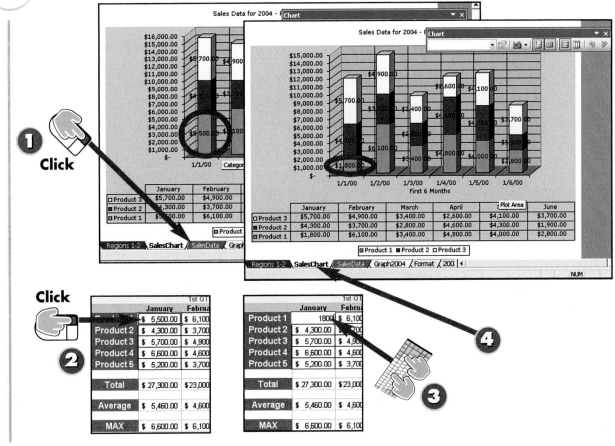

Click

Click

1 Select the worksheet tab or range that contains the charted data.

2 Click a cell that you want to alter or need to update.

3 Type in the new data and press the **Enter** key.

4 Go back to the chart and see how the edited data point has changed your chart.

End

INTRODUCTION

A chart is linked to the worksheet data, so when you make a change in the worksheet, the chart is updated. If you want to change a value in the worksheet, edit it as you do normally. The chart will be updated to reflect the change instantly. If you delete data in the worksheet, the matching data series will be deleted in the chart.

TIP

Saving changes
Make sure that you save your changes to a worksheet and chart often. You wouldn't want to lose any changes you made in case your network goes down or your computer freezes.

Changing the Chart Source Data

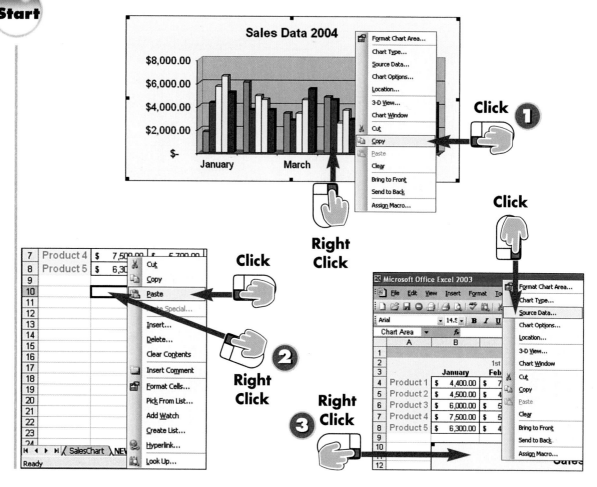

1. Right-click your current chart and select **Copy** from the shortcut menu that appears. This will copy the chart exactly.

2. Switch to the worksheet or open the file containing the new source data, right-click, and select **Paste** from the shortcut menu that appears.

3. Right-click the pasted chart and select **Source Data**.

INTRODUCTION

Suppose you just finished creating your chart in exactly the way you intended it, and your boss tells you that the data he gave you was incorrect, and hands you a file with the corrected data on it. Was all the time you spent on your chart for nothing? Of course not! Simply tell Excel what you want the new data source to be, and you are ready to go.

TIP

Adding and excluding data

Changing the chart source data is similar to adding or excluding data from your chart. See the task that follows for more information on altering the source data within your worksheet.

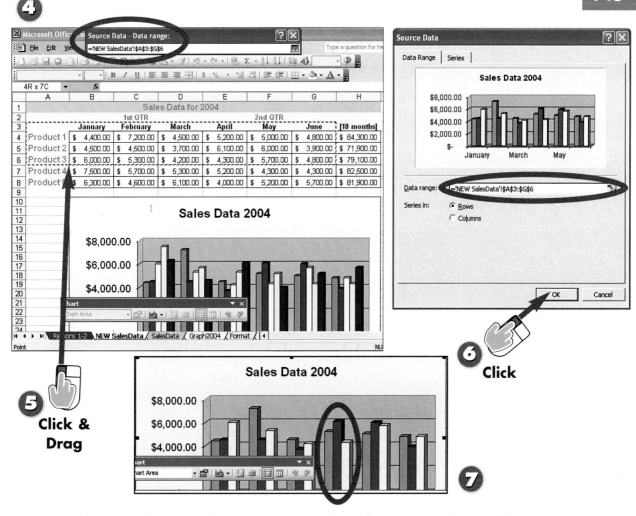

④

**Click &
Drag**

⑤

Click

⑥

⑦

④ Excel jumps to the original data-source worksheet. If the source data workbook is not open, the **Data range** field in the Source Data dialog box will appear blank.

⑤ Click and drag to select the new data source cells (for example, from five products to three); simultaneously, the Source Data dialog box shrinks to show the data.

⑥ When you release the mouse button, the **Data range** list box in the Source Data dialog box displays the new source data range; click **OK**.

⑦ The chart is updated to reflect the new data source. If you need to change some chart options, refer to the task "Altering Chart Options" earlier in this part.

End

Updating source data

A chart's source data can be kept in another worksheet. If you make changes to this source data, Excel will ask you whether you want to update the chart data or keep the data the same as the last time you worked on the chart. If you work in the chart without the source data worksheet open, you might get a reference error message indicating that you need to open the source data worksheet.

Move and resize charts

To move the chart, click the chart, hold the mouse pointer on the chart, and drag it to a new location. To resize the chart, click the chart border and drag it to resize it.

Adding Data to Charts

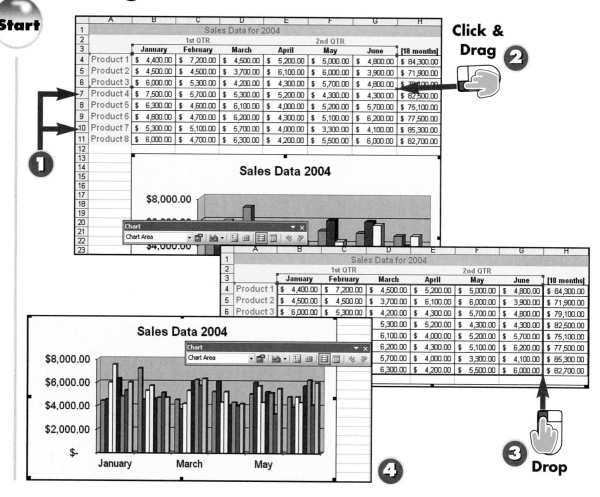

Start

Click & Drag 2

3 **Drop**

4

1. Add the new data that you want to include in your chart to the original worksheet and click directly on your chart to see what data is currently referenced in the chart.

2. Click and drag the blue chart data line to include the newly added data.

3. Drop the chart data line in the new location.

4. The chart automatically updates to include the new data.

End

TIP

Excluding chart data
You can click and drag the blue chart data line to exclude data in your chart. Simply drag the blue line so that the data you want to exclude is no longer contained within the chart.

Adding a Legend

Start Right Click

Click ②

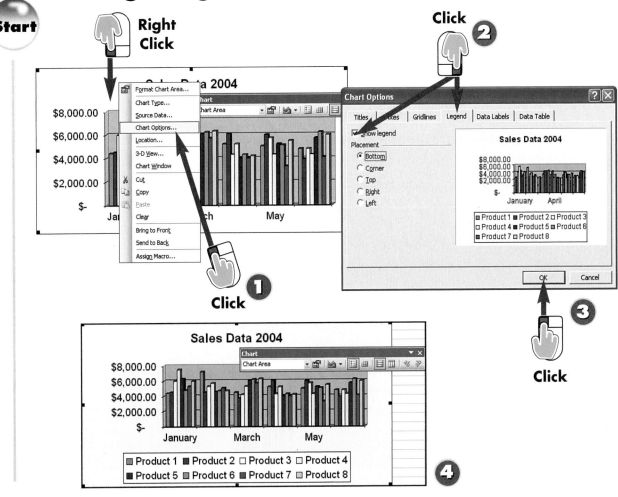

Click ①

Click ③

Click

④

① Right-click the plot area or chart area and select **Chart Options** from the shortcut menu to open the Chart Options dialog box.

② Click the **Legend** tab and click the **Show legend** check box to mark it. Then, see how altering the **Placement** options affects your chart in the preview area.

③ Click **OK**.

④ The legend is inserted in the chart.

End

A *legend* helps to makes sense out of all the data points and colors in a chart. If you didn't have a legend added when you initially created your chart, you can easily add one later.

Using the Legend button
You can also click the **Legend** button on the Chart toolbar to insert a default legend (to the right of the chart).

Formatting legends
Right-click the legend and choose **Format Legend** from the shortcut menu. From the dialog box that appears, you can alter the patterns, fonts, and even the placement of the legend.

Working with Graphic Objects

You can draw in a worksheet or on a chart using one of several Excel drawing tools. You can add a picture you draw yourself, insert a picture from another file, add an organization chart, as well as ClipArt, AutoShapes and WordArt. Charts, pictures, clip art, and drawn items are all considered graphic *objects*.

In addition to inserting objects, you can resize and move them. You can also format them and delete objects.

Inserted Graphic Objects

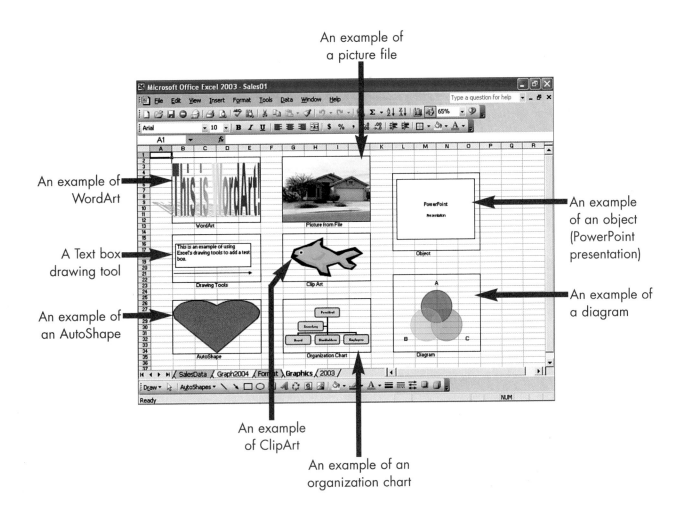

An example of
a picture file

An example of
WordArt

A Text box
drawing tool

An example of
an AutoShape

An example
of an object
(PowerPoint
presentation)

An example of
a diagram

An example
of ClipArt

An example of an
organization chart

Using Drawing Tools

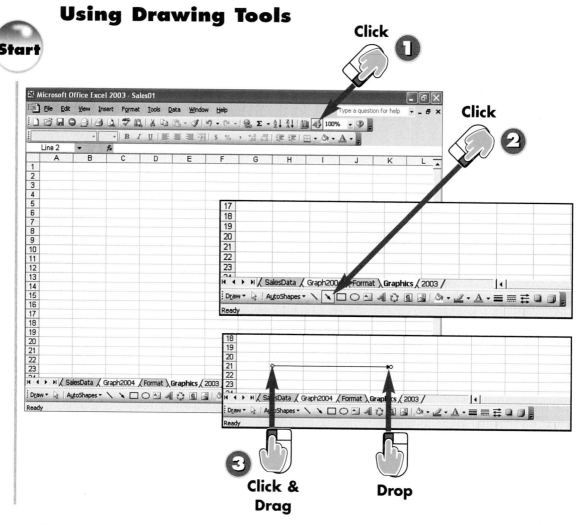

Start

Click ①

Click ②

③

Click & Drag

Drop

① Click the **Drawing** button on the Standard toolbar. The Drawing toolbar appears above the window's Status bar.

② Click any of the drawing tools' buttons—for example, the **Arrow** button on the Drawing toolbar. The mouse pointer turns into a plus sign.

③ Click and drag in the chart to draw an arrow; release the mouse button when the arrow is the length you want it to be (the pointer end will be at the point of release).

INTRODUCTION

Excel has drawing tools that you can use to draw on a worksheet or chart sheet (that is, a worksheet that contains only a chart). In this task, you'll learn about the advantages of using Excel's drawing tools to help point out information on a worksheet.

TIP

Color and style
Click the **Line Color** and **Line Style** buttons in the Drawing toolbar to change the color and style of the lines used to draw objects.

TIP

Text boxes
A text box is an object that contains text. You can move a text box, resize it, and even add formatting options.

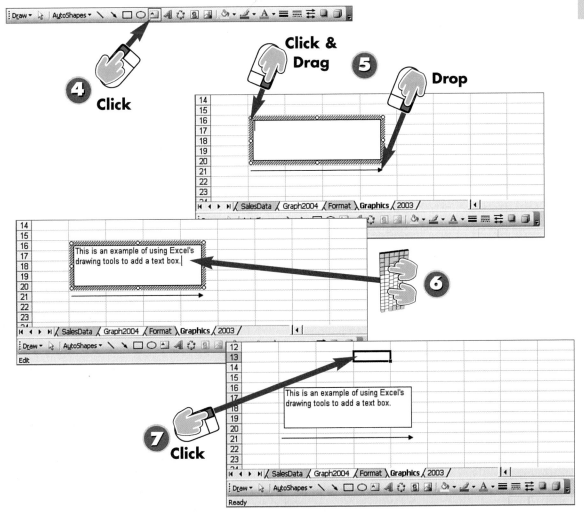

4 As another example, click the **Text Box** button on the Drawing toolbar. The mouse pointer turns into an insertion pointer.

5 Click and drag in the worksheet to draw a text box; release the mouse button when the box is the size you want it to be.

6 Type the text you want to enter in the text box.

7 Click anywhere outside the chart area to see how your drawings look.

End

Inserting Clip Art

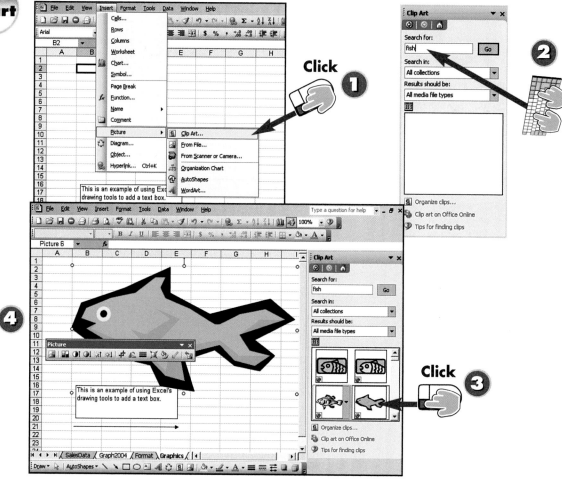

Start

Click ❶

❷

Click ❸

❹

End

① Open the **Insert** menu, choose **Picture**, and select **Clip Art** to open the Clip Art task pane.

② Type a description for the clip art you are looking for in the **Search for** text box, and press **Enter** (or, click the **Go** button).

③ If Microsoft has clip art that matches the description you typed, it is displayed in the Clip Art task pane. Click an image in the results list to insert it into your worksheet.

④ The clip art is inserted into your worksheet. (You might need to move or resize the image; see the tasks "Moving an Object" and "Resizing an Object".)

Clip art adds visual interest to your Excel worksheets. With Microsoft clip art, you can choose from numerous professionally prepared images, sounds, and movie clips. After you have added graphics, you can move them around in the worksheet and even assign text wrapping. (Be aware that the first time you try to use Microsoft's clip art, you might be asked to set up your collections and organize your clips. Make sure you do this.)

Using the Picture toolbar

When you insert a piece of clip art, the Picture toolbar appears; it contains tools you can use to crop the picture, add a border to it, or adjust its brightness and contrast.

Inserting a Picture from File

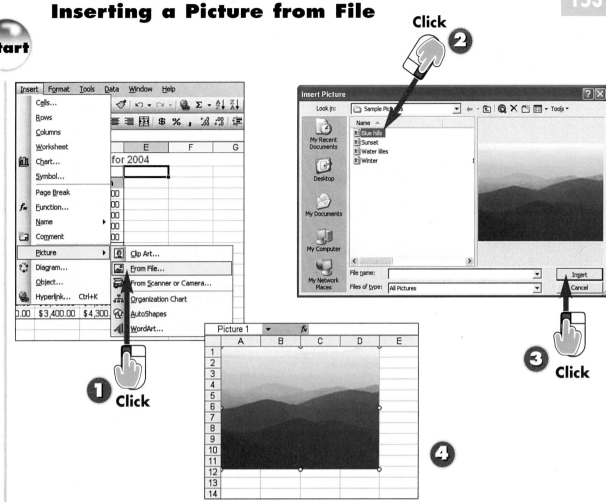

1 Open the **Insert** menu, choose **Picture**, and select **From File** to open the Insert Picture dialog box.

2 Locate the file you want to use and click it to see a preview (you might need to select **Preview** from the dialog box **Views** button).

3 Click the **Insert** button.

4 The image is inserted into your worksheet.

End

With digital cameras and sharing pictures online becoming more popular, there will certainly be times when you want to insert a picture file into a worksheet. You can insert all types of graphics files: Windows Metafiles, JPEG files, PNGs, Macintosh PICT files, Kodak Photo CD files, and many more.

Inserting other things

You can insert clip art by opening the **Insert** menu, choosing **Picture**, and selecting **Clip Art**, and then searching through the Clip Art task pane to find the image you want. You can also choose **Insert, Picture, Organization Chart** to insert an organization chart ready for you to input information. When you insert a picture, the Picture toolbar appears; it contains tools you can use to crop the picture, add a border to it, or adjust its brightness and contrast.

Adding an Organization Chart

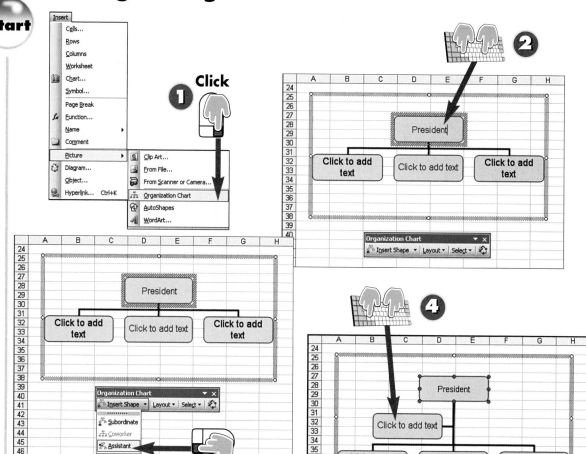

Start

Click 1

2

Click 3

4

End

1. Open the **Insert** menu, choose **Picture**, and select **Organization Chart** to insert an organization chart into your worksheet, and to display the Organization Chart toolbar.

2. An organization chart containing dummy text is inserted into your worksheet. Click a chart box and type over the dummy text with your own text.

3. To add a subordinate, co-worker, or assistant, click the appropriate chart position. Then click the down arrow next to the **Insert Shape** button on the toolbar.

4. The new chart box containing dummy text is added to the chart. Click the chart box and type over the dummy text with your own text.

INTRODUCTION

Excel lets you insert an organization chart directly into your worksheet. You can insert the chart and then add the appropriate information, in a manner very similar to inserting a table and adding data in Word or PowerPoint.

TIP

Placing new chart boxes

When adding a subordinate, co-worker, or assistant chart box, click the chart box with which the new chart box should be associated *before* choosing the desired option from the Insert Shape drop-down list. For example, if you're adding an assistant, start by clicking the chart box for the person to whom that assistant will report. If you make a mistake, click the new chart box and drag it to the correct chart position.

Inserting an AutoShape

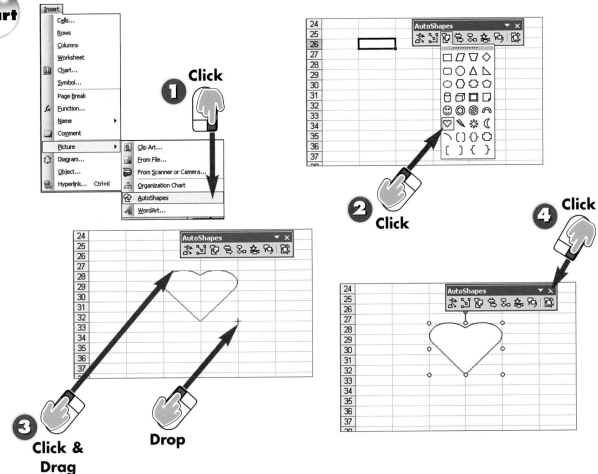

Click ①

② **Click**

③ **Click & Drag** **Drop**

④ **Click**

End

① Open the **Insert** menu, choose **Picture**, and select **AutoShapes** to display the AutoShapes toolbar.

② Click on an AutoShape button, such as the **Basic Shapes** button, on the toolbar and select from the different shape options (here, **Heart**).

③ The mouse pointer changes to a plus sign. Click and drag the pointer to draw the object at the desired size; then release the mouse button.

④ The new shape is added, complete with sizing handles. Click the **Close** (×) button on the AutoShape toolbar to close it.

INTRODUCTION

There are numerous predesigned shapes, called *AutoShapes*, that Excel allows you to add to your worksheets. For example, you can insert any one of the following AutoShapes into your worksheet: Lines, Connectors, Basic Shapes, Block Arrows, Flowchart, Stars and Banners, Callouts, and more.

Resizing and moving objects
Move the mouse over an object border; the pointer becomes a four-headed arrow and you can move it (see the "Moving Objects" task); a two-headed arrow allows you to resize it (see the "Resizing Objects" task).

Formatting AutoShapes
To format your AutoShape, right-click the object and select **Format AutoShape** from the shortcut menu. Click the **Colors and Lines** tab and choose from the various colors, line types and arrows.

Inserting WordArt

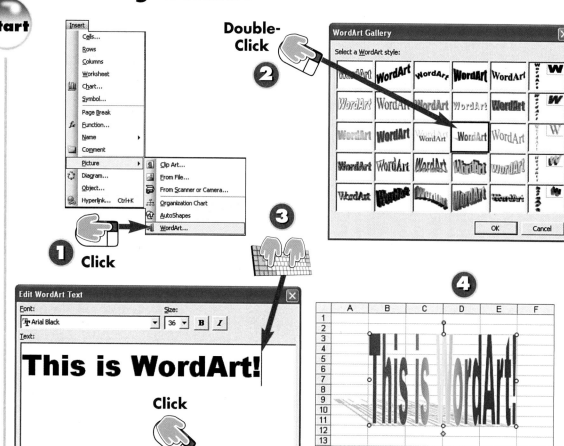

1. Open the **Insert** menu, choose **Picture**, and select **WordArt** to open the WordArt Gallery.

2. Double-click on the WordArt style you want to use to open the Edit WordArt Text dialog box.

3. Type your text into the **Text** box, and click **OK**.

4. The WordArt text is inserted into your worksheet.

WordArt is a text-based object that Microsoft provides to apply special effects to text. You don't have to add these text effects manually; the different styles of WordArt are indeed the text effects themselves.

Formatting WordArt

Once your WordArt is inserted into your worksheet, the WordArt toolbar appears (while the WordArt object is selected). You can use the various buttons on the toolbar to edit the text, alter the style, format the text, and add more WordArt.

Inserting a Diagram

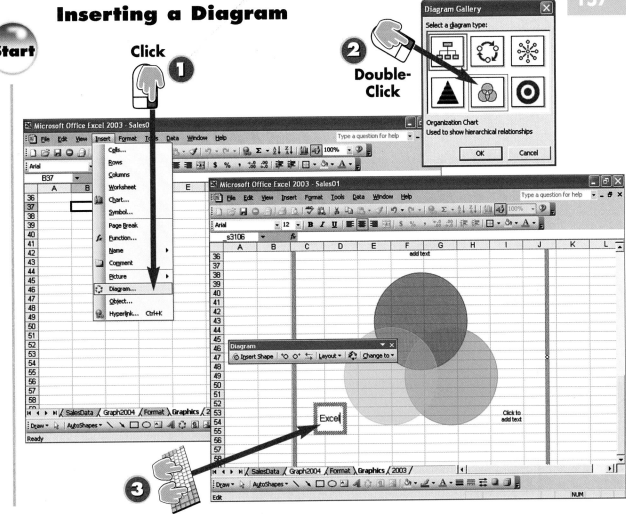

1 Open the **Insert** menu and choose **Diagram** to open the Diagram Gallery dialog box.

2 Double-click the desired diagram type; a diagram of that type containing dummy text is inserted into your worksheet.

3 Click each instance of dummy text and type over it with text of your own.

Excel lets you insert diagrams directly into your worksheets. You can insert the diagram and then add the appropriate information, in a manner very similar to inserting an organization chart and adding the data.

Inserting an organization chart

You can choose to insert an organization chart from the Diagram Gallery or open the **Insert** menu, choose **Picture**, and select **Organization Chart** to insert an organization chart ready for you to input information.

Inserting an Object

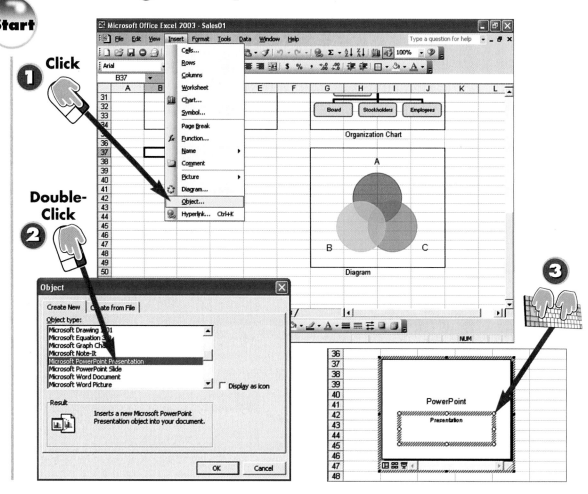

Start

Click
1

Double-Click
2

3

End

1 Open the **Insert** menu and choose **Object** to open the Object dialog box.

2 Scroll through the **Object type** list and double-click on the object you want to insert—for example, **Microsoft PowerPoint Presentation**.

3 Edit the object according to the individual object properties (in this example, as you would when creating a PowerPoint presentation).

INTRODUCTION

In addition to inserting all the different types of graphic objects that you've learned about in this part, you can also insert objects that aren't as commonly added to Excel worksheets. For example, you can insert a media clip, a PowerPoint slide, a Microsoft Works chart, a video clip, and much more.

TIP

Inserting clip art
You can insert clip art by opening the **Insert** menu, choosing **Picture**, and selecting **Clip Art**. Search through the Clip Art task pane; when you find a piece of art you like, click it to insert it.

Selecting an Object

Start

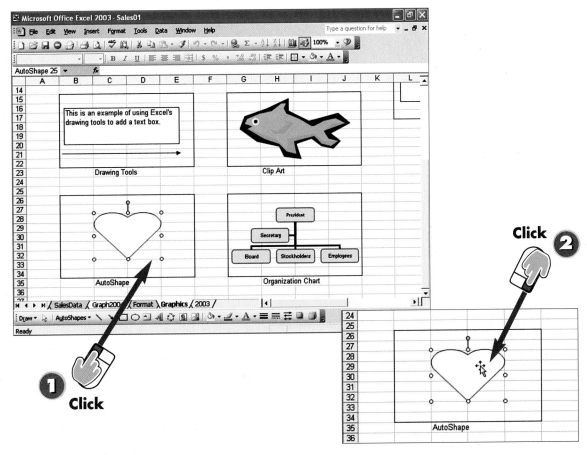

Click ②

Click ①

1. Click the object you want to select; selection handles appear around the edges of the object.

2. Move the mouse over the object border; the pointer becomes a four-headed arrow and you can move it; a two-headed arrow allows you to resize it.

End

INTRODUCTION

As you have seen, you can add charts to a worksheet, draw objects, insert pictures, and more. Each of these items exists on a separate layer on top of the worksheet and is generically called an *object*. As you will discover in the next several tasks, you can format, move, resize, and delete objects; first, however, you must select the object you want to modify.

Selecting multiple objects
To select multiple objects, click the first object, press and hold down the **Shift** key, and click on the second object. Continue until all the objects you want are selected.

Reselect
If you select a cell instead of an object by accident, try again—this time, making sure to put the pointer right on the edge of the object. Alternatively, click the **Select Objects** button on the Drawing toolbar and then click the object.

Formatting an Object

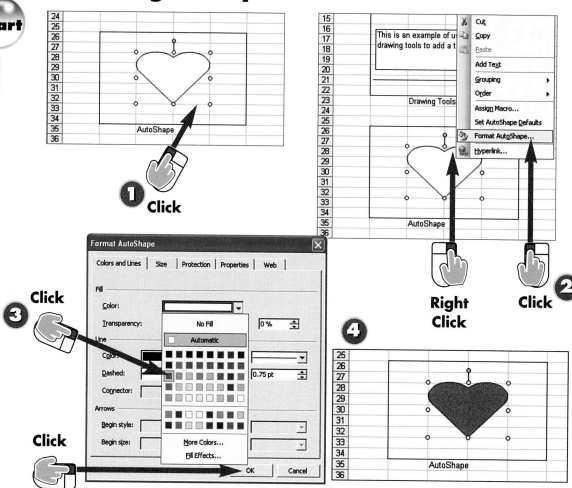

Click

3

Click

Right Click

Click 2

4

1. Click the object you want to format; selection handles appear around the edges of the object.

2. Right-click the object and select **Format [object name]** (here, AutoShape) from the shortcut menu.

3. A Format [object name] dialog box opens. Click the available tabs and alter the formatting options and click **OK**.

4. The formatting changes are applied to the object.

Formatting
You can also double-click directly on the object to auto-matically open the Format dia-log box associated with it.

Moving an Object

Start

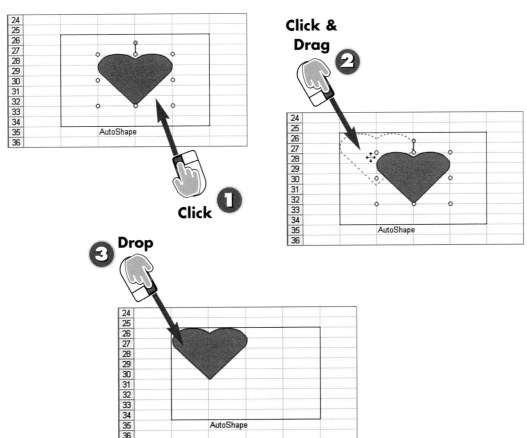

Click & Drag 2

Click 1

Drop 3

1. Select the object you want to move; selection handles appear around the edges of the object.

2. Click directly on the object or its border (not the selection handles) and hold the left mouse button while dragging the object to the new location.

3. Release the mouse button to drop the object in the new location. The object is moved.

End

INTRODUCTION

When you draw an object on or add an object to a worksheet, you might not like its placement. Perhaps the object obscures the worksheet data, or maybe it needs to be moved a little closer to (or farther away from) the data. Fortunately, you can easily move an object.

TIP

Copying objects
To copy an object, press and hold down the **Ctrl** key on your keyboard as you drag; a copy of the original object will be moved, with the original remaining intact where it is.

TIP

Moving an object to another worksheet
Select the object, and then open the **Edit** menu and choose **Cut**. Move to the new sheet or workbook, click in the spot where you want the object to appear, and then open the **Edit** menu and choose **Paste**.

Resizing an Object

Start

Click
①

②

③ Click & Drag

Drop

④

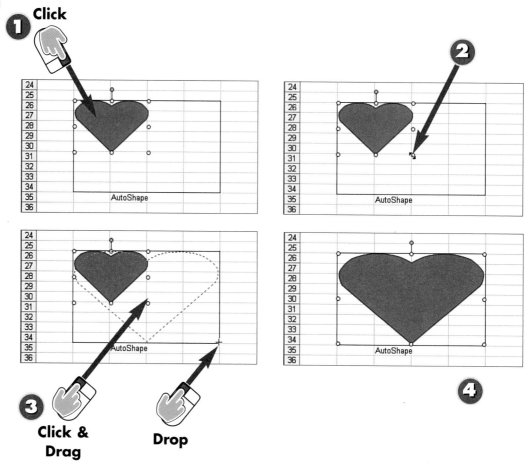

① Select the object you want to resize; selection handles appear around the edges of the object.

② Move the pointer over one of the selection handles (here, a corner handle). When the pointer is in the right spot, it changes to a two-headed arrow.

③ Click on the handle, drag it, and release the mouse button when the object is the desired size.

④ The object is resized.

End

If an object is too big (or too small), change the size. You can modify any type of object, including a picture you have added, a chart, or a drawn object. In addition, you can continue to resize the object over and over until it is the size you want.

Corners versus sides
Dragging the sides increases or decreases the height or width of an object, while dragging the corners increases or decreases the height and width of an object at the same time.

Resizing proportionally
If you hold the **Shift** key down while dragging a corner, the image enlarges or decreases in proportion.

Deleting an Object

Start

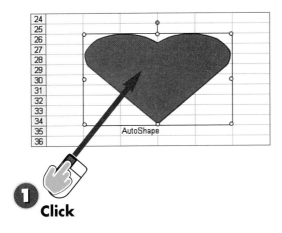

1 Click

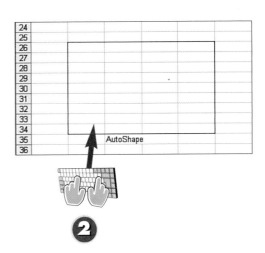

2

1 Select the object you want to delete; selection handles appear around the edges of the object.

2 Press the **Delete** key on your keyboard. Excel deletes the object.

End

INTRODUCTION

As you experiment with charts, drawings, and pictures, you may go overboard, or you might make a mistake and want to start over. In any case, if you add an object and no longer want to include it, you can delete it, as described here.

TIP

Undoing a deletion
If you delete an object by accident, click the **Undo** button on the Standard toolbar to undo the deletion.

Working with Data Lists

You can use Excel for more than totaling numbers; Excel can also be used as a simple data management program. Using it, you can keep track of clients, products, orders, expenses, and more. You can set up a data list and use some of Excel's data list features, including sorting, subtotaling, and filtering.

A *data list* is a set of related information about a particular person, transaction, or event. One piece of information is a *field*, and one set of fields is called a *record*. In an Excel data list, you enter the column headings for the fields, and the records in the rows. One way to enter these records is by using a data list *form*.

Ordering Records with Data Lists

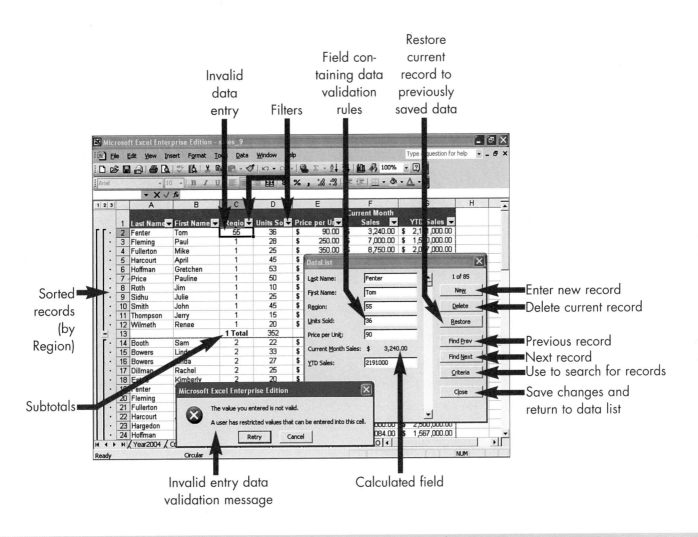

Invalid data entry

Filters

Field containing data validation rules

Restore current record to previously saved data

Sorted records (by Region)

Subtotals

Enter new record

Delete current record

Previous record

Next record

Use to search for records

Save changes and return to data list

Invalid entry data validation message

Calculated field

Entering Worksheet Data Using a Data List Form

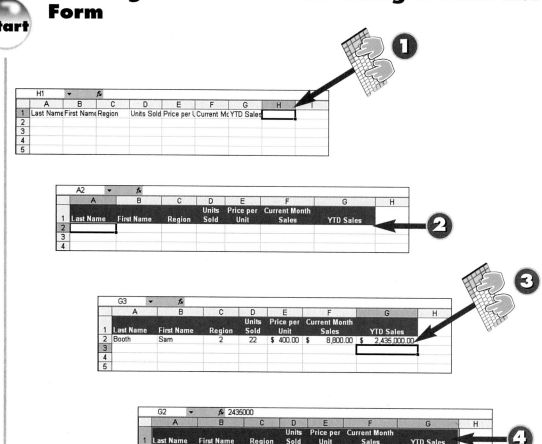

Start

1. Type a *unique* heading for each of the columns you want in your data list. (Excel can get confused if you use the same label in more than one column header.)

2. Select all the headers and format them so they will stand out from the regular listed data (perhaps adding some cell color and changing the font color).

3. Type a sample row of the data you will be inputting with your form. Your columns can include calculated fields (A × B = C) and numeric styles (Currency).

4. Select the cells that you want to use to establish the data list. Include at least one regular row of cells (with or without data) along with your data list labels.

If you like the regular worksheet style of entering data, you can enter data directly in the cells. Simply select each cell and type an entry, doing so for each record you want in your worksheet. If you prefer to concentrate on one record at a time, however, you can display a *data list form* onscreen and enter the records in that form (as covered in this task). This will be easier on your eyes and can help to keep you from getting lost in the data.

TIP

Total sales
Notice how the Current Month Sales field on the data list form doesn't allow you to enter information. This is because it is a *calculated field* (meaning that it contains the answer to Units Sold × Price per Unit = Current Month Sales). To keep from entering invalid data into particular fields, create validation rules (see the following task).

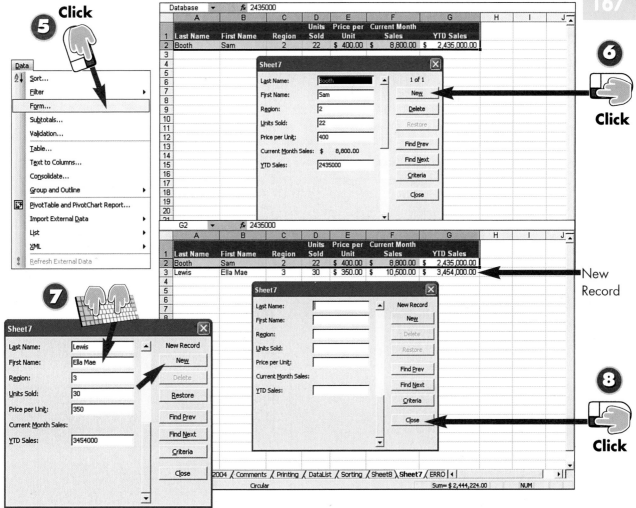

5 Open the **Data** menu and choose **Form**. A form, or Range Criteria, dialog box appears displaying the selected cells as data labels and the row as the first record.

6 Click the **New** button; the form changes to display blank fields, ready for the entry of a new record.

7 Type the data for a new record into the data list form boxes, pressing **Tab** to move from field to field. Then, click **New** to enter the data and clear the form.

8 Either enter another new record on the data list form or click the form's **Close** button when you finish entering data.

End

Record order
You don't have to enter records in any particular order. You can later sort or filter your records to display as necessary. See "Sorting Data List Records" and "Filtering Data List Records" later in this part for more information.

Correcting typos
If you make an error when typing your records and you are still working on that record in the form, you can click the field containing the error and use the Delete or Backspace key to edit your entry. To edit a record in the worksheet, double-click the cell you want to edit, make the change, and press **Enter**. To learn to modify a data list entry with a form, see "Modifying a Data List Record" later in this part.

Checking Form Entries with Data Validation

Start

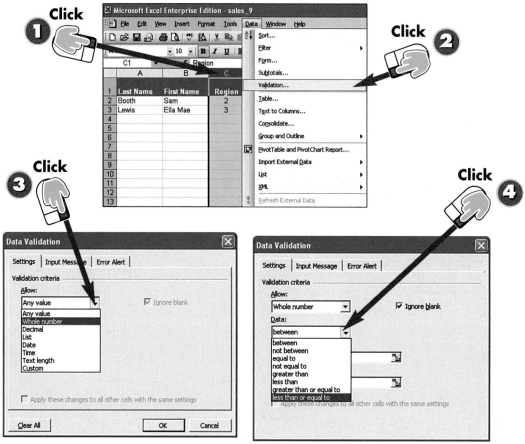

1 Click the column header for the data list field to which you want to apply a data-validation rule (for example, column **C** for **Region**).

2 Open the **Data** menu and choose **Validation** to open the Data Validation dialog box.

3 Click the **down arrow** next to the **Allow** field and select **Whole Number** (sales regions are whole numbers, never anything else).

4 Click the **down arrow** next to the **Data** field and select **less than or equal to** (sales regions are less than or equal to the total number of regions).

You might find that as you enter records into your data list, you inadvertently make some mistakes. For example, suppose your company has only five sales regions, and you keep entering numbers that can't possibly be an actual sales region, such as 6 or 55. If you set a *data validation rule* for this scenario, Excel will automatically inform you when you make this type of error.

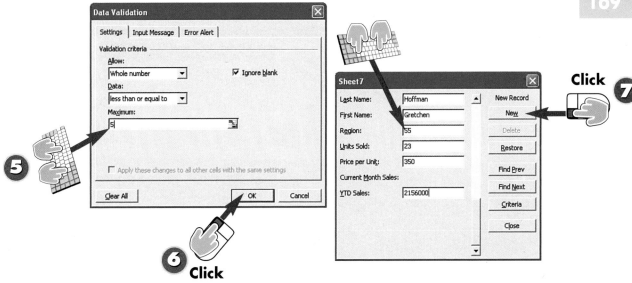

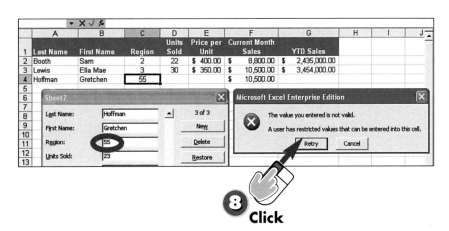

⑤ Type the number in the **Maximum** field (in this case, **5** is the maximum number of regions).

⑥ Click the **OK** button to accept your validation rules; in addition, this will accept Excel's default validation error message (see the tip "Altering the error message" on this page).

⑦ Using the form, type a new data list record (see the preceding task), but this time type an incorrect entry, such as **55**, in the **Region** field. When you're finished, click the **New** button.

⑧ Excel selects the cell with the invalid data and alerts you of your error. Click the dialog box's **Retry** button and repeat step 7, entering a valid value in the **Region** field. **End**

Altering the error message

You can alter Excel's default validation error message in the Error Alert tab of the Data Validation dialog box. Here, you can alter the error alert style, title, and error message. This is convenient when people who aren't familiar with your data list form enter incorrect data, because it enables you to tell them specifically what they need to correct. For example, you could tell them that you only have a total of five regions, and that the number they entered is invalid.

Using input messages

In addition to validation rules and error messages, you can add input messages directly in your data list. An input message looks like a permanently viewable comment in your data list. For example, you could include an input message that indicates to the person entering data that the **Region** field only accepts whole values between 1 and 5. That way, the user will think twice before entering an invalid number.

Searching for a Data List Record

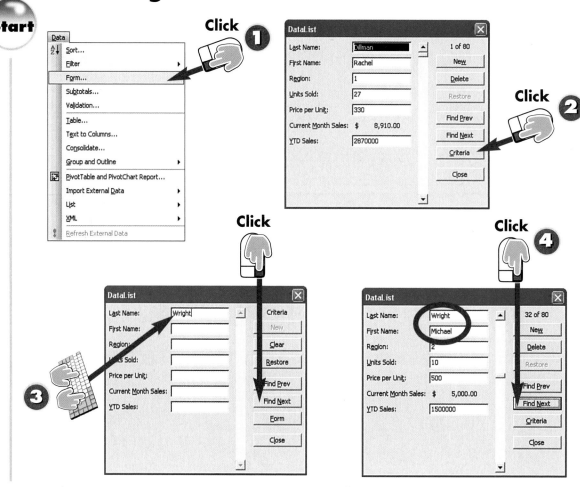

Click ①

Click ②

Click ③

Click ④

---

① Unless it's already open on your desktop, choose **Data**, **Form** to open the data list form for the worksheet data list you already created.

② Click the **Criteria** button.

③ The form becomes blank, awaiting your entry of the search criteria. Type the data (last name, for example) you are searching for, and click the **Find Next** button.

④ Excel displays the first matching record. If multiple records have the same data, click **Find Next** to see more records.

End

Rather than wasting time looking through each row in a worksheet to find the information you want, why not search for the specific record in your data list? You can limit the search to a specific field using the data list form. For example, if you are trying to find information on a particular sales representative, you could search on her last name.

Scrolling to search

In addition to looking through the data list and using criteria to locate a record on your data list form, you can scroll through the list of records on your form. The problem with this is that the records aren't sorted in any particular order. See the task "Sorting Data List Records" for more information about sorting records.

Modifying a Data List Record

Start

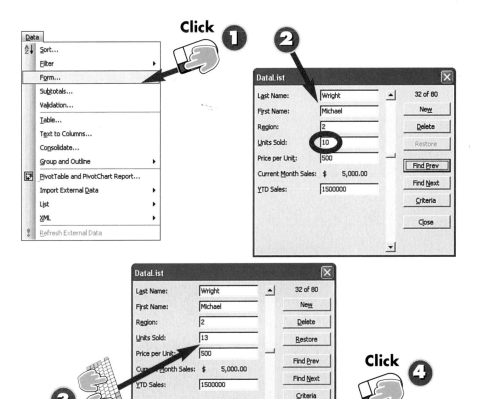

Click ❶ ❷

Click ❹

❶ Unless it's already open on your desktop, choose **Data**, **Form** to open the data list form for the worksheet data list you created in the task "Entering Worksheet Data Using a Form."

❷ Follow the steps in the preceding task to find the record you want to modify (in this example, **Michael Wright**).

❸ Select the entry in the field you want to modify, and type over it (in this example, increase the value in the **Units Sold** field from **10** to **13**).

❹ Click the **Close** button to accept the change and return to the worksheet data list; the change will be reflected in your worksheet.

End

Deleting a Record from the Data List

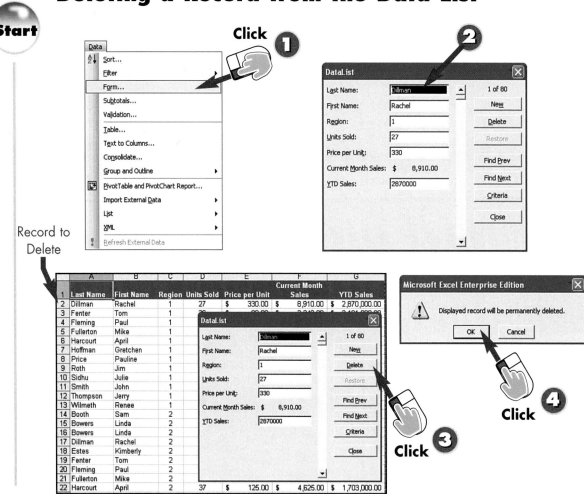

Start

Click ①

②

Record to Delete

Click ③

Click ④

End

① Unless it's already open on your desktop, choose **Data**, **Form** to open the data list form for the data list you created in the task "Entering Worksheet Data Using a Form."

② Follow the steps in the task "Searching for a Data List Record" to find the record you want to delete.

③ Click the **Delete** button in the data list form to permanently remove the record from the data list.

④ Excel warns you that the record will be permanently deleted from the data list. If you don't want to delete the record, click **Cancel**; otherwise click **OK**.

If a record is no longer valid, you can delete it. That row and all its corresponding data are removed from the worksheet. Be warned, though, that if you use the data list form to delete a record, you cannot undo the deletion. Be sure you're deleting the correct record before you confirm the deletion, and consider making backups of the data list on a regular basis so you can recover deleted records in the event of an error.

Deleting within a worksheet

To delete a record in the worksheet, rather than in the data list form, select the row containing the record and then choose **Edit**, **Delete**. The row and the information it contains are deleted from the worksheet, and will no longer display in the data list form. To undo a row deletion, use the Undo button on the Standard toolbar.

Sorting Data List Records

Start

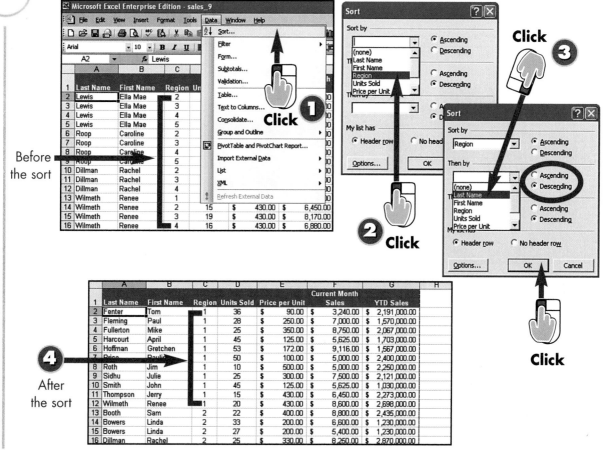

Before the sort

After the sort

Click ... **Click** ... **Click** ... **Click**

1 Choose **Data, Sort** to open the Sort dialog box (the active cell must be somewhere in the data list on the worksheet).

2 Click the **down arrow** next to the **Sort by** field and choose from the list that appears. Then, click the corresponding **Ascending** option button to select it.

3 Click the **down arrow** next to the **Then by** field and choose from the list. Then, click the corresponding **Ascending/Descending** option and click **OK**.

4 Excel sorts the entire data list using the criteria you selected; for example, first by Region and then by Last Name within each region.

End

It's easy to change the order of your data list. If, for example, you want to alphabetically arrange the names in a data list of sales representatives, you can sort on the Last Name field. Alternatively, you might want to arrange the names of your sales representatives by region; in that case, you could sort by both the Region and Last Name fields.

Minimizing the sort
If you don't select the area of the data list that you want to sort, Excel sorts the entire list. You can, though, sort only on a particular number of records by first selecting the records in the data list and then following the steps in this task.

Filtering Data List Records

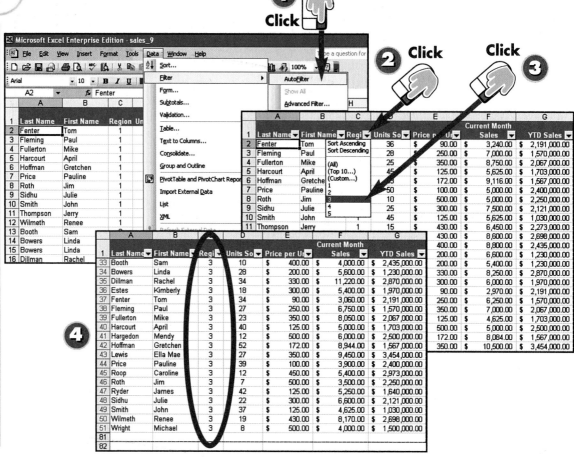

Click

Click

Click

④

1 Choose **Data**, **Filter**, **AutoFilter** to add drop-down arrows to each field header.

2 Click the **down arrow** next to the column you want to use for the filtering criteria.

3 Specify what records you want to match. You can select a particular value, **Top 10**, **All**, **Custom**, or a specific record type in that field (for example, **3**).

4 The data list displays only those records that meet your criteria. Filtered data displays a blue arrow instead of the default black.

End

You might not always want to display all records in a large data list. Instead, you might want to work with just a set of records—for example, all sales representatives in Region 3. When you want to work with a sub-set of records, you can filter the data in a data list. All the records remain in the data list worksheet, but only those meeting the criteria you select are displayed.

Redisplaying all records
To display all records again, choose **Data**, **Filter**, **Show All**. Alternatively, click the arrow with the different filter color and select **All** from the drop-down list.

Removing a Data List Filter

Start

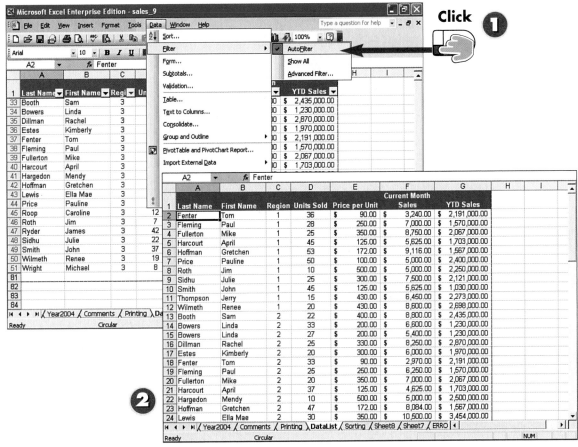

Click 1

1 Choose **Data**, **Filter**, **AutoFilter**.

2 The arrows on the column headers disappear, and the entire data list is again visible.

End

If you have filtered your data list in order to view only particular records, most likely only a subset of your data will be displayed in the worksheet. To avoid confusion, turn off the AutoFilter option when you finish working in a worksheet, so all the data is again viewable. Otherwise, the next time you open the worksheet, you might not remember that there is additional data.

Leaving on AutoFilter
Alternatively, leave on the AutoFilter, but select **(All)** in each of the AutoFilter drop-down lists to display all records in the data list.

Working with Data List Subtotals

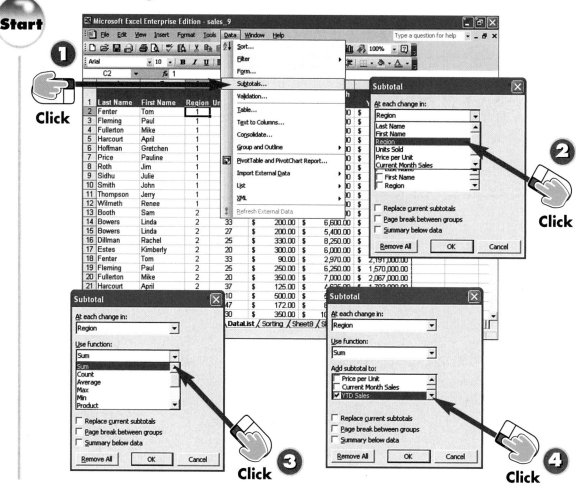

Start

Click ... **Click** ... **Click** ... **Click**

① After you've sorted your data (see the task "Sorting Data List Records"), choose **Data**, **Subtotals** to open the Subtotal dialog box.

② Click the **down arrow** next to the **At each change in** field and select the field you want to subtotal.

③ Click the **down arrow** next to the **Use function** field and select the type of function you want performed on the selected field.

④ In the **Add subtotal to** list, click the check box next to the field to which you want to add the subtotal. Uncheck any other fields to avoid subtotaling each field.

Subtotals are an easy way to summarize data in a list. You might, for example, want to total all sales by a particular region and then view a grand total. Or, you might want to total sales by sales representative. You can sort and then subtotal on any field in the data list, as long as the data in that field is of a type that can be "totaled." For this task, first sort the data in ascending order by region; then add subtotals for the year-to-date sales according to region.

More sort options

To sort your data list, you can also choose **Data**, **Sort**, select the field (**Region**) to sort by, specify how you want to sort (**Ascending** or **Descending**), and click **OK**. Refer to the task "Sorting Data List Records" for more information.

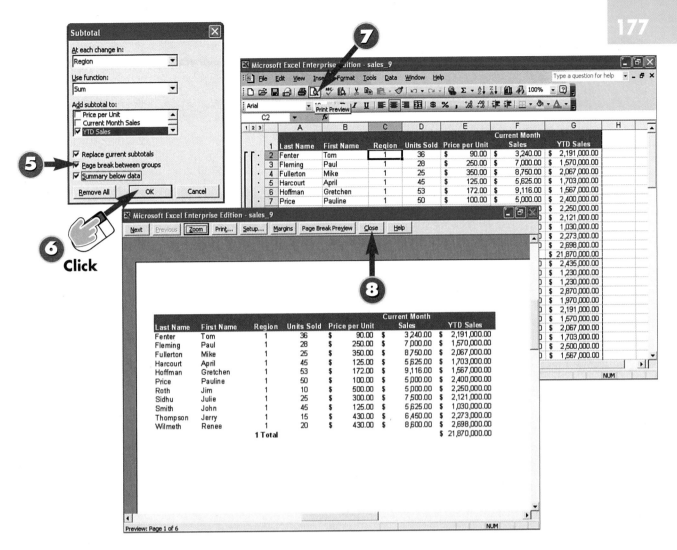

5. Click **Replace current subtotals** if data list has subtotals; **Page break between groups** to put subtotals on a new page; **Summary below data** to add subtotal summaries.

6. Click **OK**. Excel inserts a subtotal row for each time the selected field changes, performs the SUM function on the column and adds a grand total at the end of the data list.

7. Click the **Print Preview** button on the Standard toolbar.

8. The Print Preview window opens, providing a better look at your data after subtotals have been added (click **Close** to return to the worksheet).

End

Multiple subtotals
You can check more than one check box in the **Add subtotal to** list box to have Excel calculate the function on each selected field. For example, you could have a subtotal on current month sales and units sold.

Removing subtotals
To remove the subtotals, choose **Data**, **Subtotals** and click the **Remove All** button in the Subtotal dialog box.

No fields selected
If there is only one field available to you in the Subtotal dialog box, that means you need to select the entire data list in the worksheet before you complete step 2. This tells Excel which fields you want to include in the sort.

PART 9

Printing in Excel

Print Preview mode in Excel is a very convenient way to prepare your worksheets for printing, without having to print numerous copies of a worksheet to "get it right." Using Print Preview mode, you can access all the printing options, and even make changes that will be saved with your worksheet in case it's printed again in the future.

In Excel, you can print your worksheets by using a basic printing procedure, or you can enhance the printout with several print options. Options for setting up the printed page include orientation, scaling, paper size, and page numbering. You can use these options to change how the worksheet is printed on the page (across or down) or even so that your multi-page worksheet prints on a single page.

Sheet options control what elements of your worksheet are printed—gridlines, notes, row headings, and so on. You might want to make some changes to these options depending on how you want your printout to look. Another common change is to repeat column or row headings on a multi-page worksheet. On worksheets that span two pages, the information on the second page might not make sense without proper headings.

Print Preview Printing Options

Moves you to the next page in the worksheet (can also press the [page down] key)

Moves you to the previous page in the worksheet (can also press the [page up] key)

Toggles the worksheet data in and out of magnification

Opens the Print dialog box

Opens the Page Setup dialog box tabs (Page, Margins, Header/Footer, Sheet)

Toggles the margin lines display for the page (top, bottom, left, right), header, footer, and columns

Displays the worksheet when in Page Break Preview

Returns you back to the Normal worksheet view

Provides help with printing questions

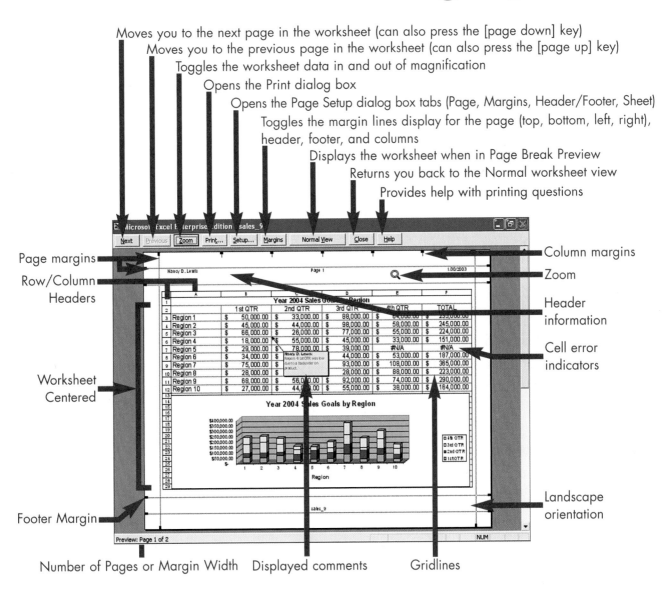

Page margins

Row/Column Headers

Worksheet Centered

Footer Margin

Column margins

Zoom

Header information

Cell error indicators

Landscape orientation

Number of Pages or Margin Width   Displayed comments   Gridlines

Using Print Preview

Start

Click ①

Click ②

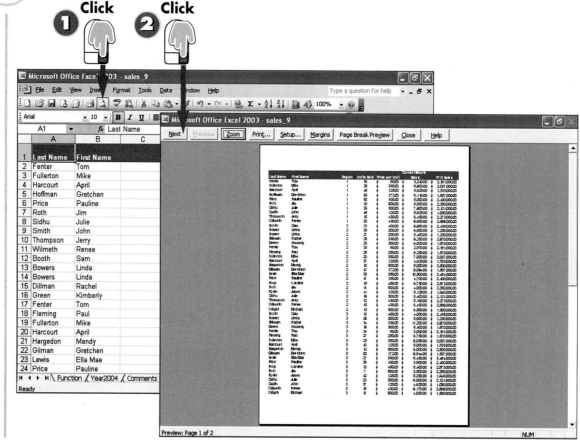

① With the worksheet you want to print open on your desktop, click the **Print Preview** button on the Standard toolbar.

② The Print Preview window opens, displaying the worksheet in Print Preview mode. Click the **Next** button to move to the next page in the worksheet.

INTRODUCTION

Worksheets with lots of data can generate large print jobs, possibly containing hundreds of pages. Waiting until all these pages are printed to verify that the information is printed correctly can cost a lot in both time and printing supplies. To help prevent printing mistakes, use Print Preview to ensure that all the necessary elements appear on the pages being printed.

TIP

Page Break Preview Button
Click **Page Break Preview** to see exactly what is selected to print (in the print area). If you haven't set the print area, see "Setting the Print Area." If you were already in Page Break Preview view when you clicked the Print Preview button, the toolbar button will display Normal view instead, which will display your entire worksheet (regardless of whether you have set the print area).

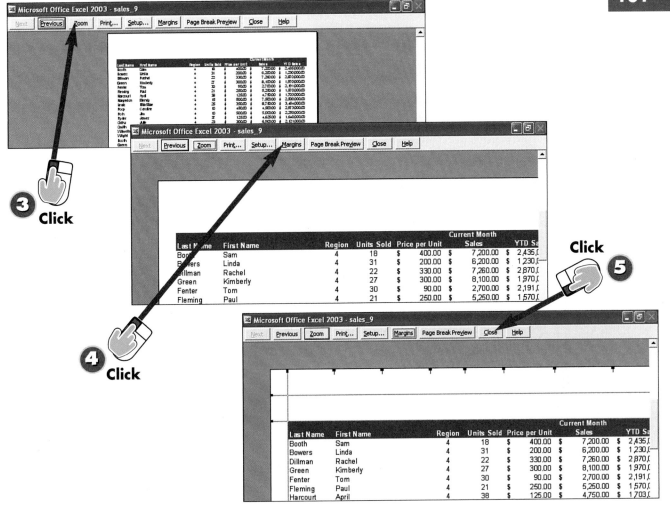

3 Click the **Zoom** button to increase the viewable size of the worksheet in Print Preview mode. (Click **Zoom** again to return to the original page size.)

4 Click **Margins** to toggle between displaying the margin indicators, which you can drag to set more or less of your worksheet to print.

5 Click the **Close** button to return to the worksheet's Normal view.

End

Setup Button in Print Preview

Click the **Setup** button to open the Page Setup dialog box. Use the **Page** tab to alter the page orientation and scaling (see "Printing Portrait or Landscape Orientation" and "Printing a Worksheet on One Page"). Use the **Margins** tab to alter the margins or center your data horizontally and vertically (see "Centering a Worksheet on a Page"). Use the **Header/Footer** tab to add a header and footer (see "Adding Headers and Footers"). Finally, use the **Sheet** tab to alter the gridlines and row and column headers (see "Printing Gridlines and Row/Column Headers"), cell comments (see "Printing Cell Comments"), cell errors (see "Printing Cell Error Indicators") and print repeating titles (see "Printing Repeating Row and Column Titles").

Setting the Print Area

Start

Click ❶ ❷

Click ❹ ❸

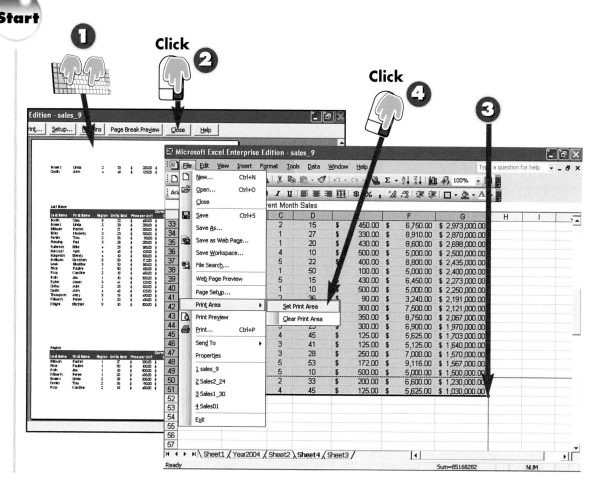

❶ In Print Preview mode, press the **page down** key on your keyboard to move through your worksheet to see what your printed worksheet will look like.

❷ Click the **Close** button to return to Normal view so you can set your print area.

❸ Select the exact cells you want to print (in this example, all the cells in the first two tables in this worksheet).

❹ Open the **File** menu, choose **Print Area,** and select **Set Print Area** to store the print area as part of the worksheet. Only the cells in the print area will print.

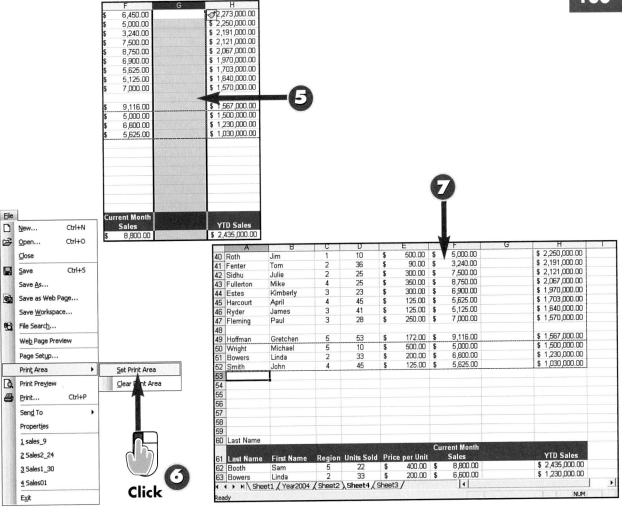

5 Insert a row or column into your worksheet (refer to the first task in Part 8). Parts of the table now fall outside the current print area.

6 To reset the print area to include the new row or column, again open the **File** menu, choose **Print Area,** and select **Set Print Area**.

7 Your new print area is stored as part of this worksheet.

End

Long and short dashes
The long dashed lines in your worksheet indicate the print area, and the smaller dashed lines indicate the current page margins. If your print area data (long dashed lines) falls outside the current page margins (short dashed lines), you will need to alter the page margins (see the next task).

Clearing the print area
If you only need to set the print area to print a portion of data in your worksheet once, you will probably want to clear the print area after you print. Open the **File** menu, choose **Print Area**, and select **Clear Print Area**.

Setting Page Margins

Start

Click ❶

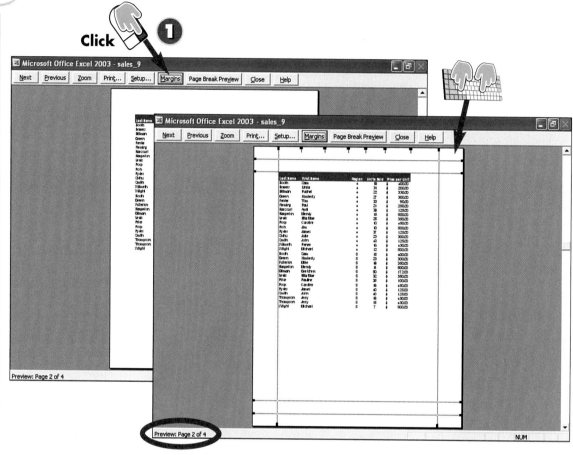

❶ When in Print Preview mode, if you have a page that displays some carryover data from another page, click the **Margins** button.

❷ Excel activates Print Preview's margin lines. Press **page up** or **page down** to display the page in your worksheet on which you want to fit all the data.

Margins affect where data is printed on a page. They also determine where headers and footers are printed. Occasionally, margins might need to be changed to make room for a letterhead or logo on preprinted stationery. When in Print Preview mode, Excel allows you to alter your column widths and margins simultaneously.

TIP

Print Preview Button
Click the **Print** button to open the Print dialog box (refer to the task "Printing Worksheets").

Drop

Click & Drag

Click & Drag

Drop

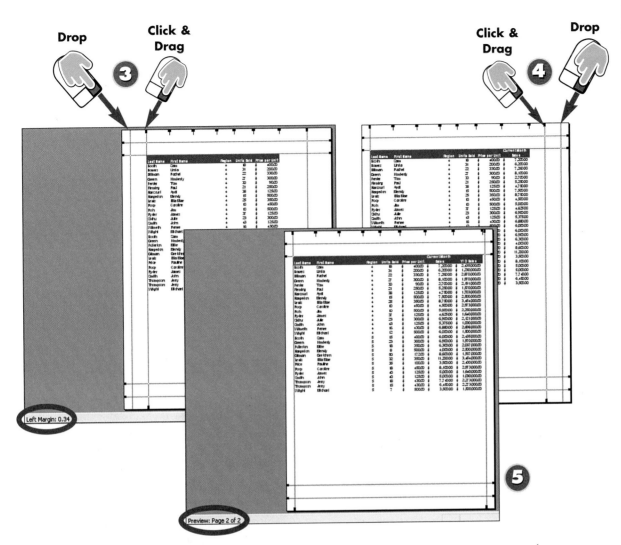

Left Margin: 0.34

Preview: Page 2 of 2

3 Drag the **Left Margin** line from the default 1'' to 0.34'' (you can see the exact measurement in the bottom-left corner of the screen).

4 Click and drag the **Right Margin** line from the default 1'' to 0.34'' (again, you can see the exact measurement in the bottom-left corner of the screen).

5 Thanks to the margin change, the total number of pages to print is reduced from four to two.

End

Entering specific margins

TIP

There might be times when you need to set your worksheet margins to a specific measurement. Perhaps your worksheet data is being placed in a binder, and you need to have a left margin of 1.25''. You can alter this in Print Preview mode, or choose **File, Page Setup**, click the **Margins** tab, and alter the margins as necessary (Left, Right, Top, Bottom, Header, Footer). Click the **OK** button to return to your worksheet or **Print** to print immediately.

Removing margin indicators

TIP

If you no longer want to see the margin lines in Print Preview mode, click the **Margins** button on the Print Preview toolbar again to turn them off.

Inserting Page Breaks

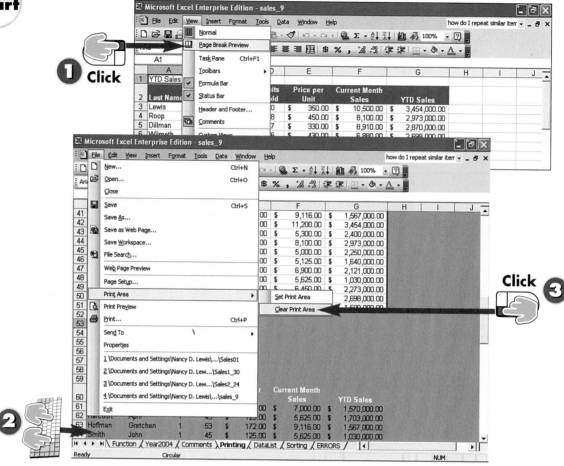

1. Open the **View** menu and choose **Page Break Preview** to change to Page Break Preview mode.

2. Press the **page up** and **page down** keys on the keyboard to move through your worksheet in Page Break Preview. Notice that cells outside the print area are grayed out.

3. Open the **File** menu, choose **Print Area**, and select **Clear Print Area** to eliminate any current print area settings.

INTRODUCTION

When a worksheet page is filled to the margins with data, Excel automatically inserts a page break for you. There may be times, however, when you want to insert a page break manually. For example, if you are creating a report with multiple topic sections, you might want each topic to begin on a new page. Inserting a page break enables you to print each page separately, and the best way to insert page breaks is using Page Break Preview view (instead of Normal view).

TIP

Removing page breaks
To remove a page break, place the active cell so that one of the cell borders is touching the page break line. Then, open the **Insert** menu and choose **Remove Page Break**. (You can also do this in Normal view.)

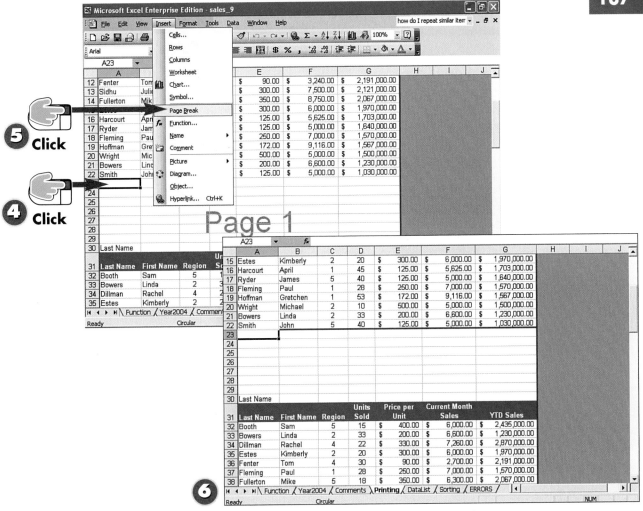

4 Click the cell below and in the left-most column in which you want to insert a page break.

5 Open the **Insert** menu and choose **Page Break** to insert the page break.

6 The page break is inserted.

End

Working in Page Break Preview Mode

Start

Click

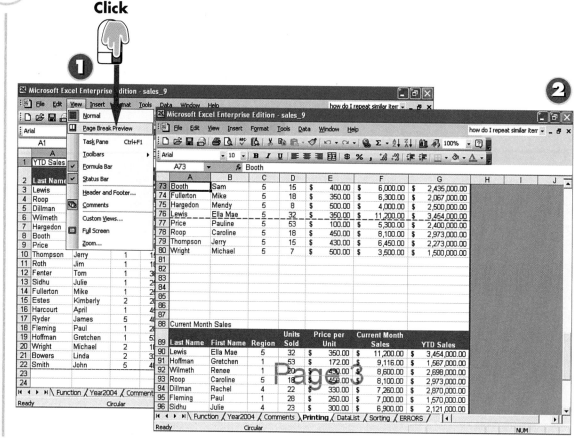

1 Choose **View, Page Break Preview**. If a print area has been set, it is displayed; if not, the entire worksheet is displayed.

2 Move through the worksheet to find page breaks (if any). Naturally occurring page breaks appear as blue dashed lines, and inserted page breaks appear as solid blue lines.

TIP

Clearing the print area
If you only need to set the print area to print a portion of data in your worksheet once, you will probably want to clear the print area after you print. Open the **File** menu, choose **Print Area**, and select **Clear Print Area** to clear the previously set print area.

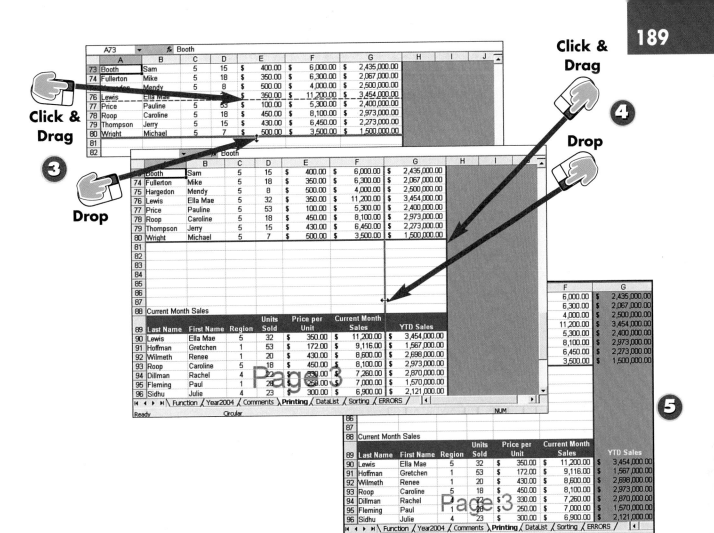

Click & Drag

Drop

③ **Click & Drag**

Drop

④ **Click & Drag**

Drop

⑤

③ To move a page break that is poorly placed, click and drag it to a better location. (Moving a *natural* page break changes it to an *inserted* break—solid-blue.

④ To exclude a column or data to the right of your set print area, click and drag the vertical page break.

⑤ The excluded column outside the print area is grayed out.

End

Removing a page break
To remove a page break in Page Break Preview mode, click and drag the page break line off to the right/left/top/bottom of the worksheet.

TIP

Printing a Worksheet on One Page

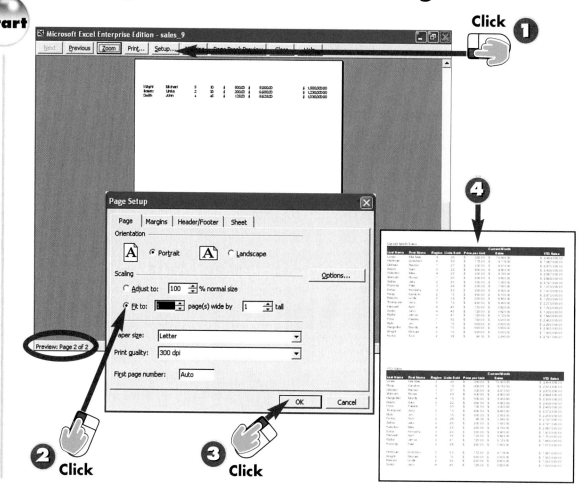

Start

Click ①

② Click

③ Click

④

① View your worksheet in Print Preview mode. If only a few rows of data spill onto a second page, you can alter the page scale; click the **Setup** button to begin.

② In the Page tab of the Page Setup dialog box, click the **Fit to 1 pages(s) wide by 1 tall** option button. (To fill more than one page, type the number of pages here.)

③ Click **OK**.

④ Your worksheet appears in Print Preview mode, all on one page. Notice that the scaling change reduced the total number of pages to print from two to one.

End

By default, Excel prints your worksheet at a scale of 100%. You can decrease this percentage if you want to fit more data on a page, or increase it to fit less data on a page. In addition, you can have Excel fit your entire worksheet on one page. (If your worksheet is large, the data might become too tiny to read when scaled down.)

Changing from letter to legal
To choose a different paper size for your printout, click the **Options** button in the Page Setup dialog box. The scaling setting automatically adjusts to the selected paper size.

Returning to the default scale
When you want to return the preview of your worksheet to the default scale, click the **Adjust to** option button in the Page Setup dialog box and type **100** into the **% normal size** field.

Printing in Portrait or Landscape Orientation

Start

Click ①

Click ② ③

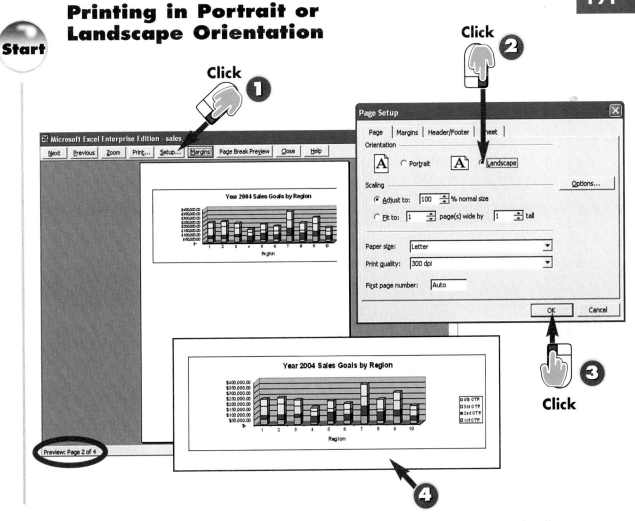

Click

---

① View your worksheet in Print Preview mode. If your worksheet is too wide to fit all its columns on a single page in Portrait mode, click the **Setup** button.

② In the Page tab of the Page Setup dialog box, click the **Landscape** option button.

③ Click **OK**.

④ Your worksheet appears in Print Preview mode, Landscape orientation. Notice that the orientation change reduced the total number of pages to print from four to two.

End

INTRODUCTION

Depending on the data in your worksheet, you might want to change its orientation from Portrait (vertical, the default) to Landscape (horizontal).

TIP

Switching back to Portrait

You can easily switch your worksheet back to Portrait orientation by following the steps in this task, selecting the **Portrait** option button in step 2.

Centering a Worksheet on a Page

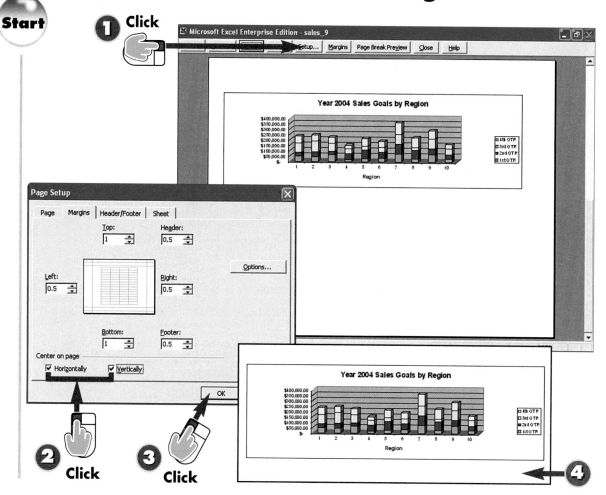

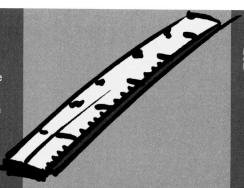

1. View your worksheet in Print Preview mode. If the data in your worksheet appears toward the top or on the far left of the page, click the **Setup** button.

2. Click the **Margins** tab in the Page Setup dialog box, and click the **Horizontally** and/or **Vertically** checkboxes in the **Center on page** area.

3. Click **OK**.

4. Your worksheet appears in Print Preview mode, centered.

End

INTRODUCTION

If you want a cleaner, more professional looking printout for a presentation, you might want to center your worksheet data on the page before you print it. This is a particularly good idea if you plan to print your worksheet on one page.

TIP

Centering vertically or horizontally
You don't have to center your data both vertically and horizontally. You can choose one or the other, depending on how you want your printed worksheet to look.

Printing Gridlines and Row/Column Headers

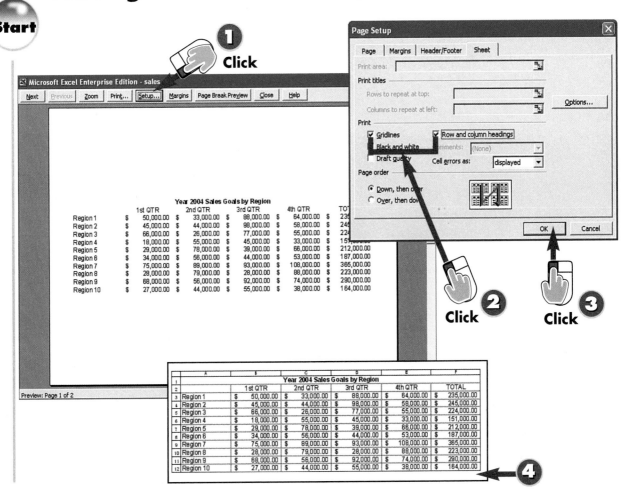

1. View your worksheet in Print Preview mode. If no gridlines or row/column headers appear, click the **Setup** button.

2. Click the Sheet tab in the Page Setup dialog box, and click the **Gridlines** and **Row and column headings** checkboxes in the **Print** area to select them.

3. Click **OK**.

4. Your worksheet appears in Print Preview mode, with gridlines and row/column headers visible.

End

INTRODUCTION

By default, Excel doesn't print worksheet gridlines or row/column headers. You can, however, instruct Excel to print them. Gridlines help you read information in a printed worksheet, keeping rows and columns of data visually organized. Row and column headers can help you quickly find data in your worksheet.

TIP

Repeating titles
Displaying row and column headers is not the same as printing repeating titles. Repeating titles are column headers and row headers that you have assigned in your worksheet. For more information, see the task "Printing Repeating Row and Column Titles" later in this part.

Printing Cell Comments

Start

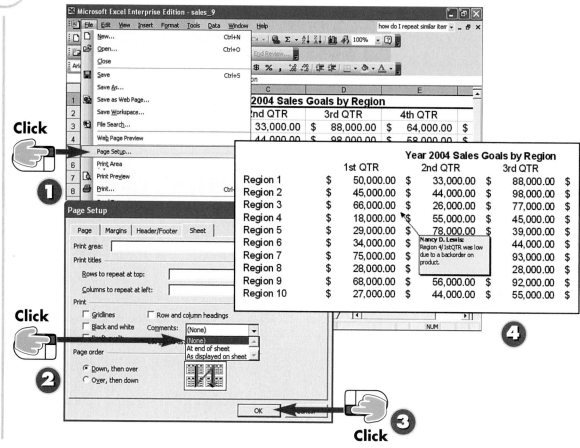

Click

1

Click

2

Click **3**

4

1. Choose **File**, **Page Setup** and click the **Sheet** tab in the Page Setup dialog box.

2. Click the **Comments** field **down arrow** and choose either **At end of sheet**, to print the comments, **As displayed on sheet**, or **(None)**.

3. Click **OK**.

4. View your worksheet in **Print Preview** mode to review the comments as display in your worksheet (as in this example) or at the end of your worksheet. **End**

Printing Cell Error Indicators

Start

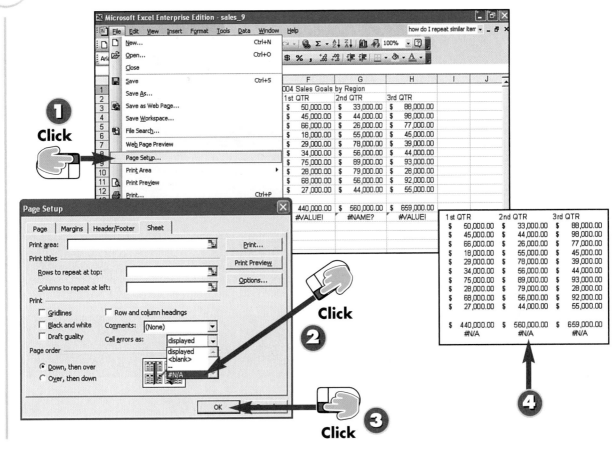

Click 1

Click 2

Click 3

Click

4

1 Choose **File**, **Page Setup**, and click the **Sheet** tab in the Page Setup dialog box.

2 Click the **down arrow** next to the **Cell errors as** field and choose **displayed**, **<blank>**, **--**, or **#N/A** depending on how you want errors to be displayed.

3 Click **OK**.

4 View your worksheet in **Print Preview** mode to review how cells containing errors are displayed.

End

INTRODUCTION

When you print worksheets for friends or colleagues (or even yourself), calculation errors that appear on your worksheet can create a negative impression, which is why they're not printed by default. If you want these errors to be visible in your printout, however, you can display them, or replace them with any of the following: <blank>, --, or #N/A.

TIP

Errors that print
All the error messages explained in Part 5 (**#DIV/0!**, **#Name?**, **#Value!**, **#REF!**, and Circular Reference errors) will print in this task, except the ##### error (unless your columns are too narrow in the printed version).

Printing Repeating Row and Column Titles

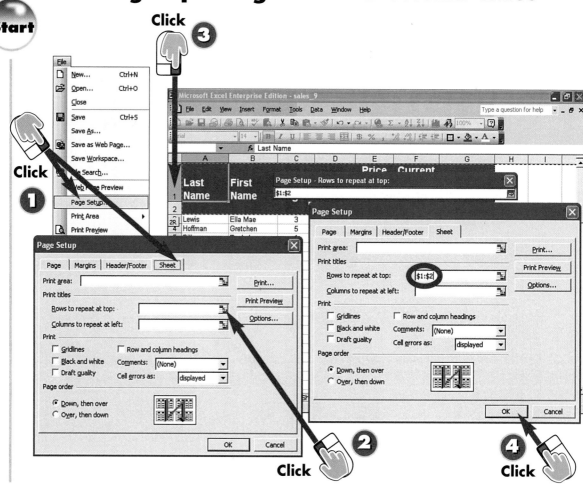

1 Choose **File**, **Page Setup**, and click the **Sheet** tab in the Page Setup dialog box.

2 Click the **Rows to repeat at top** selection box in the **Print titles** area. Excel shrinks the Page Setup dialog box, making your focus the worksheet on your desktop.

3 Click the row containing the titles that you want to repeat on each page of your worksheet, and press **Enter** to reopen the Page Setup dialog box with your selection inserted.

4 Click **OK**. If you like, view the worksheet in Print Preview mode to get an idea of what your printed worksheet will look like with repeating row headings.

End

You might have noticed that when a worksheet spans multiple pages, it is difficult to keep the column and row titles organized. A quick way to rectify this is to make particular titles repeat on each page of the printed worksheet. In this task, you'll learn how to make row headers repeat.

TIP
Repeating titles in Print Preview
You cannot assign repeating titles while you are in Print Preview mode; you must be in the worksheet view and select **File**, **Page Setup**.

TIP
Repeating column headings
To repeat column headings across several pages, follow the steps in this task, but click the **Columns to repeat at left** selection box in step 2. Then, click the columns you want to repeat, and proceed as normal.

Adding Headers and Footers

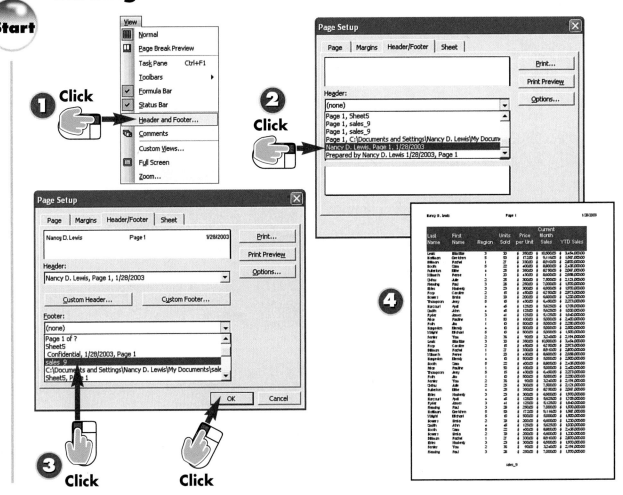

1. Choose **View, Header and Footer** to open the Page Setup dialog box with the Header/Footer tab displayed.

2. Click the **down arrow** next to the **Header** field and scroll through the header options. If you see one you like, click it to see what it looks like.

3. Click the **down arrow** next to the **Footer** and scroll through the footer options. If you see one you like, click it to see what it looks like. Then click **OK**.

4. If you like, view the worksheet in Print Preview mode to get an idea of what your printed worksheet will look like with headers and footers.

End

TIP

Creating custom headers and footers
You can create your own custom header or footer by clicking the appropriate **Custom Header** or **Custom Footer** button in the Page Setup dialog box. A separate Header or Footer dialog box will appear, allowing you to click a button to place text or any the following fields in the header/footer: Page number, Total Pages number, Date, Time, Path & Filename, Filename only, tabs, and insert graphic objects. For example, you could add page numbers and the total page count to the header or footer.

Printing Worksheets

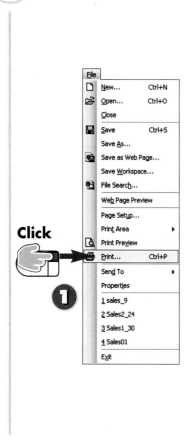

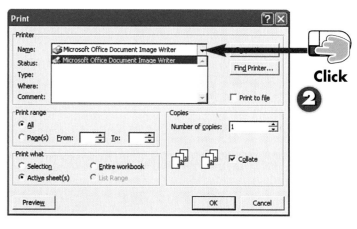

Click

2

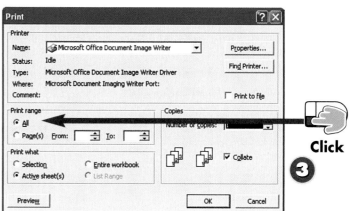

Click

Click

3

1 Choose **File**, **Print** to open the Print dialog box.

2 Click the **down arrow** next to the **Printer Name** field to choose the printer or fax you want to use.

3 In the **Print range** area, click **Page(s) From** and **To** and type the pages you want to include in the range (for example, from 2 to 5), or keep the **All** (default).

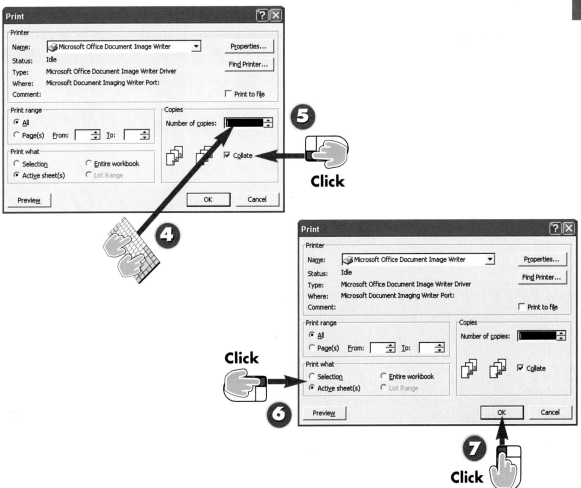

4 Type the number of copies you want to print in the **Number of Copies** field, which defaults to **1**.

5 If you want the printed pages to be collated, click the **Collate** checkbox to select it.

6 In the **Print what** area, click either **Selection** (only selected cells), **Active Sheet(s)** (currently sheets), or **Entire workbook** (all worksheets and chart sheets).

7 Click **OK** to send your printout to the printer. Alternatively, click **Preview** to preview your printout; then click the **Print** button on the Print Preview toolbar.

End

TIP

Vertical or horizontal page order
If you are working with a large worksheet, you can specify the page order by which your worksheet is printed. Open the **File** menu and choose **Page Setup**, and select the **Sheet** tab. Review the options of **Down, then over** (default) and **Over, then down** in the Page order area of the Page Setup dialog box. This is convenient if you have numerous columns that you want printed according to a specific row header.

TIP

Canceling printing
Click the **Cancel** button to cancel printing. Alternatively, if you've already sent the workbook to the printer, double-click on the Printer icon in the system tray (to the left of the clock on the taskbar) and click **Cancel**.

Advanced Excel and Web Features

Throughout this book, you have learned about features in Excel that help you accomplish tasks and make your work easier. This part takes you a step further so that you can copy and link data with other documents, import and export data, and even automate repetitive tasks with macros.

Numerous Excel features can make working with the Internet and the Web easier and more convenient. This part covers Excel Web features, such as saving an Excel workbook as a Web page and opening it up in a browser, and adding URLs and all kinds of hyperlinks to your worksheets. In addition, you can edit and remove hyperlinks using the Hyperlink dialog box. You can even add email hyperlinks and send your worksheets as email messages.

To use the Web and Internet features in Excel, you need to have access to the Internet. You might have an account with an online service (for example, America Online), with a local Internet service provider (ISP), or in a corporate setting, where you have to log in to the network to gain Internet access. In any case, it would be a good idea to connect to the Internet to perform the tasks in this part.

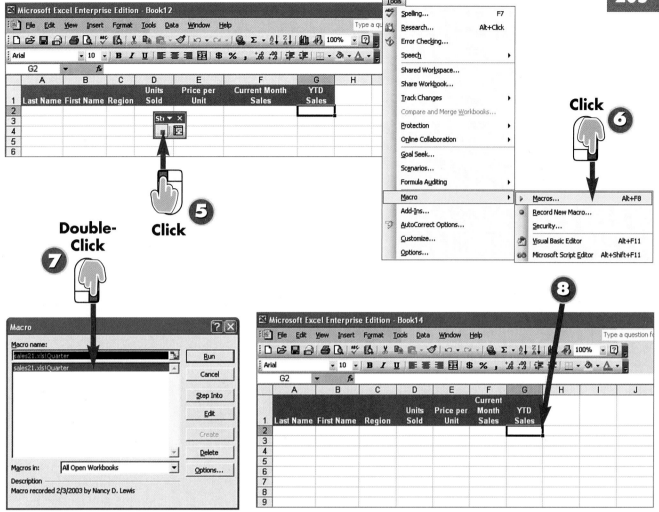

5. When you've completed all the actions that you want the macro to perform, click the **Stop Recording** button on the Macro toolbar.

6. To run the macro you created, open the **Tools** menu, choose **Macro**, and select **Macros** (or press **Alt+F8**) to open the Macro dialog box.

7. Double-click on the macro's name to run it. (Notice that in this case, the macro's name contains the name of the workbook you were using when the macro was created.)

8. Excel runs the macro—in this case, automatically creating a new workbook, and adding and formatting the text you specified.

Everything records

Keep in mind that when the macro is recording, everything you do is recorded. For example, if you page down through a worksheet, that will happen when you run the macro later.

Adding macros to your toolbars

Macros are also items that you can add to your toolbars to make it easy to launch them. To do so, click the **More Buttons** down arrow on the right-most side of the Standard toolbar, and click the **Add or Remove Buttons** command. Then select the Commands tab on the Customize dialog box and choose **Macros** from the **Categories** list. Finally, choose the macro for which you want to create a button in the **Commands** list.

Saving Data to Use in Another Application (Exporting)

Start

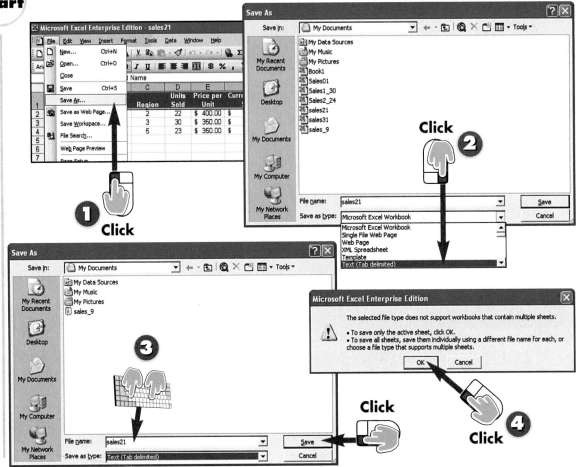

With the worksheet that contains the data you want to save for export displayed onscreen, open the **File** menu and choose **Save As** to open the Save As dialog box.

The Save As dialog box opens. Click the **down arrow** next to the **Save as type** field and choose **Text (Tab delimited)** from the list that appears.

Type a name for the file in the **File name** field (or keep the current workbook name) and click the **Save** button.

Excel notifies you that only the active worksheet—not the entire workbook—will be saved in the manner you've specified. Click **OK**.

INTRODUCTION

You might find that the data you've entered into your worksheet would be useful in another Office application. For example, you might want to upload the regional sales data you've entered in to Excel to an Access database (which has more extensive reporting tools), or use it in a Word mail merge. Thanks to Excel's *exporting* capabilities, you can. In this task, you'll learn how to save your Excel worksheet data in a *tab delimited* format that other applications can use, and to see what that data looks like in another application (here, Word). (*Delimiters* are the items that separate one field of data from the next, and can be tabs, semicolons, commas, spaces, or other types.)

TIP

Exporting workbooks
To export an entire workbook, you must save each worksheet in the workbook individually if you want them to be tab delimited.

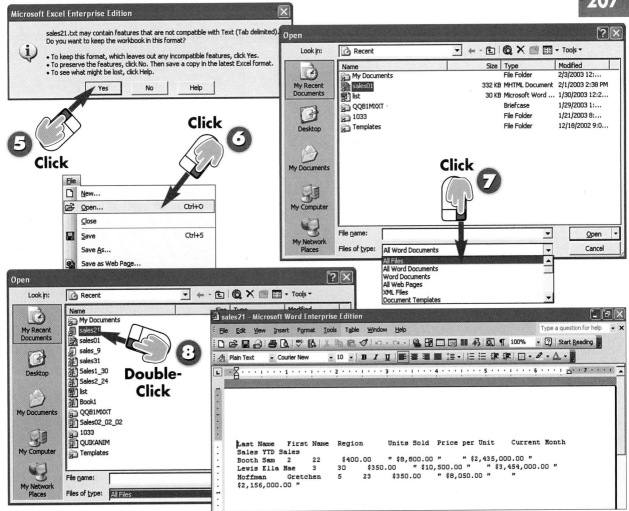

5 Excel warns you that the worksheet might contain some features (such as formatting) that cannot be retained when the sheet is saved in the new format. Click **Yes** to continue.

6 In another application, for example, Microsoft Word, open the **File** menu and choose **Open**.

7 The Open dialog box opens. Click the **down arrow** next to the **Files of type** field and choose **All Files** from the list that appears.

8 Double-click on the file you saved in step 3 to see what the tab-delimited file looks like in Word.

Exporting formatting

When you create a tab-delimited file for use in other applications, the *data* in the cells is the important information you are saving to export. The formatting in the cells (bold, blue, italic, and so on) is not saved because it is not necessary to the data.

Incompatible features

Some examples of incompatible features are data formatting (color, font, and so on) and numeric styles (currency and the like). If the numeric styles can't be saved as a number format, they may be saved in quotes as "text data" instead of numeric data.

Calculations lost

If there were any calculations performed in a cell to derive a number, only the actual number will be saved—not the formula, function, or cell references. So, if cell **F2 ($8,800.00)** is actually **=SUM(D2*E2)**, only the **$8,800.00** is saved.

Using Data from Another Application (Importing)

Start

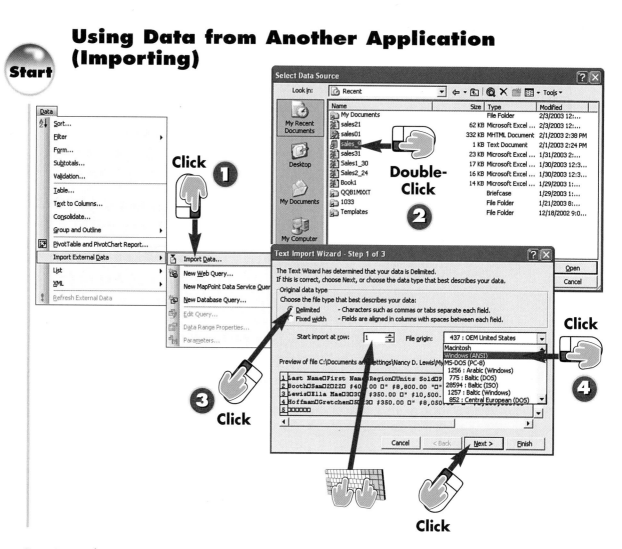

① Open the **Data** menu, choose **Import External Data**, and select **Import Data** to open the Select Data Source dialog box.

② The Select Data Source dialog box opens. Locate and double-click on the *text-based* file you want to import; Office launches the Text Import wizard.

③ Click the **Delimited** option (because it describes the data in the file you are importing), and type **1** in the **Start import at row 1** spin box (for the entire file).

④ Click the **File origin** down arrow and choose **Windows (ANSI)** (because it originated on a Windows operating system platform). Then, click the **Next** button.

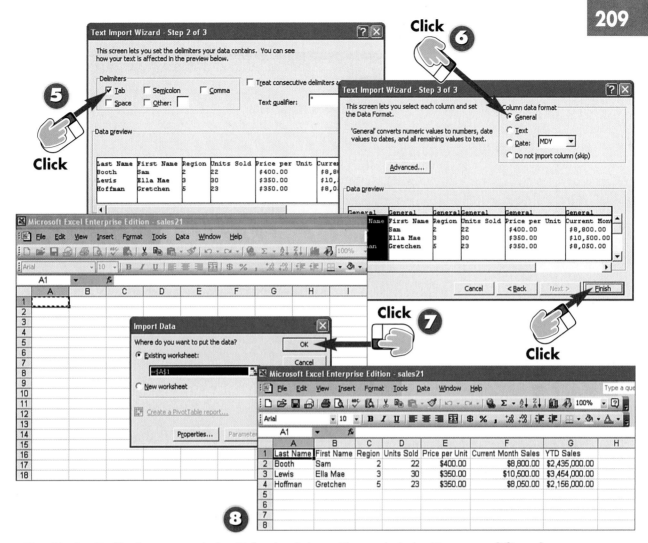

5 Under **Delimiters**, mark the **Tab** check box. Then, click the **Text qualifier down arrow** and choose **"**. Preview the file in the **Data preview** area; if OK, click **Next**.

6 Depending on your data type, choose **General**, **Text**, **Date**, or **Do not import column (skip)** in the **Column data format** area. Then, click **Finish**.

7 Click the **OK** button in the Import Data dialog box to place the data in the existing worksheet beginning with cell **A1**.

8 The data is inserted.

End

Delimiters and qualifiers

Delimiters are the items that separate one field of data from the next, and can be tabs, semicolons, commas, spaces, or other types. *Qualifiers* are the items that qualify data as text, and can be double, single, or no quotes.

External Data toolbar

The External Data toolbar opens automatically when you import data in this fashion. You can use the buttons on the toolbar, or close the toolbar and work with the new data in your worksheet.

Saving a Workbook as a Web Page

Start

Click ①

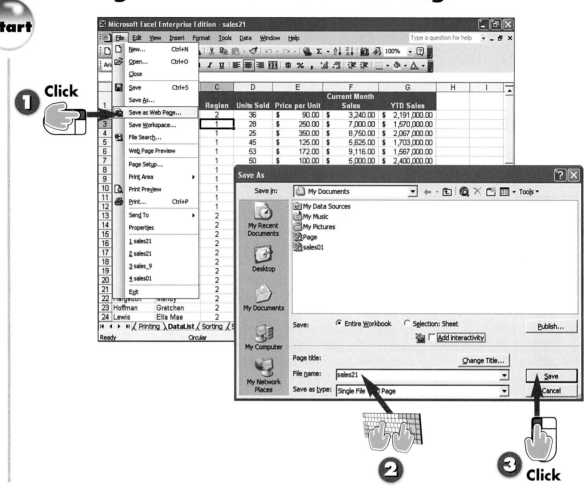

②

③ **Click**

① With the Excel workbook that you want to save as a Web page displayed, open the **File** menu and choose **Save as Web Page** to open the Save As dialog box.

② In the **File name** field, type a descriptive name for the file you want to save (for example, **Sales21**).

③ Click the **Save** button. The workbook is saved as a Web page (that is, an HTML file), and the filename you assigned appears in Web page's the title bar.

End

INTRODUCTION
To use your Excel workbook as a Web page, you must first save it in the correct file format—HTML. Excel enables you to save your workbooks in HTML format. In addition, you can reopen the Excel workbooks you save in HTML format in Excel, and then use Excel's various features to edit your Web page.

TIP
Saving workbooks versus worksheets
Instead of saving the default entire workbook as a Web page (the default), you can select the **Selection: Sheet** option button to save only the active worksheet as a Web page.

TIP
Custom views
Custom views are one element that will not save in an HTML file. If you try to save an Excel workbook containing custom views as a Web page, you may receive an Excel message about this; click **Yes**.

Viewing Your Workbook as a Web Page

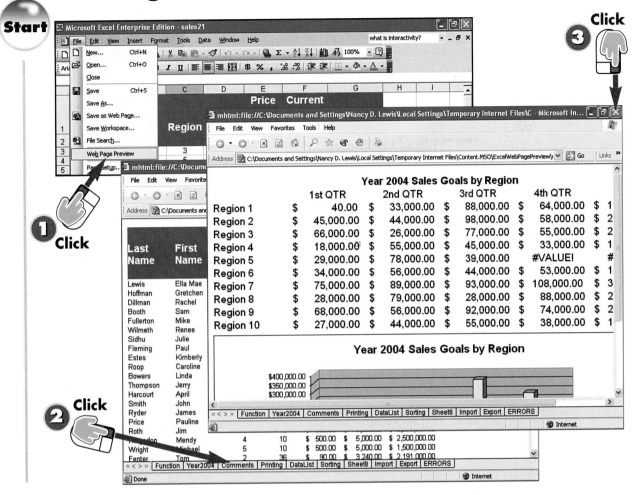

1 With the workbook that you want to preview displayed onscreen, open the **File** menu and choose **Web Page Preview**.

2 The workbook is opened in your computer's default Web browser. Click the tabs at the bottom of the browser window to move through the worksheets.

3 Click the **Close** (×) button in the browser window to close the browser and return to the original Excel workbook.

End

Excel enables you to convert the workbooks and worksheets you create into Web pages (discussed in the previous task). Before you do, however, it's a good idea to preview the workbook or worksheet you want to save as a Web page so you can see how it will look.

Browser buttons and links

Notice that the Web browser acts just like it is displaying an active Web page. The workbook filename is in the title bar, and the Explorer bar buttons are active.

Online comments

If you have comments in a document that you publish to a Web page, you can move the mouse pointer over the comment indicator (the red bracket in the upper-right corner of the cell) to display the comment in a ScreenTip.

Adding Email Address Links to Worksheets

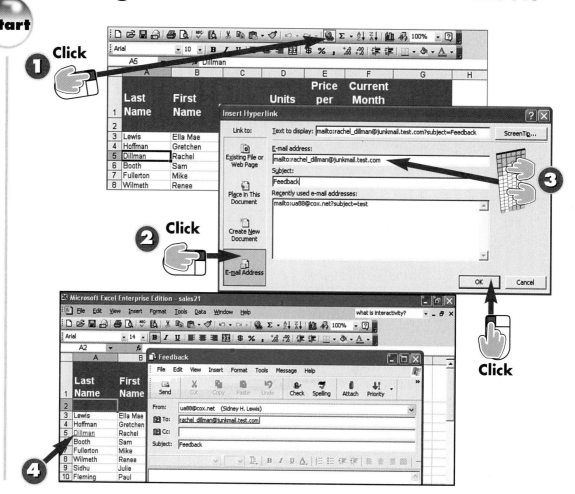

1. Click a cell (blank or one with data) in the worksheet where you want to add an email address link and click the **Insert Hyperlink** button on the Standard toolbar.

2. The Insert Hyperlink dialog box appears. Click the **E-mail Address** option in the **Link to** area.

3. In the **E-mail Address** field, type the desired email address. You can also add a **Subject** line that will fill in for the user automatically. When you're finished, click **OK**.

4. The text in the active cell becomes an email link (if the cell was blank, it is filled with the email address). When this link is clicked, an email message window opens.

End

Suppose you're creating a report for your customers to read, and want them to email you as soon as they finish it to let you know their thoughts. In that case, you can add an email link to the document, which they can use to start an email message addressed to you. Email links appear in a different color from the regular text and are underlined, making them easy to identify. In addition to making text or cell data into an email link, you can click any other object and create a link. For example, you could make a piece of clip art, a chart, or a comment a link.

TIP

mailto:
Notice that as soon as you type the @ symbol in the **Address** field in step 3, **mailto:** is placed at the beginning of the email address. This indicates that the link is an email link, not a Web address (URL).

Typing Web (URL) Links Directly into a Worksheet

Start

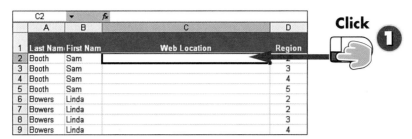

Click

1

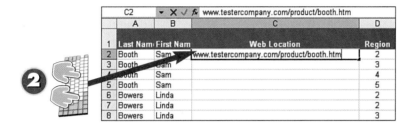

2

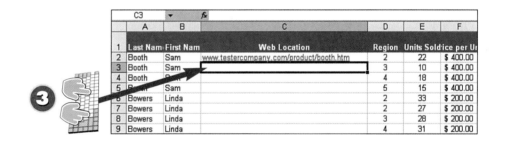

3

1 Click the cell in the worksheet where you want to type a URL that will act as a link.

2 Type the URL directly into the cell.

3 Press the **Enter** key; the URL automatically becomes a link, also called a *hyperlink*. When this link is used, a browser window opens containing the page referenced by the URL.

End

TIP

Removing hyperlinks
If you are typing a hyperlink into a worksheet as an example and don't want it to be an active link, move the mouse pointer over the link, right-click it, and select **Remove Hyperlink** from the shortcut menu.

Inserting a Web (URL) Link into a Worksheet

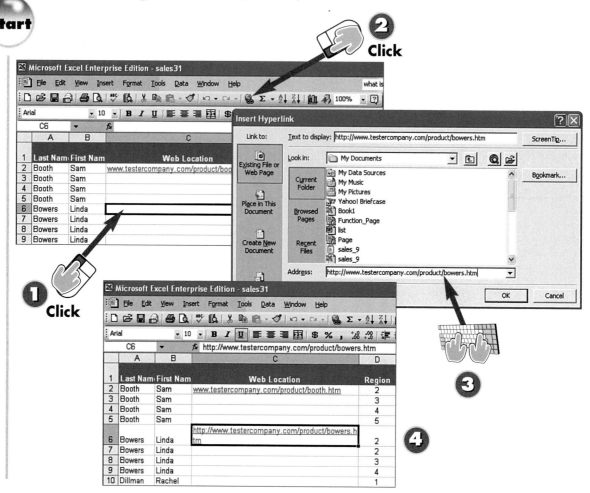

1. Select the cell in which you want to place a URL link.

2. Click the **Insert Hyperlink** button on the Standard toolbar to open the Insert Hyperlink dialog box.

3. In the **Address** field, type the desired URL, and click **OK**.

4. The cell you selected in step 1 now contains a URL link. When this link is used, a browser window opens containing the page referenced by the URL.

End

As you learned in the preceding task, a URL is a unique way of identifying a Web page's location. Excel lets you insert URL links directly into your worksheets in much the same way you insert email address links; after you insert a URL link, anyone reading the worksheet can use the URL link to view the page it references (see the task "Linking to the Web in a Document" later in this part to learn how).

Browsing the Web

If you cannot remember the URL you want to add to your worksheet, you can use the **Insert Hyperlink** button on the Standard toolbar to open the Insert Hyperlink dialog box. There, you can browse Web pages or use recent links to locate and add the correct address.

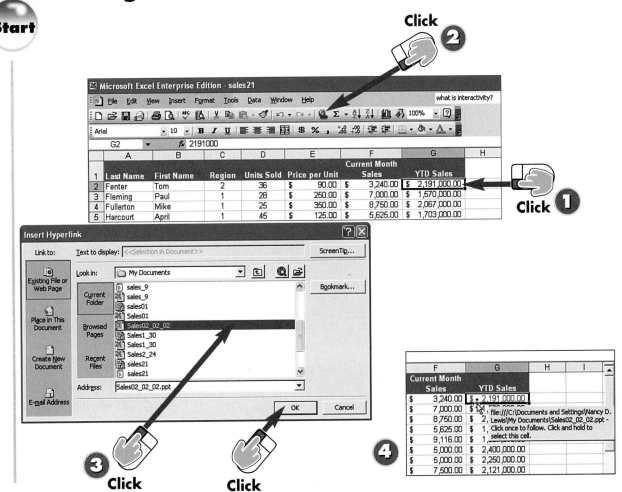

1. Select the cell in which you want to place a document hyperlink.

2. Click the **Insert Hyperlink** button on the Standard toolbar to open the Insert Hyperlink dialog box.

3. The Insert Hyperlink dialog box opens. Locate and select the file you want to link to (it can be any type of file) and click **OK**.

4. The cell you selected in step 1 now contains a hyperlink; when you move your mouse pointer over the link, the location of the linked file is displayed in a ScreenTip.

INTRODUCTION

There may be times when creating an elaborate worksheet that you will want to add a link that takes you or the reader to some other pertinent file. For example, you might add a monthly report presentation link to your sales worksheet so that anyone reading the sales worksheet can use that link to immediately view the monthly report presentation.

TIP

Locating recently used files
If the folder list in the Insert Hyperlink dialog box doesn't show the document you want to link to, try clicking the **Recent Files** option to locate the document. If it has been a while since you last used the file you're looking for, click the **down arrow** next to the **Look in** field to find the folder in which the document is stored.

Linking to the Web in a Worksheet

Start

Click 1

2 **Click**

1 In Excel, click a URL to link to the Web page associated with that link.

2 Your default Web browser opens and displays the Web page. Either click the **Close** button on the document window to close the browser or press **Alt+Tab** to toggle back to your original document.

End

TIP

Returning to your worksheet
If you have finished browsing the Web, you can click the Web browser's **Close** (×) button to close the browser and return to the original Excel worksheet, or click the browser's Back button until you return to Excel. In addition, you can click the workbook's taskbar button to make it the active window.

Updating a Link

Right Click

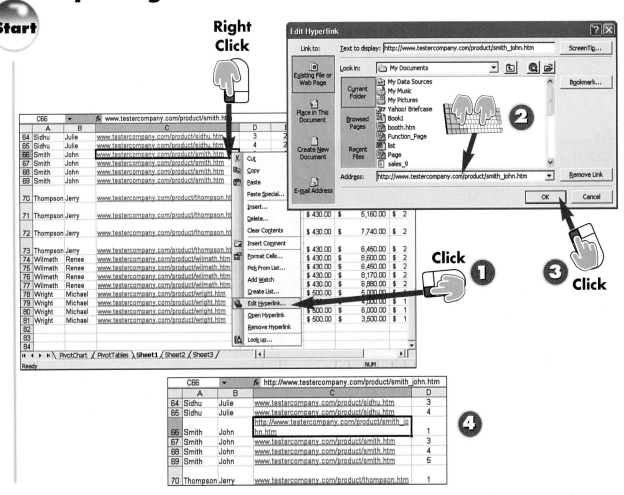

Click ①

③ Click

②

The link is updated. ④

① Right-click the hyperlink that needs to be edited and choose **Edit Hyperlink** from the shortcut menu that appears to open the Edit Hyperlink dialog box.

② Locate the page to which you want to link or, if you know the page's correct URL, simply type it in the **Address** field.

③ Click **OK**.

④ The link is updated.

End

Chances are, at some point you'll mistype a URL, email address, or document file location while creating a hyperlink and need to edit it. Alternatively, the URL, email address, or document file location associated with a hyperlink may change. Either way, you'll need to edit the hyperlink for it to function properly.

Clicking and holding

TIP

If you want to make an edit to a link directly within the cell that contains the link, you must first click and hold the mouse pointer in the cell. (A ScreenTip pops up with this information in case you forget.)

Removing a Link

Start

Right Click

1 Click

2

1. Right-click the hyperlink you want to remove and choose **Remove Hyperlink** from the shortcut menu that appears.

2. The original link text remains, but no longer acts as a hyperlink. (You can tell because the text is no longer underlined or a different color.)

End

If you refer to a particular URL, email address, or document file location in a report but don't want people to link to it, or if you decide you no longer want a particular hyperlink in your worksheet, you can remove it. When you remove a hyperlink, the link text or object remains, but clicking it has no effect.

TIP

Using the Undo command
If you remove a hyperlink but decide you want to put it back in your worksheet, click the **Undo** button on the Standard toolbar; the hyperlink will be restored.

Emailing a Workbook or Worksheet

Start

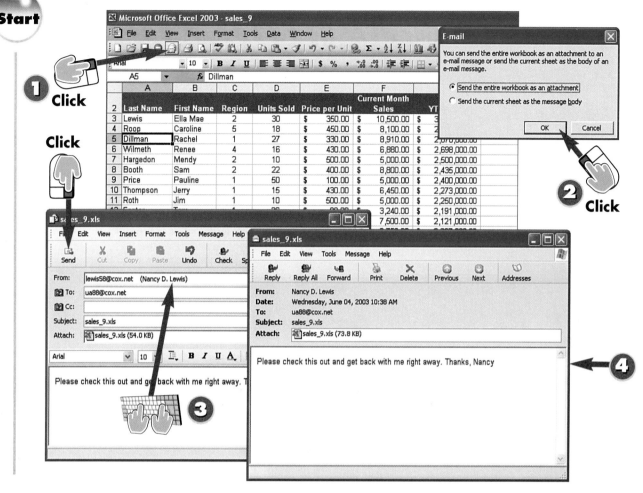

Click

Click

Click

1. With the workbook displayed onscreen, click the **E-mail** button on the Standard toolbar. If the sheet has not been saved, it will appear as the message body.

2. If you have saved, specify whether you want to send the entire workbook as an attachment or send the current sheet as the body of the email message and click **OK**.

3. When a new email message window appears, type the recipient's email address in the **To** field, any necessary text in the message body, and click **Send**.

4. When the recipient of your message receives and opens it, she will view the workbook as an attachment or the worksheet directly in the email message.

End

Excel has an E-mail button on its Standard toolbar that will let you immediately send a workbook as an email attachment, or a worksheet as the body of an email message. You will find this feature handy if you want to get quick feedback on a worksheet you are working on with a colleague.

TIP

Subject filename
Notice that the filename of the workbook or worksheet is added by default to the Subject line in the email message. You can change it by clicking in the Subject area and typing a different subject.

Setting Up Speech Recognition

Start

Click ①

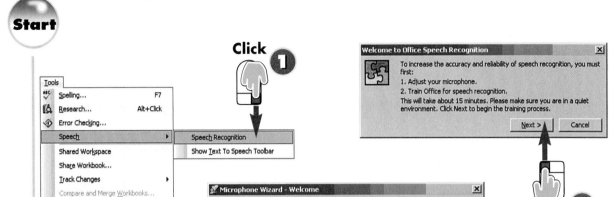

Click ②

Click ③

① In Excel, open the **Tools** menu, choose **Speech**, and select **Speech Recognition**.

② The Welcome to Office Speech Recognition dialog box informs you that Office will adjust your microphone and speech training will take 15 minutes. Click **Next**.

③ The Microphone Wizard—Welcome page opens, providing useful information about adjusting your microphone. Read it, and click **Next**.

INTRODUCTION

If you like to dictate letters and memos, you'll be pleased to learn that Excel supports speech recognition. Before you can use this feature, however, you must set it up. You can do so in any Office application or by double-clicking the Speech icon in the Windows XP Control Panel. (In this task, you'll set it up from within Excel.) Before you begin, you'll need to connect a microphone and some speakers to your PC (refer to the instructions that came with those components for help).

TIP

Adjusting the microphone's sensitivity
Double-click the **Volume** icon in the system tray (on the far-right end of the taskbar, to the left of the time) to open a window that enables you to increase or decrease the microphone's sensitivity.

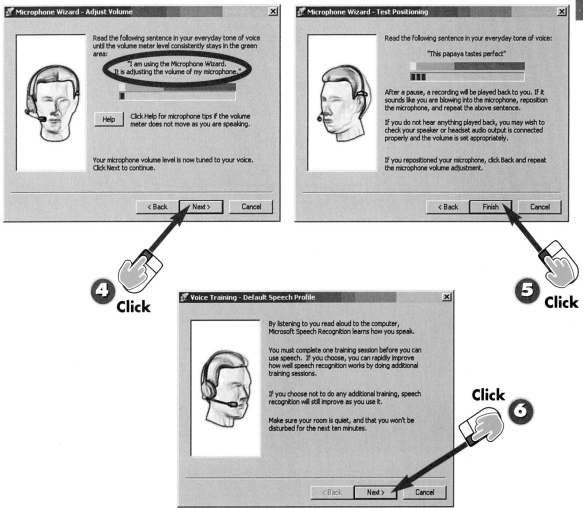

④ Repeat the text featured in the Adjust Volume page in a normal tone of voice until the volume meter level is consistently in the green. When you're finished, click **Next**.

⑤ Read the Test Positioning page aloud. If the playback recording sounds distorted, reposition the mic, click **Back**, and repeat; otherwise, click **Finish**.

⑥ The Voice Training—Default Speech Profile page opens; you must complete at least one training session before using the Speech Recognition feature. Click **Next**.

TIP

Mistakes and stops
If Excel stops highlighting text while you are reading, you probably missed a word, read too quickly, or pronounced something incorrectly. Simply take a couple breaths and begin again where the highlighting left off. If you don't recognize a word in the text, or aren't sure how to pronounce it, you can skip it by clicking the **Skip Word** button. To stop for a moment (for example, to answer the phone), click the **Pause** button. (A **Resume** button will appear for you to click when you are ready to continue.)

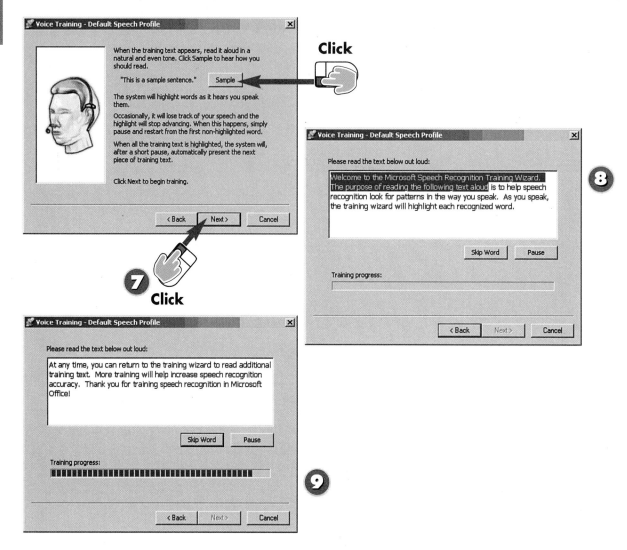

Click

Click

7 The Voice Training Wizard coaches you to read the training text in subsequent pages in a clear, natural tone. Click **Sample** to hear an example, and click **Next**.

8 Read the displayed text aloud; the text you've read will become highlighted as you go.

9 Continue to read the displayed text aloud, moving through each passage. (Notice the Training progress bar moves as you proceed.)

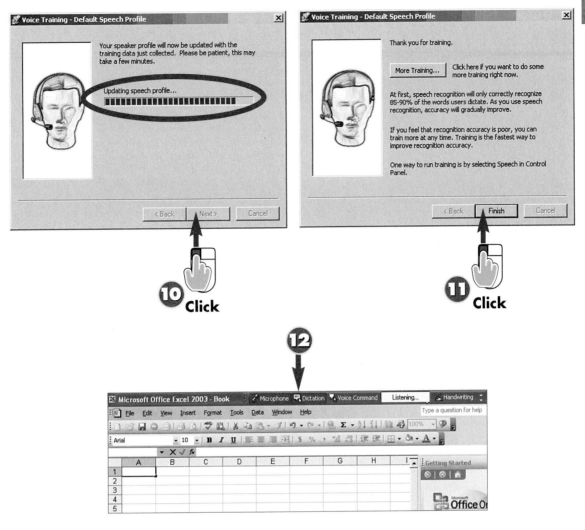

(10) After you finish reading all the passages, your speech profile is updated.

(11) Click the **Finish** button. (Note that if you decide to click the More Training button, refer to the task "Getting Additional Speech Recognition Training.")

(12) The Voice Training Wizard closes, returning you to your application window. A Language bar is added to the window's title bar, which you can click and drag to other locations on your desktop.

End

Getting more training
Click the **More Training** button in the screen in step 11 to read additional passages aloud, which will make the speech-recognition feature more accurate.

Setting up multiple speech profiles
Other people who use your computer can set up their own speech-recognition profiles. To do so, they must choose **Tools**, **Speech** to activate the Language bar, click the **Tools** button in the Language bar, and select **Options** from the list appears to open the Speech Properties dialog box. There, they click **New** button to initiate a new speech profile. Once multiple speech profiles are set up, you can select your own by choosing **Tools**, **Current User**, and the appropriate user name.

Getting Additional Speech Recognition Training

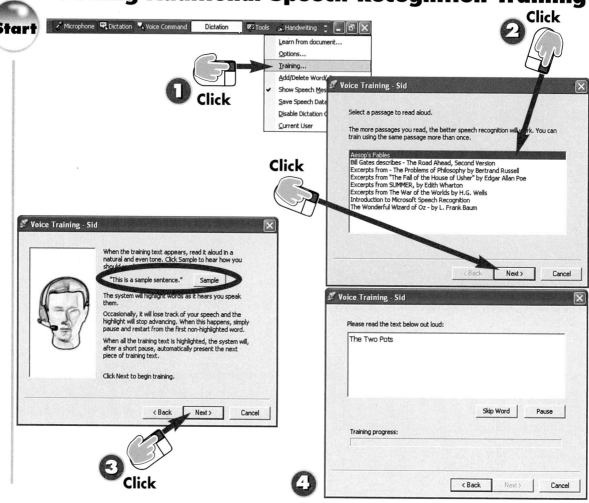

1. Click **Tools** on the Language bar and select the **Training** command.

2. Select the speech passage you would like to recite and click **Next**.

3. On the introductory page, read the sample sentence to adjust your speech and microphone sound, and then click **Next**.

4. Read the displayed text aloud as you did in the preceding task, and then click **Next** until your last screen asks you to click Finish.

End

Dictating Your Text and Data

Start

Click ①

Click ②

Click ④

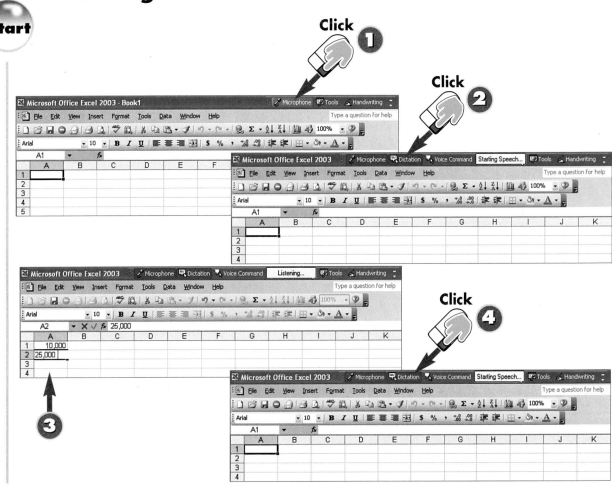

① Click the **Microphone** button on the Language bar. (If the Language bar isn't displayed, open the **Tools** menu and choose **Speech**.)

② Click the **Dictation** button on the Language bar.

③ Say the words you want to appear in your worksheet.

④ To stop dictating, click the **Dictation** button; then click the **Microphone** button (or say "microphone") to turn off the microphone.

End

INTRODUCTION

The whole point of using Excel's Speech Recognition feature is so you can speak into your microphone, rather than typing, to input data into Excel. You do so using the Dictation command. Simply say the numbers or words you want to enter into a cell. To accept your data, say "enter," or say "backspace" as many times as needed to delete characters.

TIP

Adding punctuation and nonprinting characters
To add punctuation to your document, simply say the name of the mark you want to add. For example, to add a comma, say the word "comma." To move to a new line, say "new line"; to begin a new paragraph, say "new paragraph" or "Enter." You can also issue the following self-explanatory commands: "Tab," "space," "up," "down," "left," and "right."

Using Voice Commands

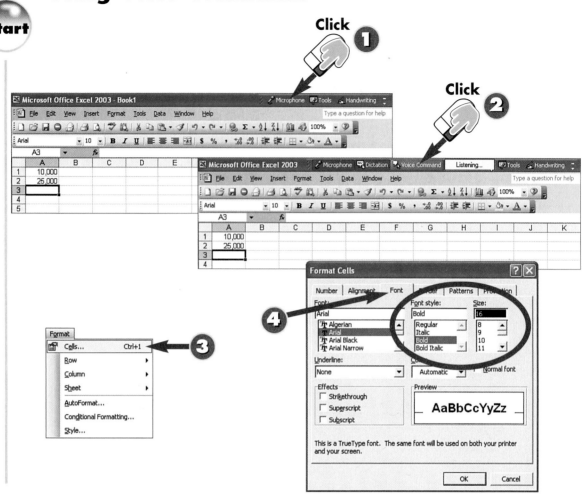

1. If the microphone is not already in use, click the **Microphone** button on the Language bar to activate it. (If the Language bar isn't displayed, select **Tools**, **Speech**.)

2. Click the **Voice Command** button on the Language bar (or say "voice command").

3. Say the name of the menu you want to open—for example, "Format." Then say the name of the command you want to issue, such as "Cells."

4. The Format Cells dialog box opens. Say the name of the tab you want to use, such as "Font." Then, say the name of the option(s) you want to activate.

Talking to the task pane

You can choose commands on a task pane by saying the full name of the desired link. For example, in the New Document task pane in Excel, you could say "From existing workbook" to create a new workbook from an existing workbook.

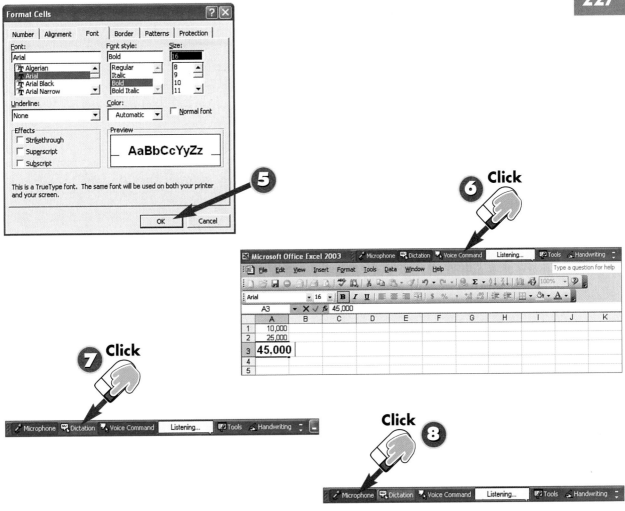

5 Say "OK" to process your commands, or "Cancel" to cancel them.

6 To turn off the Voice Command feature, click the **Voice Command** button.

7 To return dictating, click the **Dictation** button (or simply say "dictation").

8 As you dictate, changes you made using the Voice Commands feature will be active. When finished, say "microphone" or click **Microphone** to turn it off.

End

Talking to the toolbar

To access buttons on a toolbar, you must first know the exact names of each button. Simply move the mouse pointer over each of the toolbar buttons to become familiar with them. When you are ready to access a toolbar button, click the **Voice Command** button (or say "voice command") and say the name of the button. For example, to begin typing underlined text, say "underline," then "dictation," and then say the words you want to appear underlined in your document. If you make any errors, you can always switch back to the "Voice Command" feature and say, "undo."

Glossary

A

absolute cell reference   An entry in a formula that does not change when the formula is copied to a new cell. In certain formulas, you might want an entry to always refer to one specific cell value.

active cell   The cell currently selected in an Excel worksheet.

active worksheet   The worksheet currently selected in an Excel workbook.

adaptive menus   Menus that change to show the commands you use most often.

alignment   The way text lines up against the margins of a page. For example, justified text lines up evenly with both the left and right margins.

ANSI   American National Standards Institute. An organization that develops standards for computers.

application   A program that is used on your computer.

arguments   Words, phrases, or numbers you enter in a statement to modify the formula or function operation.

arrows   Items that can be clicked on in scroll bars to move throughout a workbook.

AutoFill   A feature in Excel that will automatically fill in a series of information. For example, if you type **January** and **February** and select continuous empty cells, Excel will automatically fill them with the next logical option (March).

AutoText   A feature that automatically corrects mistyped text. You can also use AutoText to invent a string of characters that automatically corrects itself to a word or phrase. For example, Word comes with AutoText that automatically corrects "teh" to "the."

axes   See *category axis* and *value axis*.

B

browser   A tool that lets you view documents on the Internet.

bullet   An object, such as a circle or square, used to set off items in a list.

C

category axis   The y-axis on a chart.

cell   An area in an Excel worksheet or a Word table that holds a specific piece of information.

cell pointer   A white cross-shaped pointer that appears over cells in the worksheet. You use the cell pointer to select any cell in the worksheet.

cell reference   The designation formed by combining the row and column headings. For example, A8 refers to the cell at the intersection of column A and row 8.

chart area   The area in a chart that contains information about the data that is being graphed.

chart   A graphic representation of a selection of Excel workbook cell data.

Clip Gallery A collection of clip art, pictures, sound files, and video clips you can use to spruce up Office documents.

Clipboard Information that is cut or copied resides in this location in the Windows operating system. This information can be accessed from the Clipboard task pane.

column A vertical set of cells designated by an alphabetical header: A, B, C, and so on.

comment A way to attach information to individual cells without cluttering the cells with extraneous information. A red triangle indicates that a cell contains a comment.

conditional statement A function that returns different results depending on whether a specified condition is true or false.

context menu See *shortcut menu*.

cursor The location of where you last entered text. This is a flashing bar in some applications. *See also* insertion point.

D

data label A label for a data series in a chart.

data list A set of related information about a particular person, transaction, or event. One piece of information is a *field*, and one set of fields is called a *record*.

data range The range for a data series in a chart.

data table A table in a chart that lists the data being graphed.

data validation The process of making sure that data is accurately entered into a form for a data list.

data The information you work with in an Excel spreadsheet, including text, numbers, and graphic images.

datasheet A grid of columns and rows that enables you to enter numerical data into a chart.

dependents Cell references that depend on a formula or function.

dialog box Any of the information boxes that appear during the installation or use of an application and require input from the user.

docked toolbar Any toolbar that is attached to one of the four sides of an application window.

document window The window that controls the individual documents within an application window.

drag-and-drop To move an object (an icon, a selection of text, a cell in an Excel worksheet, and so on) by selecting it, dragging it to another location, and then releasing the mouse button.

drop-down list A list of choices presented when you click the arrow to the right of a field in a dialog box.

E

embedded object   This is when a source and destination file aren't linked, which means that when one object is updated, the other is not. The embedded object is physically included in the document to which it belongs.

equation   A formula or function used in Excel to perform calculations.

export   To put the data in your application into a format that other applications can use.

external data   Data from a location other than the application you are currently working in.

F

field   A place where you enter data in a data list or a data element on a form.

file   Information you enter in your computer and save for future use, such as a document or a workbook.

filter   A method in Excel for controlling which records are extracted from the database and displayed in the worksheet.

floating toolbar   A toolbar that is not anchored to the edge of the window, but instead displays in the document window for easy access. In addition, you can drag a floating toolbar to your Windows desktop.

font   The typeface, type size, and type attributes of text or numbers.

footer   Text or graphics that appear at the bottom of the page of a document or worksheet.

form   A window you can create in Excel that you can use to add data list records.

Format Painter   A tool that enables you to quickly format data exactly like other data.

format   To change the appearance of text or numbers.

formatting   Applying attributes to text and data to change the appearance of information.

Formula bar   This is where Excel calculation and formatting elements are listed.

Formula palette   A list of formulas that are usable in Excel.

formulas   In Excel, a means for calculating a value based on the values in other cells of the workbook. Formulas can also include values entered by the user.

function   A built-in formula that automatically performs calculations in Excel.

G

graphics   Images that come in all shapes and sizes. Typical graphics include clip-art images, drawings, photographs, scanned images, and signature files.

grid   The relation of rows to columns.

gridlines   Lines that separate the cells in a printed workbook.

H

handles The small, black squares around a selected object. You use these squares to drag, size, or scale the object.

header Text or graphics that appear at the top of every page of a document or a workbook.

highlight (1) A band of color you can add to text by using the Highlight tool on the Word toolbar. (2) When you select text to format or move, you are selecting, or "highlighting," the text.

hyperlinks Text formatted so that clicking it "jumps" you to another, related location.

I

I-beam The shape of the mouse pointer when you move over a screen area in which you can edit text.

import To bring data into an application from another application.

indent An amount of space that an object, usually text, is moved away from the left margin.

Insert mode This is when the new text you enter moves the text that was previously in the same location to the right.

insertion point The blinking vertical bar that shows where text will appear when you type. The insertion point is sometimes called a *cursor*.

Internet A system of linked computer networks that facilitates data communication services such as remote login, file transfer, electronic mail, and newsgroups.

J-L

justify Aligning text so it fills the area between the left and right margins.

landscape This is the wide view of a printout.

legend This is a way of understanding the elements in a chart and what they represent.

link This is a representation between a linked object and a source object. If one of the objects is altered, the other is altered as well.

M

macro A method of automating common tasks you perform in applications such as Excel. You can record keystrokes and mouse clicks so they can be played back automatically.

margins The space around the top, bottom, left, and right side of a page. This space can be increased or decreased as necessary. This can also be the location where elements such as headers and footers are located.

merge A feature that enables you to combine information, such as names and addresses, with a form document, such as a letter.

mixed cell reference   A single cell entry in a formula that contains both a relative and an absolute cell reference. A mixed cell reference is helpful when you need a formula that always refers to the values in a specific column, but the values in the rows must change, and vice versa.

N

negation   This is making a number a negative number.

noncontiguous range   A range of cells that is linked through the use of the Ctrl key on the keyboard, but that is not necessarily in a straight row or column.

O

objects   Any element (workbook, chart, picture, and so on) that can be linked or moved in your workspace.

operator   This is an item that is used to perform a calculation in a formula or function.

Overtype mode   A setting that makes new text you enter replace the text that was previously in the same location.

P

page setup   The way data is arranged on a printed page.

path   A way to identify the folder that contains a file. For example, **My Documents\Letters\Mom.doc** means the document Mom.doc is stored in the Letters folder, which is stored in the My Documents folder.

plot area   The area where the data from a worksheet is plotted in a chart.

pop-up menu   See *shortcut menu.*

portrait   The tall view of a printout.

precedents   The cell references that are linked to make up a function or formula calculation.

print area   The area you select in Excel to print only.

program window   The application window.

Q–R

qualifier   An element that separates delimited fields (for example, quotation marks around imported or exported data in a file).

range   A cell or a rectangular group of adjacent cells in Excel.

range coordinates   These identify a range. The first element in the range coordinates is the location of the upper-left cell in the range; the second element is the location of the lower-right cell. A colon (:) separates these two elements. The range A1:C3, for example, includes the cells A1, A2, A3, B1, B2, B3, C1, C2, and C3.

range reference   A range of cells is indicated with a range reference. This includes the upper-leftmost cell in the selection, a colon, and the lower-rightmost cell in the selection. For example, the range reference for cells F9 through G2 would be F9:G2.

record   A row in a data list.

reference   A means for addressing something in a specified context. For example, in Excel, "A1" is a reference to the cell at column A, row 1.

relative cell reference   A reference to the contents of a cell that Excel adjusts when you copy the formula to another cell or range of cells.

repeating titles   This is when you select a row and or column of headers to repeat on each page of a printed worksheet.

Replace   A command on the Edit menu you can use to replace text with different text automatically. This feature can also be used with codes such as tabs and paragraph marks.

revision marks   Another name for the tracked changes you see onscreen.

row   A horizontal set of cells in Excel designated by numeric headers: 1, 2, 3, and so on.

ruler   A means for judging distances of where objects are in relation to the page. Appearing horizontally across the top of a page and vertically along the side of a page in Word, rulers also display page margins and tab settings.

S

sans serif   A class of fonts that don't have "tails" on the letters, such as Helvetica and Arial.

scale   You can increase or decrease the scale of objects or worksheets in Excel to make items fit in locations.

scientific notation   This is when you exponentiate large numbers to the power of 10. For example, 1,000,000 is actually 10 to the 5th power.

ScreenTip   Notes that display on your screen to explain a function or feature.

search criteria   A defined pattern or detail used to find matching records.

select   To define a section of text so you can take action on it, such as copying, moving, or formatting it.

series   This is when data follows a typical pattern. For example, 1st Quarter, 2nd Quarter, 3rd Quarter, 4th Quarter or 401, 402, 403, and so on.

serif   A class of fonts that have "tails" on the letters, such as Times New Roman and Courier.

sheet tabs   The tabs that you click to move through the worksheets in a workbooks.

sheet   *See* worksheet.

shortcut key   A keyboard combination that provides a quick way to execute a menu command. For example, Ctrl+S is a shortcut key for File, Save.

shortcut menu   The menu that pops up when you right-click an object. This menu changes according to the context of the task you are trying to accomplish.

sort   A function that rearranges the data in a list so it appears in alphabetical or numerical order.

source data   Where the data in a spreadsheet originated.

status bar   A place at the bottom of each Office window that tells you information about your documents and applications, such as whether you are in insert or overtype mode.

strikethrough   A font option that appears if the text is marked out with a dash mark (for example, ~~strikethrough~~).

style   A named collection of formatting settings that you can assign to text. For example, the Normal style might use the Times New Roman font at 11 points with standard margins.

subcategory   This is when you indent cells within a column to make the initial item in the list the main category.

submenu   A list of options that appears when you point at some menu items in Windows XP and in applications designed for use with Windows XP. A small, right-pointing arrowhead appears to the right of menu items that have submenus.

subtotal   A feature in Excel data lists that enables you to calculate subtotals on grouped data.

system tray   The area on the right side of the taskbar that displays the programs loaded into memory for use.

T

tab delimiters   These are the items between fields of data when importing and exporting data; for example, a colon, comma, or quote mark.

tab stop   An element that you place in your ruler to enable you to add space and alignment between your tabs. For example, you could add a right, center, or left aligned tab stop.

tab   An element that allows you to separate objects with a precise amount of space (such as one inch), something that using the spacebar can't do.

table   A series of rows and columns. The intersection of a row and column is called a *cell*, which is where you type text and numbers.

taskbar   This is the bar along the bottom portion of the screen displaying a Windows XP operating system where the Start button appears.

task pane   Another way for you to quickly perform common tasks in Excel, get help, find files, and much more. Also, as you continue working in Excel, additional task panes become active depending on what tasks you are performing.

template   Predesigned patterns on which documents and workbooks can be based.

text wrapping   This is when text automatically flows to the next line below the line without having to force the text to the next line (carriage return/Enter key).

toggle   The process of turning an option switch from On to Off (Yes to No).

trace   To follow a formula or function to see where the cell references start and end. *See also* dependents and precedents.

transpose   To flip information. For example, you can transpose column headers with row headers to read a worksheet differently.

truncate   To cut off or to shorten.

U–V

URL   A Uniform Resource Locator is a link to an addressable location on the Internet.

validation   See *data validation*.

value axis   The x-axis on a chart.

W

Web   Also known as the World Wide Web; a hypertext-based document retrieval system with machines linked to the Internet. This enables you to view documents, especially ones that are graphical in nature.

wizard   A Microsoft element that walks you through a procedure with a set of steps that tell you what you need to do.

workbook   An Excel document that contains one or more worksheets or chart sheets.

worksheet   In Excel, the workbook component that contains cell data, formulas, and charts.

Index

D

Merge and Center button (Formatting toolbar), 82

MIN function, 101, 106

minimizing workbook size, 5

mixed cell references (formulas), 100

modifying
chart options, 138-139
records in data lists, 171

mouse, shortcut menu access, 13

Move or Copy dialog box, 36

moving
charts, 135
data within worksheets, 58
graphic objects, 151
objects within worksheet, 161
worksheets, 36-37

multiple applications, switching between, 29

multiple objects, selecting, 159

multiple speech profiles (speech recognition), 223

multiple workbooks
switching between, 29
viewing, 31

multiple worksheets
cell referencing, 112-113
switching between, 30

N - O

Name command (Insert menu), 110

naming
cells, 110
ranges, 110
workbooks, 24

navigating
command menus, 12
worksheets via scroll bars, 5

New button (Standard toolbar), 27

Number format, applying to worksheets, 77

numbers
charts, formatting, 142
formatting options, 75-80

Object command (Insert menu), 158

objects
copying, 161
deleting, 163
formatting, 160
inserting, 158
moving within worksheet, 161
resizing, 162
selection handles, 159

Open button (Standard toolbar), 28

Open dialog box, 28

opening
new files (task panes), 16
workbooks, 28

order of operations (formulas), 107

organization charts
chart boxes, adding, 154
chart boxes, moving, 154
inserting, 153-154

orientation (cells), 86

overriding worksheet data, 8

overwriting
formulas, guidelines, 48
worksheet data, 48

P

Page Break Preview, manipulating, 180, 188-189

Page Break Preview command (View menu), 186

U - V

worksheets

X - Y - Z